Jewish Communities on the Ohio River

Ohio River Valley Series

Rita Kohn, Series Editor

Jewish Communities on the Ohio River

A HISTORY

Amy Hill Shevitz

THE UNIVERSITY PRESS OF KENTUCKY

Publication of this volume was made possible in part by a grant from the National Endowment for the Humanities.

Scholarly publisher for the Commonwealth,
serving Bellarmine University, Berea College, Centre
College of Kentucky, Eastern Kentucky University,
The Filson Historical Society, Georgetown College,
Kentucky Historical Society, Kentucky State University,
Morehead State University, Murray State University,
Northern Kentucky University, Transylvania University,
University of Kentucky, University of Louisville,
and Western Kentucky University.

Editorial and Sales Offices: The University Press of Kentucky
663 South Limestone Street, Lexington, Kentucky 40508-4008
www.kentuckypress.com

Library of Congress Cataloging-in-Publication Data

Shevitz, Amy Hill, 1953-
Jewish communities on the Ohio River : a history / Amy Hill Shevitz.
p. cm.
Includes bibliographical references and index.
ISBN 978-0-8131-2430-8 (hardcover : alk. paper)
1. Jews—Ohio River Region—History. 2. Jews—Ohio River Region—Politics and government. 3. Jews—Ohio River Region—Social life and customs. I. Title.
F520.6.J5S54 2007
977.00492'4—dc22

2007014320

Member of the Association of
American University Presses

Contents

Series Foreword

The Ohio River Valley Series, conceived and published by the University Press of Kentucky, is an ongoing series of books that examine and illuminate the Ohio River and its tributaries, the lands drained by these streams, and the peoples who made this fertile and desirable area their place of residence, of refuge, of commerce and industry, of cultural development, and, ultimately, of engagement with American democracy. In doing this, the series builds upon an earlier project, *Always a River: The Ohio River and the American Experience*, a multifaceted project sponsored by the National Endowment for the Humanities and the humanities councils of Illinois, Indiana, Kentucky, Ohio, Pennsylvania, and West Virginia, with a mix of private and public organizations.

Each book's story is told through the men and women acting within their particular time and place. Each directs attention to the place of the Ohio River in the context of the larger American story and reveals the rich resources for the history of the Ohio River and of the nation afforded by records, papers, artifacts, works of art, and oral stories preserved by families and institutions. Each traces the impact the river and the land have had on individuals and cultures and, conversely, the changes these individuals and cultures have wrought on the valley with the passage of years.

Jewish Communities on the Ohio River: A History is a vibrant mosaic of twenty-four communities embedded along the length of the Ohio River. Despite "imprecision in the term 'small town,'" Amy Hill Shevitz draws us into her sense of "small" and ultimately helps us envision the bits and pieces as an image of how and why the Ohio River Valley and the concomitant flux and flow of Jewish in-migration, settlement, and out-migration have affected each other and the larger American and Jewish stories over three centuries. Shevitz rightfully avers that "the study of small-town Jewry is critical to understanding the American Jewish experience to the fullest." In so doing, we gain a fuller understanding of the Ohio River Valley. Shevitz provides both a horizontal and vertical depiction. Her style makes this book intriguing to the general public while contributing substantially to regional scholarship.

As a durable companion to Darrel E. Bigham's *Towns and Villages of the Lower Ohio* (University Press of Kentucky, 1998), *Jewish Communities on the Ohio River*, too, is a benchmark work based on thorough, impeccable research. Shevitz integrates newer interpretations within older assumptions, thus showing how historians grow within their contexts. She probes questions important to deciphering how a religious and cultural group factors into the importance of small towns as an American phenomenon.

Throughout the pages of *Jewish Communities on the Ohio River*, we hear the voices of people who stir our imagination. We experience their lives up to the present, with descendents arranging their Ohio River Valley memories into a mythic "old country" framed by closeness, warmth, supportiveness, and the transplantation of "old friendship networks into new settings."

Rita Kohn
Series Editor

Preface

In the spring of 1977, I went with some acquaintances to visit an old Jewish cemetery tucked away on a hill beyond a side road in Marietta, Ohio, the town where I grew up and to which they had moved from Pittsburgh a few years earlier. There were only six gravestones, and the names on them ranged from the familiar—some family members in their eighties still lived in town—to the irretrievable, with stones so worn that we could not make out the Hebrew inscriptions. I took some of the names and dates to the local public library to see if I could find something about them from obituaries published in the local newspaper. There they were. From 1907: Morris Miller, the "aged Jew," who died when his junk-peddling wagon was hit by a train at a crossing just around the corner from my parents' home. From 1934: Harold Ginsburg, killed in an oil well explosion only three weeks after his wedding.

These obituaries suggested the existence of a community now dissolved, its people dispersed. I was eventually able to re-create much of this community's history and life, and the resulting article was published in 1979. Much later, when I was back in graduate school studying American history, my original story of a small river town's Jewish past was still piquing interest, and I was asked to expand my local project to a regional one. Thus "Jewish Communities on the Ohio River" became my doctoral dissertation and, now, a book for the University Press of Kentucky's Ohio River Valley Series.

Without a specific external motivation, I might not have chosen to undertake this particular study. But the start of the project coincided with my move from the East Coast to the West, and the questions I needed to address turned out to be extremely relevant to my immediate experience: How do Jews and Jewish communities differ in different parts of the country? Can we ascertain why? In addition to studying the Ohio River Valley, I turned my scholarly attention to the Jews of Oklahoma (the first phase of my cross-country journey) and then to the Jews of Southern California. My intellectual journeys have been enhanced and invigorated by my physical journeys.

My research was supported in part by several sources: a Graduate Student Senate Research Grant and a Graduate College Student Research Presentation Award from the University of Oklahoma, the Loewenstein-Wiener Fellowship in American Jewish Studies from the American Jewish Archives at Hebrew Union College in Cincinnati, and the Finkelstein Fellowship in Jewish Studies at the University of Judaism in Los Angeles.

Many, many individuals have been important resources for me on this project. I would like to thank the following for their help via personal correspondence: Robert Beren (Wichita, Kansas, formerly of Marietta, Ohio), Darrel Bigham (Evansville, Indiana), Dr. Jules Duga (Columbus, Ohio, formerly of Bellaire, Ohio), Nancy Ehrmann (Randolph, Massachusetts, formerly of Portsmouth, Ohio), Jerome Endich (Steubenville, Ohio), Howard Epstein (Atlanta, Georgia), Henny Evans (Gallipolis, Ohio), Mary Freedman (Steubenville, Ohio), Rita Goldhoff (Cincinnati, Ohio), Rabbi Shoshana Kaminsky (Ambridge, Pennsylvania), Herman Landau (Louisville, Kentucky), Beverly Levine (Cincinnati, Ohio), Miriam Levite (Clearwater, Florida, formerly of Steubenville, Ohio), Ned Lewison (Baltimore), Rabbi Daniel Lowy (Wheeling, West Virginia), Michael Mearan (Portsmouth, Ohio), Anne Mintz (Forbes and Company, New York), Phil Thuma (Ironton, Ohio), Martin Weill (Ironton, Ohio), and Lee Shai Weissbach (Louisville, Kentucky).

The following granted me personal interviews, either face-to-face or by phone: Rabbi Arthur J. Abrams (Evansville, Indiana), Rabbi Shalom Bell (Sewickley, Pennsylvania), Sharon Bogarad (Weirton, West Virginia), Barb Feige (Pittsburgh), Alvin Fineman (Chester, West Virginia), Leila Beren Jacoby (Encino, California, formerly of Marietta, Ohio), Louise Kline (Portsmouth, Ohio), Bernard Levi (Boca Raton, Florida, formerly of Portsmouth, Ohio), Ruth Baldauf Levi (Blowing Rock, North Carolina, formerly of Henderson, Kentucky), Rabbi Richard Levy (Los Angeles), Rachel Kleiman Lichterman (Parkersburg, West Virginia, formerly of Marietta, Ohio), Rabbi Shimon Paskow (Woodland Hills, California), Robin Riback (Union of American Hebrew Congregations [now Union for Reform Judaism], New York), Helen Josephy Robeson (White Plains, New York, formerly of Marietta, Ohio), Judith Ross (Pittsburgh), Herschel and Elsa Rubin (East Liverpool, Ohio), Joyce Rubin (Los Angeles, formerly of Cairo, Illinois), Leon Rubin (Boca Raton, Florida, formerly of East Liverpool, Ohio), Janey Solomon (Cairo, Illinois), Paul Tobin (East Liverpool, Ohio), Susan Warshaw (Portsmouth, Ohio), Elizabeth Weinberg (Louisville, Kentucky, formerly of Madison, Indiana),

Marian Weinberg (Newton, Massachusetts, formerly of Martins Ferry, Ohio), Max and Florence Weinstein (Naples, Florida, formerly of Portsmouth, Ohio), Steve Weinstein (New York, formerly of Portsmouth, Ohio), Sylvia and Louis Zell (Sewickley, Pennsylvania), and Nancy Zymelman (Rockville, Maryland, formerly of Maysville, Kentucky).

Many archivists and librarians at public and private institutions were very helpful; I would like to give special mention to Kevin Proffitt and his staff at the American Jewish Archives. Elizabeth Stein Schneiderman helped with research at Harvard Business School. Cynthia Goldstein copyedited for me.

I need to give very special acknowledgment and thanks to several people who were particularly important to me while I was on this intellectual journey. First is my father, Dr. Robert S. Hill, emeritus professor of political science at Marietta College, who manned the scholarly home base in the Ohio River Valley. I had the outrageous good fortune to come to know Dr. David W. Levy during my sojourn in Oklahoma; he has been a remarkable teacher, an insightful and respectful advisor, and a constant friend (in spite of the birds). Finally, I must thank my husband, Rabbi Dan Shevitz, with whom I moved across the country from Boston to Oklahoma City to Los Angeles, and with whom I look forward to many new adventures. In the immortal words of Baron Hugo: this is a great relationship.

The Ohio River Val
INDIANA
ILLINOIS
N
W
E
S
Wabash R.
Great Mia
Ci
Lawrenceburg
Madison
Kentucky R.
New Albany
Louisville
Mississippi R.
Mount Vernon
Evansville
Henderson
Owensboro
Ohio R.
Cairo
Cumberland River
KENTUC
Paducah
Tennessee R.
0
25
50
100

ey
East Liverpool
Aliquippa
Ambridge
Pittsburgh
Allegheny R.
Steubenville
Weirton
PENN.
OHIO
Wheeling
Bellaire
Monongahela R.
Muskingum R.
Scioto R.
Ohio R.
Marietta
Parkersburg
nnati
Newport
gton
Pomeroy
Little Kanawha River
Gallipolis
Portsmouth
Kanawha River
Ironton
Ashland
Huntington
WEST VIRGINIA
Big Sandy R.
Tug Fork R.
Y
150
200
Miles
Map Design by Todd Mitchell

Introduction

This is a study of Jews in specific small-town communities in a specific place across time. Twenty-four communities, strung along the entire length of the Ohio River, from the confluence of the Allegheny and Monongahela rivers to the junction with the Mississippi, constituted the area of my research: Ambridge and Aliquippa, Pennsylvania; East Liverpool, Steubenville, Bellaire, Marietta, Gallipolis, Ironton, Pomeroy, and Portsmouth, Ohio; Weirton, Wheeling, Parkersburg, and Huntington, West Virginia; Ashland, Newport, Covington, Owensboro, Henderson, and Paducah, Kentucky; Madison, Evansville, and Mount Vernon, Indiana; and Cairo, Illinois. Pittsburgh, Cincinnati, and Louisville, while not subjects of this study in and of themselves, are integral to it as regional Jewish centers.

There is, I admit, a certain imprecision in the term "small town." Scholars, journalists, government officials—all have used different criteria at various times. Historically, there is a subjective dimension to these definitions; as the size of the biggest cities increases, perspectives change. What might have seemed like a thriving metropolis of ten thousand in 1840 would probably have seemed like a small town to most Americans even in 1940 and certainly in 2005. Also, for a highly urbanized group like American Jews, a place might seem small that is not so perceived by, for instance, white Protestants, who would make up the overwhelming percentage of the community.

Almost all of the towns in my study currently have a population of less than 50,000; most are under 25,000 and always have been. The exceptions are Evansville, Indiana; Owensboro, Kentucky; and Huntington, West Virginia. Owensboro and Huntington have populations of around 50,000, and Evansville of 120,000. They are major regional centers, but not quite major cities, and in any event their Jewish populations have never been large.

In all of these towns, the Jewish population rose, at some point, to a level where communal organization could be—and was—attempted. In only a few did the Jewish population ever exceed one thousand, and only in Evansville did it remain above one thousand for a significant length of time. On the other hand, this is not a story of Jews in towns with only one or two Jewish families. There were numerous towns on the Ohio where Jewish residents numbered two dozen or less; it is impossible to say what percentage of such isolated Jews affiliated with the nearest community, though we know that many did. (Tables of estimated populations, both general and Jewish, appear in the appendix.)

The study of small-town Jewry is critical to understanding the American Jewish experience to the fullest. This has been masterfully demonstrated by Lee Shai Weissbach in his book *Jewish Life in Small-Town America*, which came out just as I was finishing my manuscript. Weissbach's book is a study of the patterns of small-town Jewish life across the country, primarily during the late-nineteenth-century mass Jewish immigration. "Small communities have always been fundamental features in the American Jewish landscape," he writes. "These communities played a crucial role in American Jewish settlement and mobility patterns not only in the era of mass migration, but before and after as well. Indeed, even while a huge proportion of America's Jews lived in major Jewish centers, throughout the late nineteenth century and into the twentieth, the vast majority of the country's individual Jewish communities were, in fact, smaller ones in less prominent cities and towns. It would be a mistake to think that the full story of the American Jewish experience can be told without considering the history of small-town Jewish life."[1]

As Weissbach points out, American Jews have always been urban dwellers in a much higher proportion than the population as a whole, but, especially in the nineteenth century, a significant minority lived at least for a time in a small town. Small-town Jews adapted and accommodated in ways different from urban Jews. Their relations with non-Jews were perforce different, given their numbers; for example, they felt a greater need to present Judaism in terms that non-Jews could understand. Yet not all small towns were alike. The experience of Jews in predominantly Protestant towns located in rural areas was in many ways distinct from that of Jews in ethnically and religiously diverse industrial towns. The exceptions to patterns are intriguing, too, and demonstrate the irreducible and unpredictable effect of individual personalities and group interests. From the point of view of the study of American Jewish history, local studies can both help clarify national patterns and provide greater nuance.

The Jewish communities studied here developed and lived in the context of a specific region. From the colonial era through the nineteenth century, white Americans sensed that the Ohio River Valley was a special place, particularly in terms of the development of American democracy. "There will be no rubbish to remove before you lay the foundations," wrote Manasseh Cutler in 1787 of the upcoming project of settling the Ohio River Valley; both geographically and morally, "the seat of [American] empire" would be on the Ohio. To Frederick Jackson Turner, who tended to identify regions with sequential frontiers, the Ohio River Valley was the first place to manifest what he identified as "the Western point of view," an outlook that is capitalist, democratic, antiaristocratic, antihierarchical, innovative, and individualist.[2] The sense of having once been an important frontier still colors Ohio River Valley life. In Marietta, which constantly advertises its role as the first permanent organized settlement in the old Northwest Territory, the designation "Pioneer" is attached to everything: a savings bank, a bakery, a preschool, a Cadillac dealership.

But this aspect does not, of course, exhaust the possibilities for the Ohio River Valley's regional identity. In a 1909 lecture, "The Ohio Valley in American History," Turner made a more useful observation: "The Ohio Valley is . . . not only a commercial highway, it is a middle kingdom between the East and the West, between the northern area, which was occupied by a greater New England and emigrants from northern Europe, and the southern area of the 'Cotton Kingdom.'" Turner was neither the first nor the last to observe that a variety of factors influenced the development of the Ohio River Valley, but the observation is critical.[3]

The Ohio River has always functioned as both a border and a seam. The present study's focus on towns directly on the river reflects an implicit understanding of the centrality of the river, as both physical and economic entity, in the development of the region. The Ohio has the unique characteristic of having been a politically charged border between slave and free states. Thus the region has felt the impact not just of market forces and natural forces (especially flooding) but also of the heritages of slave labor versus free labor societies and of different forms of government organization.

Yet, as a seam, the river joined the cultural forces of the Upper South and the Deep South coming in from one direction and the Yankee influences coming in from another. Reflecting geopolitical realities, river towns on the north bank participated in the creation of midwestern culture, being among those "communities of the Old Northwest [where] the birth of bourgeois society had been natural and inevitable." The Midwest, particularly its small towns, was *the* middle-class frontier of the nineteenth and early twentieth centuries. But if much of the Ohio Valley is midwestern, southern influences blunted its development into the sort of Yankee diaspora that much more of the Midwest was. The Ohio River Valley was a unique cultural meeting ground.[4]

To what extent has region shaped the American Jewish experience? And to what extent are broader, even national, similarities with respect to other variables (such as community size or economic role) more compelling? The question of the relationship of regionalism to the American Jewish experience is vigorously debated by scholars. This prompts the question of the coherence of the Ohio River Valley as a region. The multistate Ohio River Valley project, of which this book is part, took as its starting point the recognition that "whereas in a previous generation the Ohio River was . . . 'a pregnant term with which to conjure,' we seem to have largely lost a regional consciousness in our own time."[5] But in the nineteenth century, when Jews first settled in the Ohio River Valley, this regional consciousness was alive and relevant.

The Jewish experience and the regional experience reflected and at times reinforced each other in the Ohio River Valley. The antebellum Ohio River Valley's meaning as a cradle of bourgeois America fit very well with the middle-class aspirations and achievements of German Jewish immigrants. Jewish population and institutions proliferated in the Midwest at a much faster rate than in the older settlements of the Northeast.

Most important, the region was increasingly influential in American Judaism. Contemporaries thought that the nineteenth-century Cincinnati Jewish community had "a spirit all its own."[6] The Ohio River Valley was crucial to the development of a new American Judaism in the mid-nineteenth century, not only in the bustling city of Cincinnati that was its center but also in the smaller river towns that shared an optimism about the Jewish future in America and participated avidly in the project of religious reform and unity.

Jews also participated in the construction of regional identity in the nineteenth century. The Jewish merchant is a stock character in popular writings about the Ohio River Valley.[7] Through their participation in the evolution of the small-town middle class, Jews in the nineteenth-century Ohio River Valley helped create a powerful model of American culture. And by building Jewish religious, social, and cultural institutions, they helped build American pluralism at the same time that they transformed Judaism into an American way of life.

Even after the nineteenth century, the effects of chain migration and regional networks of associations enhanced Jewish regional consciousness. Jews in the small river communities were part of a larger economic, social, cultural, and religious community that spanned the region; the patterns of Jewish interactions in the valley expressed a sense of connectedness that clearly defined this as a community. For Jews, who needed the contacts to maintain their Jewish lives, the Ohio River has acted more as a seam than as a border. Jews in East Liverpool and Steubenville, Ohio, keep in close touch with their relatives in Pittsburgh. Jews in Marietta, Ohio, cross to Parkersburg, West Virginia, to attend the Reform temple. Women raised in Ashland, Kentucky, live in Portsmouth, Ohio, with husbands who grew up there. A Jewish family sells its business in Henderson, Kentucky, and moves across the river to the big city of Evansville, Indiana. These intravalley and transriver connections are at least as prominent in the lives of valley Jews as are connections with large Jewish population centers inland.

All of these facets of the Jewish experience in the Ohio River Valley are exhibited within the context of Jewish community, and therefore I have paid most attention to the development of community and to the experiences of Jews in community. It is important to keep in mind that, despite a similar dynamic of Jewish settlement in towns across the Ohio River Valley, different patterns of local development reflected specific economic and cultural characteristics and created a variety of local Jewish experiences. Population and economic growth were necessary but not sufficient for the development of organized Jewish communities. An example: alike in many ways, both growing steadily, Marietta and Portsmouth fostered very different Jewish experiences in the antebellum era. Likewise, the boom-and-bust history of Madison, Indiana, in the 1830s and 1840s was reflected in its Jewish life.

The Jewish narrative of the Ohio River Valley includes the stories of German Jewish immigrants in America, of American Reform Judaism, and of small-town American Jewish culture. While reflecting the diversity of the Ohio River Valley, the stories of various towns also illustrate central issues in American Jewish history and life. For some of these communities, their significance is in their origin and early development, either in the era of central European immigration or the era of mass migration from eastern Europe. Several communities exemplify diverse paths on the often contentious road to religious adaptation and reveal the bumpy process of communal organization. The changing significance of these communities to American Jewish life as a whole is also important, for American Jewry has often undergone, and therefore been called upon to respond to, considerable demographic change. In this respect, too, one can note how Jews pioneered the minority experience in small towns, an experience that by the late twentieth century was being shared by new minorities. In many places in the Ohio River Valley, immigrant Indian and Pakistani physicians now provide a critical percentage of local health-care needs. Local industrial facilities—now owned by multinational corporations—bring foreign-born Asian and Middle Eastern engineers to town.

Floods—of people no less than of water—come and go, leaving a changed landscape. The development of Jewish communities in small towns on the Ohio was related to the development of the valley as a whole. The history of the valley set many of the conditions for—and limits on—the emergence and existence of Jewish communities. Because this is true of all the settings in which Jews have lived in their dispersion across the globe, this study may enable us to participate—at whatever modest level—in the great historical project of understanding the Jewish people.

CHAPTER 1

On the Frontier

On July 3, 1825, the small Jewish community of Cincinnati, Ohio, sent a fund-raising letter to the long-established congregation Beth Elohim in Charleston, South Carolina. Appealing for financial assistance in "the erection of a House to worship the God of our forefathers," the Cincinnatians emphasized both their spiritual closeness to other American Jews, who were all "children of the same family and faith," and their physical distance, "separated as we are and scattered through the wilds of America." "We are well assured," they noted, "that many Jews are lost in this country from not being in the neighbourhood of a congregation[;] they often marry with Christians, and their posterity lose the true worship of God for ever." The Charlestonians were being asked to contribute to the growth not only of Judaism but also of America. As the only Jewish congregation in a five-hundred-mile radius, the Cincinnatians averred, "We have always performed all in our power to promote Judaism, and for the last four or five years, we have congregated, where a few years before nothing was heard, but the howling of wild Beasts, and the more hideous cry of savage man."[1]

More than merely a dramatic fund-raising device, this letter clearly expresses the early Cincinnati Jews' consciousness of their pioneering role as Jews in America's first West. The men who composed the letter had lived in cities in Europe and in North America; their journeys down the Ohio River to Cincinnati, though no longer subject to the threat of Indian attack, were nonetheless long and rough. Cincinnati in 1825 was chronologically far beyond its beginnings as a military outpost, but it was still very far both geographically and psychically from New York and Philadelphia, with their old, wealthy, and secure Jewish populations and institutions. The Ohio River Valley in 1825 was still a *Jewish* frontier, and the Cincinnatians' letter conveys their sense of living on that frontier—on the edge, in a dangerous place where both body and soul were still potentially in peril. Yet it also suggests their optimism about a Jewish future in the West.[2]

What does it mean, America's "first West"? The classic image of the West is, of course, the trans-Mississippi region, the turf of Geronimo and Buffalo Bill, of the gold rush and the Donner party. But there were also earlier, more eastern Wests, like the frontier inhabited by Daniel Boone and Davy Crockett.

In a famous 1893 essay, "The Significance of the Frontier in American History," historian Frederick Jackson Turner crystallized a common conception of the American frontier as "the meeting point between savagery and civilization." Civilization, he argued, is an inevitable evolutionary process whereby society develops from a simple to a more complex state, of necessity expanding across the landscape. The frontier is, in Turner's words, a "meeting point" at "the outer edge of the wave" of ever-expanding civilization; it is the border between something and nothing, between complex social organization and "free land." In America, this wave of civilization "has followed the arteries made by geology" (such as rivers and mountain passes) until "the wilderness has been interpenetrated by lines of civilization."[3]

But Turner's linear model creates a false dichotomy, oversimplifying the experiences of Americans who participated in settling the continent. Previously distinct groups, coming into proximity, lived in zones of social and cultural interpenetration, where no single group was effectively in control. In North America, the struggle for control appeared in different regions at different times: between English and Indians in Massachusetts in the seventeenth century; among British, French, and Americans in the trans-Appalachian West in the eighteenth century; between Mexicans and Americans in Texas in the early nineteenth century; between white Americans and Indians west of the Rockies in the later nineteenth century. These conflicts were a result of intercultural contact and part of a complex process of mutual cultural exchange. The violence of the frontier laid bare the way in which the lives of European, white American, and Indian inhabitants were intertwined.[4]

Settlers themselves did not view their experience in Turner's terms of lines and borders. Certainly, white settlers living in the Ohio River Valley during the Revolutionary era did not see themselves as being the periphery to a center. Once they had moved into the West, they saw their settlement as being "in" American society, a society they superimposed onto a specific area of land. Despite physical proximity, the settlers defined the Indians as "out of" society, giving evidence of their understanding of themselves as occupiers. It was later generations who, ignoring the Indian presence both in fact and in white settlers' imaginations, made American expansion a story of inevitable movement rather than of slow accretion of population and gradual incorporation into an ever-larger American orbit.[5]

Since the frontier is, then, both a place and a process of encounter, a frontier—a "West"—can exist on many levels. It encompasses many cultural phenomena, and the experience differs for different populations. Certainly, the frontier as a place held one meaning for the farmer and one for the hunter—and yet another for the merchant. By 1830, for example, the Ohio River Valley was no longer a frontier, a borderland for American whites; they were securely integrated into the national metropolitan orbit physically, socially, economically, and culturally. But for African Americans, the Ohio River remained a powerful boundary and a symbol of incomplete integration. Before the Civil War, crossing the river symbolized a literal journey to freedom; in the late nineteenth and early twentieth centuries, the trip was an economic, cultural, and psychic journey from peasant agriculture in the South to modern industrial life in the North. African Americans in the Ohio River Valley created their communities in the context of this juxtaposition of freedom and oppression.[6]

The Jewish experience was also unique. The American frontier, argues Jacob Rader Marcus, founder of the field of American Jewish history, created a new Jew. "The Jew *was* different here," he writes. "He had left the 'ghetto' to become a pioneer on the American 'frontier.' . . . If to be a frontiersman is to be a man who dares to hazard, then the Jews as a whole are America's urban frontiersmen par excellence. . . . Here he could be an individual. With opportunity and achievement and the regard of others came self-respect and dignity."[7] But the influence of the frontier on Jews also operated at a deeper existential level. Throughout history, Jews have been in perpetual encounter with other peoples, experiencing changing patterns of accommodation and conflict. In a way, Jews have always lived in a borderland and have had to create Jewish identity in part through a definition of themselves relative to their experience of the non-Jewish world.[8]

The Ohio River Valley was a Jewish frontier—a borderland—long after it ceased to be a national frontier. It was a place where Jews lived between the organized Jewish society of the Atlantic coast cities and the fearful—or delightful, depending on predilection—state of galut (the psychologically loaded Hebrew term for exile). In the valley's cities, Jews experienced their own frontier of Jewish-Gentile contact; through participation in the market and in the civic life of Ohio River Valley cities and towns, they organized their environment into a place they could call home.

"The Ohio River from fifty miles above Muskingum to Scioto is most beautiful. . . . This country may, from a proper knowledge, be affirmed to be the most healthy, the most pleasant, the most commodious and most fertile spot of earth known to European people."[9] This was the promise of the Ohio Valley as one white man, expressing the hopes of many other white men and women, put it. For the European colonial powers in North America, the Ohio Valley was a land full of potential for profits from fur trapping and trading with the Indian nations. For the new United States of America, it was the first West—the first of many national frontiers inhabited by European Americans as they filled up the continent. The Ohio River played a central role in this first frontier drama as the movement of white American settlers along the Ohio established the trajectory for a new nation's occupation of an entire continent.[10]

Much of the earliest white penetration of the Ohio River Valley came from the north. The French, interested primarily in trade, explored the inland waterways between the Great Lakes and the Ohio as early as the 1670s. In the eighteenth century, British traders moved into the valley. The charters of some seaboard colonies, such as Virginia, provided them with sea-to-sea land claims; the colonies exercised these "rights" by moving westward. The Ohio Valley's Indians were also in a state of flux. The Iroquois and other groups entered the valley, both north and south of the river, in the early 1600s, and eventually pushed out the small resident population and established permanent settlements in the early 1700s.

By the early 1750s, the Ohio River Valley encompassed a network of interconnected French, British, and Indian communities, linked through commerce along the waterways anchored by the Ohio. After 1763, when France ceded its North American claims to Britain, the demand for white settlement there increased. Despite Indian resistance and British military restrictions, white migration flowed across Pennsylvania and spilled down from the mouth of the Ohio at Fort Pitt. In 1773, a British general remarked on "the growing 'spirit of emigration'" impelling more and more whites downriver, without regard for legal prohibitions and physical dangers.[11] Also in the 1760s and 1770s, an even larger population movement developed south of the Ohio River. Virginians leaving the Tidewater came through the Shenandoah Valley, the Blue Ridge Mountains, and the Cumberland Gap into the trans-Appalachian counties of Virginia, where they overcame Indian resistance by force.

White settlement of the Ohio Valley was a chaotic process. Virginia's issuance of land warrants to military veterans set off a speculative boom in western Virginia. Legal claims, often staked without an actual physical presence, were contested by those claiming squatters' rights. Freelance surveyors and explorers from Virginia also moved into the Kentucky country, claiming land and organizing settlements; Virginia formalized this claim in 1776 by creating the County of Kentucky. To complicate matters, some white squatters, in defiance of Indian reprisals and British military policy, moved onto the north bank of the Ohio. By the eve of the Revolution, European Americans were settled throughout the Ohio River Valley along with Indian communities, and the situation was highly unstable.

The Revolution cleared up some problems but created others. In the minds of the white American settlers, the concept of liberty that motivated independence from Great Britain also legitimated their desire for open access to western lands. Not surprisingly, then, the end of the Revolution and the acquisition of the trans-Appalachian West by the new United States propelled even more waves of settlers into the Ohio Valley. Operating under the Articles of Confederation, Congress established forts along the river, such as Fort Harmar, at the Ohio and Muskingum, in 1785 and Fort Steuben, about fifty miles west of Fort Pitt, in 1786. Intended primarily as bulwarks against the lingering British military threat, this network of forts encouraged migration by making it seem safer. In the spring of 1788, soldiers counted 308 flatboats passing Fort Harmar, carrying six thousand settlers, three thousand head of livestock, and 150 wagons.[12]

Virginia's program of land warrants created difficulties for white settlement. When Kentucky became a state in 1792, straightening out the land ownership situation was a huge task for the new government. There was no such correction, though, in the trans-Appalachian counties that Virginia retained. The welter of land speculation, absentee ownership, and conflicting claims led to such insecurity about land titles and availability that prospective settlers were loath to take risks there, slowing the area's development.

A different dynamic was at work north of the Ohio. In 1780, the Continental Congress decided that the new nation should take over existing states' western claims, to be "disposed of for the common benefit of the United States, and [to] be settled and formed into distinct republican States."[13] Mindful of the chaos of claims in Kentucky and western Virginia, the new national government intended to proceed deliberately with settlement of the rest of the trans-Appalachian West. In 1787, the cession of state claims complete, Congress passed the Northwest Ordinance, a plan for organizing the territory north of the Ohio River and providing for its eventual division into new states, which were to be "on an equal footing with the original States in all respects whatever."[14] This was not merely a device for doling out land. It was also a project necessary for the United States government to gain control over the West as part of establishing national sovereignty and to articulate its vision of a powerful, well-ordered, prosperous—and growing—new nation.

Thus the Ordinance of 1787 provided an interim governmental structure as the region developed from territories into states, a structure that adumbrated an ethos for American society. It provided for freedom of worship, right of trial by jury, public support of education, and abolition of slavery. American society in the Northwest Territory would be free, egalitarian, ambitious, and religiously tolerant—a fact not overlooked by Jews in the United States and Europe.

Under a preliminary law, Congress had in 1785 authorized a plan for surveying and distributing Northwest Territory land. The first area surveyed was around Fort Steuben, the so-called Seven Ranges, but land sales there were slow. In 1787, the federal government sold several large tracts of land in Ohio territory: to a Massachusetts syndicate called the Ohio Company of Associates, to the eastern-controlled Scioto Company, and to Jonathan Symmes of New Jersey.

The Ohio Company of Associates sent its settlers into the Northwest Territory on the Ohio River; in April 1788, they established the town of Marietta at the confluence of the Ohio and the Muskingum, opposite Fort Harmar. As the first permanent organized settlement in the Northwest Territory, Marietta was the center of the first local government under the Northwest Ordinance. The Symmes (or Miami) Purchase was the second area settled, farther west, at the confluence of the Ohio and Miami rivers. In contrast to Marietta's example, and contrary to the intention of the ordinance, it was settled in a thoroughly unsystematic fashion. The town of Losantiville was established on the Ohio River in 1788, reinforced by Fort Washington in 1789, and renamed Cincinnati in 1790. The ordinance's intentions also failed in the hands of the Scioto Company, which arranged to purchase land just west of the Ohio Company lands in south-central Ohio but fell victim to the financial shenanigans of its agent before the title could be secured.

Indian resistance collapsed in the Ohio territory in the 1790s and in Indiana and Illinois territories by 1820. After 1815, the migration of small-scale farmers across the Ohio River into Indiana and Illinois from the upland south—Virginia, the Carolinas, Georgia, Tennessee, Kentucky—reached major proportions. (Typical of this migration was the family of Tom Lincoln; his son Abraham was born in Kentucky, grew up in Indiana, and then moved to Illinois.)

"The Ohio Valley emerged from the Revolutionary era a distinctive region," writes historian Eric Hinderaker, "united within itself by the powerful experiences of the war years and connected with the United States at large by ties of military and economic dependency."[15] But even as settlers helped tie the Ohio Valley into the network of older states, the colonial history of the region determined the preconditions for differential development within the valley.

The interests of the Commonwealth of Virginia determined the developmental path of the region south of the Ohio, which was in any event less tied to the federal government that supervised the north bank under the Northwest Ordinance. Land speculation had left a residue of vast economic and social inequality. There was little interest among Virginia's governing Tidewater elite for developing transportation routes through the rough terrain to the commonwealth's western counties or for creating new communities there. As a result, the western Virginia counties remained a backwater, a virtual colony of the east. As a state, Kentucky retained the sense of independence it had developed when part of Virginia because of its distance from the seat of state government.

Parts of the Northwest Territory were also affected by southern inheritances. The Ohio River was critical in white migration to southern Indiana and Illinois, but few of these migrants settled on the riverbanks. Southern Indiana and Illinois, unlike southern Ohio, have few navigable streams that go inland from the Ohio for more than forty miles, making the area more appropriate for backwoods southern migrants who preferred the familiarity of subsistence life in the woods to urban life or market farming.

Cultural differences were evident within the upper Ohio River Valley too. In 1789, Arthur St. Clair, governor of the Northwest Territory, remarked,

> The reservation for the Virginia officers upon the Scioto [the Virginia Military District, a set-aside of Ohio land for Revolutionary veterans from Virginia] has turned the attention of many to that part of the country and as soon as it shall be open for settlement, a settlement will be made there where People from that state or from the District of Kentucky where they have been used to the laws & customs of Virginia will predominate. Higher up the Ohio comes the country purchased by the Ohio Company, which being composed of chiefly adventurers from Massachusetts & Rhode Island—the first inhabitants are and will be from those states. Above them are the range of townships that have been sold, and as they have become the property of People from NYork & Pennsylvania & NJersey the Settlements will be made to people from those states.[16]

As intended, the provisions of the Northwest Ordinance helped develop a political and social culture north of the Ohio River that was different from that to the south. The authors of the ordinance and the members of the Ohio Company of Associates shared a federalist mind-set that emphasized strong government, strong property rights, systematic settlement, industry, and republican virtue—in other words, a vision of a well-ordered society explicitly based on New England ideals.

These ideals faced a serious challenge. Political boundaries are artificial, and conditions in Kentucky and other parts of the south led more southerners to cross the river into Ohio. In the late eighteenth and early nineteenth centuries, conflicts arose within the population of white settlers, many of whom were squatters who had left their previous communities precisely because of a dislike of authority and a desire for autonomy. In Marietta, for instance, the governing elite of the Ohio Company struggled—unsuccessfully—to enforce their vision of social order through laws against gambling, drunkenness, cursing, disobedient servants, and Sabbath violation. Elsewhere in the Ohio country, the Northwest Ordinance's intended cultural impact was even less pronounced; society was more individualistic and localistic. This southern attitude prevailed in Cincinnati, which was by early in the nineteenth century the military and financial center of the Ohio River Valley. The city in the early national period was a playground of disorderliness, awash in taverns and other dens of iniquity.[17]

As a result of these diverse influences and cultural clashes, a hybrid culture emerged in the upper Ohio Valley by 1825.[18] The Ohio River could be a border, but it was also a seam—or, perhaps better, a blurred rather than a straight edge. The influence of north on south and vice versa would persist as much as would the distinction between north and south. The malleability of early Ohio Valley society would give many different peoples—including, soon, Jews—a hand in its formation.

By the time white Americans began flooding into the Ohio River Valley in the 1750s, Jews had lived in North America for a century. The seed of the American Jewish community was a group of twenty-three who arrived in the Dutch colonial city of New Amsterdam in 1654. Most of these twenty-three were Sephardim, Jews of Spanish origin whose families had been forced out of Spain in 1492 and Portugal in 1497 by triumphalist Catholic monarchs or whose families had publicly become Christians until they could migrate from the Iberian Peninsula to places where they could again practice as Jews. One favored destination for Sephardim was the Netherlands, especially the burgeoning mercantile port city of Amsterdam, which was also attractive to Ashkenazim, Jews whose medieval ancestors had lived in Germany, who were leaving Germany and Poland in the seventeenth century.

In the generally tolerant atmosphere of the Netherlands, Amsterdam Jews developed a full religious and cultural life and prospered economically. They participated in the burst of capitalist (or protocapitalist) activity that was feeding exploration and colonization around the globe by all of Europe's powers. Some Dutch Jews ventured off to the colonies themselves. By 1645, almost 1,500 Jews resided in the Dutch colony in northeastern Brazil, especially in the city of Recife, which had been wrested from Portugal in 1630. An old threat seemed to be catching up with them, though, as the Portuguese began to reconquer American territories, including Brazil. Most Jews headed back to Holland, but one group of twenty-three decided instead in 1654 to head for New Amsterdam, the Netherlands' North American colony.[19] Within a decade, yet another imperial power overtook them there, but one whose rule had much more beneficial consequences. In 1664, England capped a series of wars with the Dutch by capturing New Amsterdam and, in 1666, all of New Netherland, renaming both city and province New York.

By the mid-seventeenth century, capitalism and Protestantism had changed traditional English social and political attitudes. Not overlooking the potential benefit to the nation of Jewish mercantile experience (and influenced by Puritan philosemitism), Oliver Cromwell's government agreed in 1656 to readmit Jews to residence in England after an absence of more than 350 years. In the eighteenth century, England's growing religious toleration, added to the economic promise of its colonies, led more and more Jews, both Sephardim and Ashkenazim, to migrate to North America from Holland and England and their colonies, or from central Europe via Holland or England.

Most of these migrants were not wealthy; in fact, the London and Amsterdam Jewish communities encouraged their poor to emigrate. But because legal restrictions dating to the Middle Ages prevented many European Jews from entering economic fields other than trade, almost all the migrants had experience in market exchange. Many Jews who came to eighteenth-century North America were Germans from villages and small towns where Jews plied traditional trades as peddlers, shopkeepers, petty moneylenders and pawnbrokers, and cattle dealers and brokers of agricultural produce. These Jews were aware of the economic expansion going on in Europe and of the developing Jewish role in this expansion. In America, they functioned as small shopkeepers, merchants, and shippers, roles vital to the colonies' development. At various times, colonial Jewish merchants traded in—among other things—furs, liquor, soap and potash, grain, livestock, lumber, iron, rice, sugar, firearms, and slaves; they had interests in fishing, whaling, candle making, distilling, shipbuilding, and milling.[20]

Numbering at least one thousand by the mid-1700s, the Jews of British North America resided primarily in Newport, Rhode Island; Philadelphia; New York; Charleston, South Carolina; and Savannah, Georgia, and they traded up and down the Atlantic rim, including in the Caribbean, as well as back and forth to the ports of England and northern Europe. Through business and family connections—which were to a large extent identical—the Jews of colonial British North America sustained their economic and communal lives in an Atlantic context. Jewish community life was multifaceted, if limited in scope. In 1656, a Jewish cemetery was established in New Amsterdam; the first synagogue building in New York was erected in 1731. Communities throughout the Western Hemisphere assisted one another in funding synagogues, obtaining kosher butchers and kosher food, and hiring cantors, teachers, and sextons.

These Americans were pioneers of Jewish history. Free from the rigid legal and social barriers that isolated and in large part defined European Jewish society, American communities were organized on a voluntary basis. But the transition was not easy. Differences between Sephardic and Ashkenazic customs caused conflicts that had to be resolved by compromising or, in some cases, by establishing separate synagogues. Old patterns of authority did not work in the American context; attempts to enforce religious observance (especially Shabbat, the Sabbath, and kashrut, the dietary laws), payment of communal taxes, and acquiescence to communal leaders failed miserably. In premodern Europe, Jews conformed to the rules of the community because it was their only resource for individual needs and for protection from the depredations of the Gentile government. That was no longer the case in America.

The result, however, was not instant assimilation. The intermarriage rate between Jews and Christians in the eighteenth century was high, relative to the European experience and to all other times in American history up to the 1960s. But there were barriers to complete assimilation on both sides, from Gentiles and from Jews, many of whom were traditionally observant and valued their communal bonds. Still, American Jews—less than one-tenth of 1 percent of the population—exhibited a considerable degree of acculturation in their material and intellectual culture and comfort in associating with Christians. The formal portraits of such prominent colonial Jews as Jacob and Abigail Franks display all the wealth and culture of their economic class—and no visual hints that the subjects are Jewish.

Though primarily connected with the Atlantic trade, some colonial Jewish merchants also ventured into trading on America's frontiers, linking the North American interior to Atlantic commerce. In the mid-1700s, New York City–based Daniel Gomez traded in upper New York's Mohawk River Valley and in the wilds of central Pennsylvania. Opportunities soon presented themselves in the trans-Appalachian West. Long before actual Jewish settlement there, Jewish interests were involved. Jewish capital preceded Jewish individuals to the frontier: Jewish capital was flexible, whereas Jewish individuals preferred the psychic protection of the Jewish communities of the coastal cities.

The most active Jewish traders in the eighteenth-century Ohio River Valley were merchants based in Philadelphia, including Nathan Levy, David Franks, Joseph Simon, and Barnard and Michael Gratz. They engaged in trade and land speculation schemes throughout the trans-Appalachian West for more than half a century starting in the 1750s.[21]

The New York–born Franks was the nephew and early business partner of Levy, the first permanent Jewish resident, in 1737, of Philadelphia. Levy and Franks was soon the largest Jewish firm in Pennsylvania. Simon was an immigrant from England who, in the 1740s, moved his base of operations to the hinterland Pennsylvania town of Lancaster. There he started trading local agricultural produce to Philadelphia in exchange for imported textiles and sugar. The Gratz brothers came from southeastern Silesia, an important commercial nexus between western and eastern Europe. Members of their family had preceded them to London, providing important contacts that helped Barnard settle there in 1750. In 1753 he came to Philadelphia to join the firm of Levy and Franks. Michael arrived in America in 1759 after years trading throughout Europe and Asia.

A wide diversification of business interests was an absolute necessity for successful colonial merchants, to protect them against the consequences of the failure of any one enterprise. The Philadelphia group was indeed diversified. Simon was an arms manufacturer and dealer, iron exporter, distiller, precious metals fabricator, financier, bail bondsman, and small-scale slave trader as well as a fur trader and supplier to other western traders. Franks was an army purveyor, shipper, insurance provider, fur trader, mining investor, slave importer, land speculator, international banker, and all-purpose merchant and financier. The Levy-Franks-Simon-Gratz business interests were so structurally intertwined that it is almost impossible to follow all the various partnerships and to separate joint from individual ventures. The Levy-Franks-Simon-Gratz families were also, like other colonial Jewish families, intricately connected by marriage. In fact, the Gratzes became involved in the western trade from contacts made through Simon, a close relative of Barnard's wife.[22]

The western trade took several forms: direct trade with the Indians, supply of other Indian traders, and military supply. Jewish merchants took part in all of these. In 1760, the Philadelphia syndicate—at this point including Levy Andrew Levy (Joseph Simon's partner, nephew, and son-in-law) and William Trent (a non-Jew)—set up a trading facility at Fort Pitt, on the Forks of the Ohio, to trade with local Indians, supply white settlers, and provision the British military. By the late 1760s, the firm had become the principal supplier to

George Croghan, the leading Indian trader in the trans-Appalachian West, and its interests extended throughout the Ohio and Mississippi valleys, the Great Lakes, and the Illinois country.

The frontier trade was a risky business. Simon, Franks, and the Gratzes regularly sustained losses from Indian raids on military and trading posts that they supplied. Deploying their capital flexibly, when the western trade was disrupted by the French and Indian War, the Philadelphians shifted as much of their business commitment to other, less risky ventures as they could. The Gratzes, for example, concentrated on the Caribbean trade. Most of the risks faced by the Philadelphia Jewish merchants in the western trade were financial, but the reality of frontier life came particularly close to home when Levy A. Levy was captured by the Wyandots near Fort Pitt in 1763 and held for a short time. He soon returned to calmer eastern Pennsylvania.

If the frontier wars caused some financial hardships, British military needs created ample opportunity in another aspect of western trade, army supply. Here also, Jewish businessmen provided a wealth of goods and services, including foodstuffs, clothing, hardware, armaments, and transportation. During the French and Indian War, Joseph Simon was provisioner to British troops, and his firm Simon and Henry manufactured and sold rifles. The Franks family, which dealt in military supplies from as early as 1739 through the Revolution, served as England's chief agents for army supply.

The financial risk of military supply, of course, rested on the ability and willingness of governments to pay their debts. The western involvement looked as if it had the potential to pay large rewards when the crown started doling out land grants to traders as compensation for losses in the wars, similar to the compensation in land warrants given to soldiers. Though not themselves remunerated, Franks, Simon, and the Gratzes in the 1760s and 1770s became owners of considerable acreage around Pittsburgh through land transfers from George Croghan in payment of his debts to them.

Like many others, these merchants soon became involved in the flurry of land speculation. Throughout the 1770s, Joseph Simon and a non-Jewish partner, John Campbell, held mortgages on much of the land where present-day Louisville is located. The Gratzes bought and sold their own and others' land and land warrants in western Virginia and Kentucky. In the early 1770s, they and David Franks bought shares in the Grand Ohio Company and its "grand"—and ultimately unsuccessful—Vandalia scheme for the Indiana and Illinois lands, and helped finance others' involvement.

During the Revolution, the Gratzes and Simon pulled back somewhat from the western trade as a financial precaution, though they did do some business in provisioning American troops at Fort Pitt and supplying the military expeditions of George Rogers Clark in the Illinois country. Like many other American Jews, they had pro-patriot political loyalties, and they signed on to (though, like most American merchants, occasionally violated) patriot boycotts and nonimportation movements. (David Franks, however, was a loyalist, which proved the end of his career in America.)

After the Revolution, only the Gratzes retained an active interest in the Ohio Valley. When George Croghan died in 1782, Barnard and Michael Gratz were owners, through sale or bequest, of large amounts of his original property, including more than 60 percent of Croghan's original two-hundred-thousand-acre grant around Pittsburgh. They were also the executors of his estate. Michael's sons Simon and Hyman, still based in Philadelphia, financed trading ventures in Pennsylvania, Kentucky, and Indiana.

In addition to trading, the Gratzes were involved in Ohio River shipping, taking advantage of the huge increase in traffic sparked by white migration to the Ohio River Valley. In 1793, Jacob Myers, a Gratz business associate (and probably a relative), advertised in the *Pittsburgh Gazette* the availability of river transport from Pittsburgh to Cincinnati. The best advertisement that could be made for his boats was their safety: Ohio River traffic in the 1790s still fell prey to guerrilla attacks from Indians and to the predations of white outlaws. Myers's advertisement averred that he had "taken great pains to render the accommodations on board the boats as agreeable and convenient as they could possibly be made" and promised that "every person on board will be under Cover, made proof against rifle or musket balls [with] convenient port-holes to fire out of." Likewise, "conveniences [i.e., toilet facilities] are constructed in each boat so as to render landing unnecessary, as it might be at times attended with Danger."[23]

The Gratz family retained its western land interests for the long term, although not all of the investments paid off. In the mid-1770s, David Franks and the Gratz brothers invested in the Illinois and Wabash land companies, which had elaborate plans for the settlement of what became the states of Indiana and Illinois. The United Illinois and Wabash Land Companies' claims on this project were finally settled (by being invalidated) only in 1823, a great disappointment to the Gratz heirs. Barnard's daughter Rebecca wrote to her brother Benjamin while he was in Indiana in 1819, "The Illinois and Wabash claim, of which I have all my life heard so much, seemed like a romance—I never expected to see anything but maps and pamphlets of the subject. . . . But since it has proceeded so far—I catch a little of the mania and frame wishes for its success."[24] These wishes came to nothing, of course. The Gratzes did retain some land interests in western Pennsylvania until the late 1830s, gradually selling off the holdings.

So by the early national period, the financial involvement of the colonial Jewish merchant families in the Ohio River Valley had essentially petered out. All of these merchants had spent time in the valley, keeping track of their various enterprises. A sometime partner of Simon, Mordecai Moses Mordecai, and his wife, Zipporah, operated a tavern near Pittsburgh from 1775 to 1779, but they returned east. None of the members of the Philadelphia families actually lived in the valley, either before or even after the Revolution, with the exception of Benjamin Gratz, who settled in Lexington, Kentucky, in 1819.[25]

The Ohio Valley—the whole trans-Appalachian West—was not yet a place for acculturated but observant Jews. These Jews were urbanites, comfortable in the provincial European-derivative culture of America's eastern cities; they had a busy social circle and were concerned for the proper education of their children. Joseph Simon and the Gratz brothers kept kashrut and Shabbat and observed the holidays carefully, practices for which residence in Philadelphia—or in the nearby small community of Lancaster—was more congenial.

For the Gratz-Simon-Franks-Levy combine, the frontier was a place to be exploited. Its land was a commodity, not a potential home. It would be newer immigrant Jews who would form the bases of permanent Jewish communities in the Ohio Valley in the first decades of the nineteenth century. The establishment of regional markets, the rise of urban centers on the river, and the beginning of Jewish settlement in the Ohio River Valley were linked phenomena. As the region became more urbanized, more economically integrated, and solidly joined to the East Coast base of the American nation—that is, as its frontier character diminished—Jewish interests and regional opportunity coincided.

In the early nineteenth century, the Ohio River Valley was incorporated into the national framework politically, economically, and culturally. Political integration was accomplished as the territories north of the Ohio River were incorporated as states into the federal structure: Ohio in 1803, Indiana in 1816, and Illinois in 1818.

The Ohio Valley was rapidly developing a market infrastructure. Connecting Pittsburgh, Cincinnati, and Louisville to St. Louis, Natchez, and New Orleans, the Ohio River and its links to the Mississippi and Missouri rivers were the major features of this market development. Population grew and economic life diversified along this trade axis, especially after the Louisiana Purchase secured the route all the way to New Orleans and the Gulf of Mexico. In turn, transportation technology accelerated population growth and economic diversification. Steamboats appeared on the Ohio and Mississippi in 1811, making upriver transportation almost as easy as downriver. By 1820, there were sixty-nine steamboats on the river; by 1830, more than four hundred. Along the Ohio—"a river of opportunity," in historian Darrel Bigham's phrase—new transportation technology, new transportation facilities, and the spread of commercial agriculture reinforced one another.[26]

The expansion of markets also demanded increasing skills from merchants, who played several vital roles in the developing Ohio River Valley. In the late eighteenth century, merchants were a link, via material objects, with the commercial East. As settlement and activity increased, merchants also functioned as middlemen for surplus agricultural produce (and therefore also as shippers) and eventually as informal bankers, through brokering and the extension of credit.

Manufacturing developed along with trade. In Jefferson County, Ohio, for example, in the first decade of the nineteenth century, there were factory-style weaving and fulling, whiskey distilling, shipbuilding, and manufacturing of rope, iron, candles, and paper. Pittsburgh's iron rolling mills were set up in the early 1800s to minimize the need to ship heavy goods from the East. Trade, manufacture, and urbanization were the components of a dynamic synergy, especially in the valleys of the Ohio's tributaries: the Muskingum (Marietta), the Scioto (Portsmouth), and the Miami branches (Cincinnati). Even before 1820, Cincinnati had small-scale manufactures based on local products, such as a wool-carding mill, flour mills, and breweries. Each city and town developed an economy based on its unique location and resources, but commerce was the linchpin of urbanization.[27]

The market economy, with its demands for centralization and bureaucratization, stimulated the development of cities in the Ohio Valley. Pittsburgh had the advantage of its location at the confluence of the Allegheny and Monongahela rivers. Two major military roads converged at Fort Pitt, making eighteenth-century Pittsburgh a natural setting for trade and defense, a gateway between the eastern commercial cities and the trans-Appalachian frontier, and an important intraregional hub. During the large migrations to the Ohio Valley in the 1790s, local merchants outfitted the migrants, and as the migrants created new settlements in the Ohio Valley, Pittsburgh became as important to valley commerce as Philadelphia or Baltimore.

Cincinnati became the military and financial center of the Ohio River Valley after 1790, when Northwest Territory governor Arthur St. Clair moved the territorial government there from Marietta. In 1800, Cincinnati's population was only about 750, but with the coming of steamboat traffic, it expanded explosively. By 1815, the city had emerged as the most important commercial center of the Ohio River Valley; by 1830, it was the dominant city of the West, with a population of 25,000. Louisville prospered as a transshipment point around the rocky Falls of the Ohio; it grew more slowly than Pittsburgh or Cincinnati but boomed with the arrival of the steamboat, reaching a population of 4,000 in 1820 and more than 11,000 in 1830.

The success of those towns that are now major cities was not inevitable. Settlers came to the West for opportunities in towns as well as for opportunities to farm, and the ability to attract these settlers was critical to a town's success or failure. For example, the relatively late settlement in southern Indiana and Illinois and its particular conditions—that is, the dominance of agriculture and the backwoods character of residents—militated against the development of river cities despite the area's proximity to the Mississippi.

Competition for urban greatness was quite conscious—and quite fierce. In the early nineteenth century, the fiercest and most notable rivalry in the upper Ohio Valley was between Wheeling, Virginia, and Pittsburgh. Wheeling had the advantage of a deeper river channel that was easily navigable year-round, a consideration that had dictated its selection as the Ohio River terminus of the National Road in 1811. As Pittsburghers grumbled that Wheeling was only a "miserable Virginia country town," the Virginians (in the tongue-in-cheek phrase of one observer) were "doing nothing but walking about on stilts, and stroking their chins with utmost self-complacency" and civic pride. The seriousness of Wheeling's challenge was only temporary; Pittsburgh outpaced it by 1820.[28] In contrast to the rest of western Virginia, however, the northern panhandle around Wheeling did urbanize and industrialize. Before 1800, Wellsburg had some manufacturing, and an iron furnace on the site of what is now Weirton began operations in 1794. Wheeling was the panhandle's preeminent manufacturing center by the mid-1830s.[29]

Within the larger region, rivalries also flourished between Pittsburgh, Cincinnati, and Louisville, with considerable impact on the hinterlands. By 1830, some Ohio River small towns were already eclipsed by urban neighbors and settled into positions of dependency in the metropolitan area. Newport and Covington, Kentucky, opposite Cincinnati, grew only as adjuncts to the Ohio city. Jeffersonville and New Albany, Indiana, settled into the shadow of Louisville. Urban population growth rates vastly outstripped overall state rates. Between 1810 and 1830, Ohio's population grew four times, but Cincinnati's grew twelve times. Kentucky's grew 50 percent; Louisville's, 650 percent. Pennsylvania's barely doubled; Pittsburgh's tripled.

Despite the rise of large cities, the most ubiquitous urban center—the one with which Americans were most likely to be familiar—was the small town. Throughout the Ohio River Valley, numerous small towns served as regional centers for professional services, agricultural supply and trade, and, increasingly, consumer goods. Often similar in physical appearance, the towns offered typical business establishments: a town miller, blacksmith, wainwright, saloon, and dry goods store. They were centers of education and religion, diffusing standards of taste, manners, and morals to the countryside.

Towns were central to the transformation of the Ohio Valley from a frontier to an integrated part of the American nation. Merchants, tied to regional and national trade networks, linked local communities with communities and perspectives beyond themselves. With their priorities controlling local government, they were the most influential men in town, more so than the professionals—even ministers. The needs of stable community and economic development were both served by the discipline of bourgeois values.

"In no city in the Old Northwest," assert historians Andrew Cayton and Peter Onuf, "did bourgeois values take hold as early or as fully as in Cincinnati." By 1825, as Cincinnati became a manufacturing as well as a regional market center, the Ohio River Valley gave birth to the nineteenth century's classic liberal, bourgeois society.[30] This society would be particularly receptive to America's growing Jewish population. By 1830, the Ohio River Valley no longer seemed like a frontier to most white Americans. But it was just coming into its own as a Jewish frontier.

Between 1780 and 1820, the Jewish population of the United States nearly doubled. From a possible maximum of 1,500 in 1790, it expanded to a probable maximum of 2,750 in 1820.[31] At the same time, the total population of the United States increased two and one-half times, growing from 3,929,000 in 1790 to 9,638,000 in 1820, in some of the largest annual percentage growth spurts in history.

Most of the national growth was natural increase; with Europe in an upheaval of wars, only about 250,000 immigrants came to the United States between 1783 and 1815. With the decline of Atlantic commerce under international political pressures in the early national period, America was less attractive to that cosmopolitan segment of Jewry that was riding the wave of gradual modernization and emancipation in England, France, and a few parts of Germany.

But the small Jewish population of the early-nineteenth-century United States was ever more comfortable living in the American environment. In the absence of Atlantic commerce, American Jews found niches as local merchants and artisans. They rebuilt communities dislocated by the Revolution and built new ones. American culture had more and more influence on Jewish religious practice, from the architectural styles of synagogues to the adoption of written constitutions for congregational governance. Jews' confidence in America was confirmed by the fact that, despite opposition and the necessity for extensive lobbying, Jews enjoyed political equality in all but a few jurisdictions by the mid-1820s.

Colonial America's Jewish residents were true pioneers in the creation of modern Jewish identity. In historian Eli Faber's words, they were "exploring the implications of living where Jews were not the objects of debilitating hostility. They were among the first Jews in the modern world to experiment with acculturation [and] to envision a synthesis in which Jewish tradition could combine with elements of the surrounding culture without being undermined."[32] Perhaps it is not surprising that in the early national era, American Jews, being themselves on the frontier of world Jewry, were not yet on the physical frontier of the nation. But soon the urban frontier of the trans-Appalachian West began to create in Jews' minds the vision of new opportunities. At the same time, conditions for central European Jews changed in ways that motivated mass emigration. The confluence of these factors brought Jews to settle in the Ohio River Valley, to establish homes, businesses, and congregations, first in the cities and, increasingly, in the promising small towns.

In Ohio, the population doubled between 1810 and 1820, with the majority of the population in the southern river valleys. These circumstances provided the setting for the settlement of Jews in Ohio and the establishment of America's first Jewish city of the West—Cincinnati. By 1830, Cincinnati represented all the possibilities emerging in the new western urban centers. According to a contemporary observer, immigrants—at least "those classes which seek large towns" (such as Jews, though the observer did not mention them specifically)—found it "the largest, the most increasing, and the most convenient."[33] The Jewish community of Cincinnati was among those permanent cultural institutions in the West that marked the end of the frontier stage of Ohio's history.

In his seminal 1900 article, "The Jewish Pioneers of the Ohio Valley," Rabbi David Philipson undertook to find the first Jew in Cincinnati. He was able to locate one Benjamin Leib (or Lape), who, upon his death in 1821, requested a Jewish burial, but apparently Leib had not lived as a Jew, had not publicly identified as such, and had married a non-Jew and raised Christian children. Concludes Philipson, "There may have been other instances like this in the recently founded town, of Jews by birth who were not known nor recognized as such, but we possess no knowledge nor record of them." It is evident, though, that in Cincinnati, as in other cities and towns on the western frontier, Jewish business travelers sojourned in the region well before any Jews settled permanently. These transients left fleeting hints: a name in a newspaper advertisement in 1814, another advertisement for a physician and medical salesman in 1816.[34]

Cincinnati's first identifiable Jew was the English-born Joseph Jonas, a watchmaker and silversmith who, then in his mid-twenties, immigrated in 1816 and arrived in Cincinnati via Philadelphia in 1817. Like those of many immigrants, Jonas's imaginings of America were inspired by books; he claimed that he had been influenced to settle in the Ohio River Valley by descriptions of the area that he had read as a young man. At least in his later years, he viewed his Jewish pioneering in terms analogous to the visions of the Puritans: Cincinnati, in "the Great West," was "a new resting place for the scattered sons of Israel . . . [where] a sanctuary should be erected." Jonas was convinced that it would be possible to make a life as a Jew even in such isolated circumstances. In this, he set a pattern for many in small Jewish communities in the ensuing years of Jewish settlement throughout the expanding United States.[35]

Jonas apparently accepted with good graces his status as a tourist attraction for curious local non-Jews; in a famous story, he was visited by a local Quaker who, intrigued to meet a real, live Jew for the first time in her life, looked him over several times before declaring, "Thou art no different to other people!" Jonas came to a conclusion that many small-town Jews would later reach: America's opening society offered opportunities to recast the Jewish social position. "From the experience which we have derived by being the first settlers . . . ," Jonas later wrote, "we arrive at the conclusion that the Almighty will give His people favor in the eyes of all nations if they will only conduct themselves as good citizens in a moral and religious point of view."[36] In America, one need not struggle under the burden of an inherited, despicable reputation. The assumptions of equality gave the individual—and by extension the group—a blank slate. The biblical rhetoric of "finding favor" should not be misinterpreted as obsequiousness. A new society did require of Jews a new approach to life. But far from cravenly and fearfully caving in to American Protestant values, early-nineteenth-century Jews sought only the freedom offered to nearly everyone to make his own place.

Within a few years, a number of other English Jews settled in Cincinnati. Joseph Jonas's brother Abraham arrived in 1819; in the 1820s, they married sisters, Rachel and Lucia Seixas, daughters of Gershom Mendes Seixas, New York City's first professional Jewish communal leader.[37] Also among the earliest arrivals to the city, Rabbi Philipson found, were two English immigrants with some experience on the frontier, David and Eliza Israel, who used the surname Johnson in the United States. David's brother had been an Indian trader on the Whitewater River in east-central Indiana during the 1810s. After two years with him there, the Johnsons repaired to the more cosmopolitan setting of Cincinnati in 1820.

Despite the lack of a traditional minyan (quorum of ten men required for communal prayer), this small group of Cincinnati Jews held High Holidays services in the fall of 1819 and celebrated Passover together in the spring of 1820. Eighty years later, Rabbi Philipson admired the "great desire and zeal which must have possessed them to participate in such a service."[38] One need not disparage the pioneers' spiritual devotion to suggest that their zeal was also driven by their utter confidence in the future of their new settlement. Small Jewish communities organized with the expectation that they would grow; as they began the process of integrating Jewish psychic space into the physical space of the frontier, the optimism of America led them to see themselves as seeds of a greater enterprise.

Cincinnati soon fulfilled this promise. In the 1820s, migrants from Germany supplemented the small English and Dutch Jewish community. The 1825 Cincinnati city directory listed twelve individual Jewish men, of whom nine were English, one German, and two native born. Four of the men described themselves simply as merchants, and two others listed commercial specialties, auctioneer and grocer-tobacconist. Two were watchmakers, one a tailor, and one a distiller, rounding out an occupational profile that would come to be typical of nineteenth-century American Jewry.[39]

In 1824, a formal congregation, Bene Israel, was organized; in 1830, it was legally incorporated, with eighteen men listed as incorporators.[40] In 1836, the congregation dedicated its first building, the first synagogue in the Old Northwest. This was accomplished with generous financial support from Beth Elohim of Charleston, South Carolina, and other American and English congregations. That dramatic fund-raising letter of 1825, offering vicarious participation in the expansion of Judaism and of the American West, was evidently effective.

The pioneering role of Cincinnati's Jewish communal organization is even clearer when compared to the slower start of the communities in the other two major Jewish cities of the Ohio Valley, Pittsburgh and Louisville. There was a transient Jewish population in the Kentucky city even in the first decade of the nineteenth century, but it was the 1830s before there were as many as ten families. Pittsburgh's early-nineteenth-century population apparently included only a few Jews, mostly men married to Christian women. "So far as is known," a historian of Jewish Pittsburgh concludes, "not a single Jew who wished to be recognized as such lived in Pittsburgh for more than two months during the fifty years between 1788 and 1838."[41]

In the 1820s, the pace of Jewish immigration to the United States began to quicken. From about 2,700 in 1820, the American Jewish population grew by 1830 to about 4,000, including some immigrants, mostly young men, mostly from England and Holland. Immigration accelerated dramatically in the 1830s. The numbers tell the story: 4,000 Jews in the United States in 1830, and 15,000 in 1840. By the 1830s, a mass migration was underway, as central European Jews, buffeted by contradictory forces of economic and social change, sought new lives across the Atlantic.

Though Cincinnati attracted the most Jews, a small number of Jews began in the 1820s and 1830s to filter into other areas of the Ohio River Valley. According to the 1830 Ohio census, one Mordecai Levy was in Brown County, on the Ohio River east of Cincinnati; perhaps he peddled out of Cincinnati. Peter and Reuben Israel were in Belmont County, just west of Wheeling and Pittsburgh; perhaps they peddled from one of those two cities. The earliest documented Jewish residents of southeast Indiana, appearing in the 1830 census, were the Isaac Levy family of Switzerland County. The family had emigrated from Hungary and consisted of a young couple and an older one, perhaps parents of the younger. A few individual Jews may have entered what is now West Virginia as early as 1825.[42]

By 1840, there were Jews throughout the Northwest Territory, which included the Ohio River states of Ohio, Indiana, and Illinois. When later American Jews surveyed the trajectory of their acceptance into American life, the Northwest Ordinance of 1787 stood out to some as having been particularly significant.[43] Since the ordinance applied the federal guarantees on freedom of religion to this territory and to the states that would be carved from it, Jews in the Northwest Territory were from the beginning in a position of political equality. But social change in the Ohio River Valley, as well as legal change, provided the suitable context for Jewish community growth both north and south of the river in the egalitarian climate of the antebellum era.

In the early national period, it was market relations within the Ohio Valley and between the valley and the Atlantic seaboard that transformed the European Americans' frontier by decisively linking the region to the nation. Before the 1820s, Jewish merchants were on the eastern end of these links. As Jews moved west, they came to inhabit a frontier of new market encounters and new social, cultural, and religious interpenetrations. A frontier of religious and cultural pluralism emerged as the geographical frontier receded and groups met and dealt with one another in the expanding market.

As a Jewish frontier both sociologically and psychologically, the nineteenth-century Ohio River Valley was an important locus for the creation of American Jewish identity. The environment of the valley would prove particularly hospitable to a new wave of Jewish migrants to America. In the small towns there, European Jewish immigrants became American businesspeople, American bourgeoisie, American citizens, and American Jews.

CHAPTER 2

From Europe to the Ohio River Valley

Between 1750 and 1850, the political, social, and economic developments identified as modernization began to dramatically change the traditional life of European Jewry.[1] Soon, too, westward movement rearranged the demography of European Jewry, just as, beginning with the Northwest Territory, westward movement on the North American continent reshaped the United States. Together, these phenomena helped create new Jewish communities in the Ohio River Valley, for ultimately, the roots of the valley's small-town Jewish communities can be found in the small towns of southern Germany and eastern France.

The European Jews who chose migration to America in the nineteenth century were heirs to a Jewish culture that had existed for centuries in a situation of complete subservience within medieval Christendom. Medieval European Jewish society was not merely physically and socially separate from the surrounding Christian society; legally, Jews had no intrinsic rights of residence or livelihood and were subject entirely to the needs (especially economic), religious passions (or religious politics), and even mere whims of local rulers. Massacres and expulsions were tragically commonplace.

Throughout these upheavals, European Jewish communities held together because, as separate corporate entities within Christian feudalism, they were permitted to develop their own internal governance, a comprehensive system known as the kehillah. Ironically, the restrictions placed on Jews fostered an atmosphere in which self-help and provisions for mutual security sustained a strong and positive Jewish identity. The kehillah organized every aspect of Jewish life—education, social welfare, religion, communal harmony—and was the representative of the community to the Gentile authorities. Individual Jews' contact with non-Jews was perforce limited to economic and political activities; Christians seemed as alien, and as innately inferior, to Jews as Jews seemed to Christians. For premodern Jews, subservience in the temporal sphere was the price paid for living in an unredeemed world.

Better times on earth did not, of course, arrive in an instant, but Jews as a group were—again, ironically—in a good position to take advantage of new economic developments precisely because of their medieval disadvantages. Laws prohibited Christians from money lending while prohibiting Jews from virtually all livelihoods *except* money lending and commerce. It might even be said that European Jewry was protocapitalist—because Jews were permanent temporary residents, their capital had always been more liquid and their economic strategies more flexible. From the Rothschilds to the street peddlers, Jews' traditional economic activity became progressively destigmatized as money and markets expanded. "The more that money was recognized as vital to the state's economy," historian Jacob Katz explains, "the more bargaining power the Jew had."[2]

Enlightenment political philosophy and the radical spiritual individualism of Protestantism also began to slowly change Gentile thinking about the possibilities of the Jewish position in European society. By the 1770s, calls for equal Jewish civil and political rights were heard more regularly throughout Europe. Formal emancipation came to the Jews of France by acts of the revolutionary National Assembly in 1790 and 1791. By the early eighteenth century in both England and Holland, the only restrictions on Jews were those borne also by other religious nonconformists.

But for every two steps forward, there always seemed to be one step backward; a tension of acceptance and rejection characterized the precarious path of Jewish emancipation and integration at the start of the nineteenth century. Legislation might change the legal status of Jews, if in a patchwork fashion, but Gentile attitudes still molded the reality of Jewish social status. Despite the revolutionary promises, the many Jews in the eastern French province of Alsace still faced residential and occupational restrictions—and Alsace was home to the majority of French Jews. In the northeast German kingdom of Prussia, select Jews had lived since the late seventeenth century as Schutzjuden (protected Jews). Decrees of 1812 affirmed Jewish citizenship and abolished various remaining restrictions but excluded from these rights the numerous Jews in Poznań (Posen), a province in far eastern Prussia.

With the rise of Napoleon, Jews in many areas gained citizenship, though it was often a second-class version. But after Napoleon's defeat, Germany remained a patchwork of small states, most of which quickly revoked Jewish legal gains and even in some cases reimposed medieval restrictions such as residential constraints. The harshest and most insidious laws were in Bavaria. Starting in 1813, the government capped the number of Jews in each town and required Jewish communities to keep a *matrikel* (list of residents); only if a place became vacant on that list could another Jew—even one born there—qualify as a legal resident of the town. The matrikel was in place until 1861.

Jews in Poznań finally became Prussian citizens in 1848. Jews in Bohemia and Moravia were freed of marriage restrictions in 1849, though not until 1867 did the Austro-Hungarian Empire affirm basic Jewish political rights. Whipsawed for more than three-quarters of a century between competing political forces, Jews attained full legal emancipation only with Germany's unification into a single empire in 1871. By the end of the nineteenth century, German Jewry emerged as an economically successful and acculturated middle class.

The Jewish population of central Europe was distributed unevenly. Estimates for 1815 counted at least 25,000 in Alsace; about 50,000 in Hesse, the Rhein Valley, and especially the Franconian provinces of Bavaria; about 65,000 in Poznań and east Prussia; and between 500,000 and 600,000 in Austria-Hungary. Though politically separated, these various Jewish communities were all the inheritors of Yiddish-speaking medieval Jewry. (Yiddish—literally, "Jewish"—is a Germanic language with many Slavic and Hebrew loan words, written in Hebrew characters.) In particular, Alsatian Jews, under French rule since the cession from Germany in 1648, were closely connected economically, culturally, and familially with Jews still under German rule on the other side of the Rhein. As Europe modernized, Jews in all of central Europe encountered—to different degrees—new challenges to their survival skills. The inheritance of this adaptation was brought to the Ohio River Valley by young, largely German and Alsatian Jewish immigrants.[3]

The basic pattern of Jewish life in the early nineteenth century was similar throughout central Europe. Having historically been forbidden residence in cities, Jews in the early nineteenth century were concentrated in small towns and villages, in small communities—mostly of fewer than three hundred Jews—where they often constituted 10–25 percent of the population. They spoke regional dialects of Yiddish, gave their children basic Jewish educations (though with different content and expectations for boys and girls), and were generally unacquainted with—and initially not particularly interested in—the modern secular culture developing across Europe. Within their close-knit societies, Jews were socially and religiously conservative.

Their occupations were those followed by their ancestors, mostly variations on peddling and petty trade. Many Alsatian Jews were middlemen for farmers, brokering agricultural products and livestock, and in fact largely controlled the livestock trade and butchering. Earning a living involved all members of the family, and Jewish women were used to taking part in commerce.

Some Jews could not earn a living at all, with up to 20 percent subsisting as itinerant Betteljuden (beggar Jews).

When emancipation came, it was, for the bulk of the Dorfjuden (village Jews), largely a condition with only potential, not immediate, advantages. The term "emancipation" suggests a liberation that was only part of the picture, for Christian Europe was not interested in what we would today call multiculturalism. It was interested in "improving" Jews to the point of fitness for citizenship, and the strategies for "improvement" were not far from coercion. The kehillah was abolished. To gain acceptance, Jews were expected to abandon traditional commercial occupations for more "normal" and "productive" ones, such as agriculture and artisanry, and to dispense with the primitive "Orientalism" of their religious practices in order to make Judaism a Western religion—and, presumably, eventually to convert to Christianity. In the face of these attitudes, Jews took up the challenge to adapt to government demands and attain access to greater opportunities while retaining their own values and sense of identity.

One example was education. Jewish communities had always run their own educational systems. The ḥeder was the elementary school for basic instruction in Judaism. Better students went on to yeshiva, an advanced school for talmudic studies. Girls traditionally received far less education; they were generally taught a bit of Hebrew and Yiddish reading in separate schools or by tutors, often using texts specially edited for women.

Throughout the 1820s, German states attempted to enforce Jewish acculturation by making secular German elementary education compulsory for Jewish children. Jews adapted the new government requirements to their own needs by starting their own schools, which, while significantly different from traditional ḥedarim (not least in that they taught in German rather than Yiddish), still included Jewish religious instruction. In Alsace also, Jews took advantage of new opportunities for secular elementary education for both males and females. Jewish children began to attend secular secondary schools in disproportionate numbers, and yeshiva education declined rapidly. But Jews did not precipitously abandon their traditional language, only gradually adopting German or French as their primary language.

Jews also effectively resisted the demands of many emancipation laws regarding their occupations. Their resistance to the pressure to become artisans or farmers was ultimately a boon. Jewish emancipation was simultaneous with the industrialization of Europe, when the officially promoted "productive" occupations of agriculture and crafts lost status and commerce gained in importance. Jews, who had never been able to own land, were able to deploy their liquid capital into investment in the new economy; the familiar and the new were synthesized as Jews became shopkeepers, wholesalers, and manufacturers.

Religious change too was undertaken cautiously. As part of the project of "improving" Jews for integration into Christian society, reform of Jewish religious practice was either encouraged or discouraged by government intervention—whichever course the state considered would better discourage Jewish continuity. The Bavarian government at first encouraged reform, with the idea that this might make Jews more "normal" (that is, like Christians), but suppressed it in the 1840s. The opposite happened in Prussia, where an 1823 edict made Jewish religious reform illegal and an 1844 repeal of the law made it possible.

The Jewish community, itself divided on the idea of religious reform, had to find its path within the parameters set by outsiders. Sensing their own shifting cultural identity as they came into contact with European norms, many Jewish communities, large and small, experimented with modest changes to synagogue aesthetics and decorum, such as German-language sermons and formal choral—though not instrumental—music. (Traditional Jewish law forbids the playing of musical instruments on Shabbat and holidays.) But most Dorfjuden were not exposed to more thoroughgoing and ideological reforms until after 1850. In France, where Judaism was regulated through a state religious structure that already included Catholicism and Protestantism, the rural Alsatians deliberately resisted efforts at religious modernization promoted by the urban Jewish elites of Paris who dominated the establishment.

This, then, was the cultural baggage that the German and Alsatian Jews brought to America, to the Ohio River Valley. Modernization created changes that enabled young Jews to consider the possibility of a life different from that of their grandparents and even their parents. But economic, social, and political conditions continued to create enormous obstacles to realizing those possibilities. Legal emancipation, it turned out, was no guarantee of acceptance by Gentiles, or even of fair treatment. Even the mundane ambition to marry and have a family was frustrated for young Bavarian Jews by the matrikel.

One option available to Jews in some regions was migration to the city, particularly a growing regional city. Yet another option for poor and frustrated young Jews was emigration. Increasing thousands of Europeans were crossing the Atlantic to the United States; millions were reading and talking about the place. Did it make sense to wait in Europe for equality and opportunity, Jews asked themselves, given the inconsistency and ambivalence of governments and the persistent antisemitism of the Gentile populations? Or did it make sense to take advantage of the new option: life in America? For many, emigration would be their "substitute for emancipation."[4]

Between 1830 and 1914, more than 200,000 Jews from Germany entered the United States, the bulk of them in the mid-nineteenth century; the total central European Jewish immigration from 1820 to 1880 was about 150,000.[5] In the early years, the immigration was largely poor, young, single, and male. But though most migrants were poor, they were not the Betteljuden, who had the least means to plan and execute such a journey. Often, the migrants were younger sons, with a smattering of secular and Jewish education and usually a trade or experience in a family business. Families with small children were always part of the mix, as were single women, who were equally affected by economic conditions and marriage restrictions. The proportion of women increased through the years of the migration, since many women were followers rather than leaders in a family or village chain migration. Chain migrations of families were often necessary because, unlike Gentiles, Jews did not have land they could sell to finance a voyage. Someone had to go to America first and earn the money for the rest to follow. Typically, the most employable was sent first, followed by his younger teenage brothers, and then their sisters.

Non-Jewish Europeans were of course also migrating in large numbers at the same time, as populations soared and traditional farm economies collapsed. But though Jewish migration was contemporaneous with non-Jewish migration, it was a different phenomenon. The unique pressures on Jews show in immigration statistics. Jews were 4 percent of the total number of Germans who immigrated to the United States between 1830 and 1914, though they made up only about 1 percent of the German population. Specifically, Jews made up 5 percent of Bavarian emigrants, though they were only 1.5 percent of Bavaria's population. Four times as many Jews as non-Jews left Poznań.[6]

It may have been easier for young Jews to uproot themselves than it was for non-Jewish Germans who lived on the land. Though restricted in their residence, Jews had many connections to other communities through business and family. As one scholar, Steven Lowenstein, describes it, "In South Germany peddlers and agricultural middlemen traveled from village to village, buying and selling whatever they could, and often returning home only once a week. . . . Hard as this type of life could be, it broadened the geographic horizons of Jews in a way not available to non-Jews, not even to the more stationary non-Jewish storekeeper."[7] When the opportunity for migration—whether to the European cities or to America—arose, Jews could more easily envision their options. Experience left them better prepared for migration .

Jews who arrived in this wave of immigration pioneered the mercantile frontier in the Ohio River Valley's small towns. Where did they come from? Their hometowns in southern Germany and in Alsace mostly had fewer than 2,000 residents, including several hundred Jews who constituted a significant proportion of the total population. For example, Maroldsweisach in the Unterfranken province in Bavaria, home to Matthias Schloss and Mayer Seidenbach, who settled in Portsmouth, Ohio, had a population in 1837 of 550; Jews were one-quarter of the total. In Hainsfarth, in the Schwaben province in Bavaria, hometown of Simon Oberdorfer of Henderson, Kentucky, the 440 Jewish residents in 1837 were more than a third of the town's number. Likewise, Schmieheim, in Baden-Württemberg, hometown of Isaac Wolfe Bernheim of Paducah, Kentucky, and later of Louisville, was more than one-third Jewish in 1825; Buttenhausen, also in Baden-Württemberg, hometown of Isaac Weil of Portsmouth, was more than half Jewish. Many of these towns had Jewish community schools that provided at least primary secular education in the German language. For example, Gunzenhausen's Jewish school opened in 1827 with 36 students from the local Jewish population of about 250; Sarah Seidenbach of Portsmouth, Ohio, who was born in Gunzenhausen that year, probably attended in the 1830s.[8]

Statistics on the decline of the Jewish population in these towns over the nineteenth century show the dramatic effects of migration to the cities and emigration to America. By 1890, Maroldsweisach, for example, had only 39 Jewish residents in a total population of 501, and by 1910, Hainsfarth had only 91 in 999; the percentage of Jews in these villages had slipped to below 10 percent. Similar declines were evident in most Bavarian, Rheinland, and Alsatian villages.

With the influx of immigrants from German-speaking lands, the Jewish population of the United States mushroomed. From about 15,000 in 1840, it more than tripled in a decade, to about 50,000. By 1860, the numbers had increased again, anywhere between 150 percent and 300 percent; that year there were at least 125,000—and more likely 150,000 or even 200,000—Jews in the United States.[9]

Jewish settlement in the United States in the nineteenth century, outside those cities that had had Jewish communities since colonial times, tended to follow a standard pattern. A young Jewish man—or several men in partnership—would establish a store or stores, often after a period of peddling. They would bring their brothers into the business as it grew. When practical, they would marry and start families; these families would be the nucleus of Jewish communal life. Jews maintained regional and national networks of family, business, and religious connections, which supported their family formation, commercial progress, and religious life.

Jews did not choose their places of American settlement randomly. In the first half of the nineteenth century, there were very good reasons to choose the Ohio River Valley. One of those reasons was the growth of Cincinnati, which in the 1830s was the exemplar of America's urban energy in the West and home to an increasing number of Jewish permanent residents. Cincinnati's antebellum growth was directly related to its location on the Ohio River. From about 1820 through the 1850s, steamboat traffic made the city the major commercial center above New Orleans. Canals built in the 1820s and 1830s reinforced this role by easing the shipment of agricultural goods from the city's Miami Valley hinterland. Much of the city's prosperity, therefore, was related to its role as an agricultural center, especially for pork-packing plants—indeed, the city was nicknamed "Porkopolis." Heavy industries such as iron soon developed, as did the legal profession, banking, science and medicine, publishing, literature, art, and music. Cincinnati offered high-quality, progressive public education—even, after 1848, to its black citizens, though in a segregated system—and was home to a liberal Christian evangelical antislavery movement.[10]

In 1820, Cincinnati's total population was already 9,642; in 1840, it was 46,338; and in 1860, it was 161,044. Among those swelling the population were many central European (mainly German) Jewish immigrants. In 1840, there had been only about 1,000 to 1,500 Jews in the city. In 1850, there were 2,500 or 3,000, and in 1860, perhaps as many as 10,000—about 5 or 6 percent of the total population.[11]

Cincinnati's Jews were for the most part not directly involved in any of the principal industries of the city, but they developed a new one for a city on the make—the garment trade, a traditional Jewish occupation. By the 1850s, when the Singer sewing machine was introduced, Cincinnati manufactured more ready-made men's clothing than all other western cities combined, and this enterprise was dominated by German Jews. Involved in all aspects of the business—manufacture, distribution, and sales—Jews virtually monopolized the wholesale segment, owning sixty-five of the city's seventy wholesale firms. The garment business by 1860 supported—directly or indirectly—the vast majority of Cincinnati's Jews. It supplied the livelihood of many non-Jews as well, for Cincinnati garment manufacturers employed some 950 people in their factories and more than 9,000 home-based pieceworkers, mostly non-Jewish women. Significant proportions of the Jewish community made their living in other traditionally Jewish occupations, especially dry goods, liquor, and cigar making.[12]

Louisville and Pittsburgh also established themselves as important river cities in the antebellum era and began to attract Jewish populations, though they lagged behind Cincinnati in this respect. With fewer than 400 residents in 1800, Louisville was not even the largest city in Kentucky (Lexington was) until the steamboat boom of the 1820s lifted its population from 4,012 in 1820 to 11,345 in 1830. In the 1830s, there were about 15 adult Jewish men in Louisville, and by the mid-1840s, there were several dozen families. In 1860, Louisville's total population of 68,033 was still less than half of Cincinnati's; the Jewish population of more than 1,000 was a substantial increase over earlier years but still far behind Cincinnati's.[13]

Pittsburgh was even slower in its Jewish development. The general population grew substantially: from 1,565 in 1800 to more than 12,000 in 1830 and almost 75,000 in 1860. But little of this population was Jewish. In 1839, there were only 5 Jews in the city (all men), and in 1850, only about 35 men and women. The total for 1860 was probably around 350 or 400 individuals. In fact, Pittsburgh's developmental lag was related to the importance of water transportation generally and the Ohio River specifically. Cincinnati, dominating the Ohio, and Cleveland, dominating the eastern Great Lakes, gained significant Jewish population in the early nineteenth century because of the commercial attractiveness of their accessibility by water. Only in the late 1840s, when improvements to river transportation—specifically, locks and dams on the Ohio's feeders and better steamboats—were introduced did many Jews stay permanently in Pittsburgh, virtually all of them making their livings from retail, especially dry goods and clothing.[14]

In the Ohio River economy, smaller cities and towns, especially those on the north bank of the upper valley, also held some promise. The 1833 *Ohio Gazetteer* listed four river towns—Steubenville, Marietta, Gallipolis, and Portsmouth—in addition to the city of Cincinnati as among the state's major centers. In 1840, only three Indiana towns had populations over 2,500, and two of these—Madison and New Albany—were on the Ohio (the third was Indianapolis). Ten years later, these were still the three largest towns in the state, and two other river towns, Evansville and Lawrenceburg, also had grown to more than 2,500. On the south bank of the Ohio, the northwestern Virginia city of Wheeling grew by leaps and bounds in the antebellum years, from 1,500 in 1820 to 5,000 in 1830 and more than 9,000 in 1840. In 1860, with a population of 16,000, Wheeling was the second-largest city in the state, trailing only the capital, Richmond.[15]

The steamboat economy invigorated smaller places as well by integrating them into regional markets. Even the smallest villages directly on the river developed local ports that served as portals to the surrounding inland area and as stopover points for long-haul traffic. Once again taking advantage of opportunities provided by market expansion, Jewish immigrants from German-speaking countries began to settle in small towns along the Ohio River and to try their hands at business in what seemed to be a promising environment. They were familiar and comfortable with small-town life. By 1860, Jews were widely—though not evenly—settled in the valley, on both northern and southern banks, in towns of all sizes.

Jacob Rader Marcus was fond of saying that there is no such thing as "the first Jew" anywhere—there was always someone earlier.[16] This is, of course, a hyperbolic way of pointing out the difficulty of making such assignments. There was no "first" until one or more Jews settled in a town and stayed long enough to be captured by a census or other vital record, to be listed in a city directory, or to appear in a newspaper story or business advertisement.

In large part, the difficulty in identifying firsts is that so many German Jewish men (who were the majority of the early Jewish immigrants) took up itinerant peddling as their first occupation on arriving in America. Most of these were young men, ages eighteen to twenty-five, who peddled for less than five years, forming and re-forming partnerships with relatives or acquaintances. The staples of their trade were clothing, dry goods, and notions—needles, thread, buttons, lace, ribbons, and so forth. As merchants, they were the outermost edge of a complex distribution system. East Coast importers and wholesalers shipped goods to merchants and manufacturers in regional centers like Cincinnati, who in turn provided goods directly to peddlers, local retail outlets, and retail outlets in smaller towns (who also supplied peddlers as well as selling directly). Peddling was a particularly useful and viable business when a region's population was spread out in tiny villages and on isolated farms within a few days' traveling distance of supply centers. A very small town might have a general store, but nonperishables like dry goods were most efficiently supplied through the peddler's occasional visit.[17]

In some American communities, up to half of Jewish men were peddlers who were based in the town but spent most of their time on the road selling to residents of villages and farms. The job required little, if any, capital, since goods were usually provided on consignment from a wholesaler, and the expansion of the American population into new areas meant there was always a need for men who could take goods to customers. The peddling life was a crash course in American culture, as the immigrant peddler struggled with the English language and stayed overnight in the unfamiliar surroundings of whichever farm he happened to be near.

Since peddlers spent most of their time on the road, tracing their earliest sojourns is difficult or impossible. Some, such as Isaac Wolfe Bernheim of Louisville, who later became very successful, left memoirs in which they identified the areas in which they peddled.[18] Sometimes public records expose facets of this peripatetic life. A list of licenses issued to peddlers in Jefferson

County (Steubenville), Ohio, in the 1840s and 1850s includes many Jewish men who later lived elsewhere in the Ohio Valley, especially in nearby Wheeling, Virginia. Also on the list of licensees were Charles Coblenz, who later opened a store in Marietta, Ohio, and Joseph Dinkelspiel, who later lived in Marietta; Madison, Indiana; and Louisville, Kentucky.[19]

But many peddlers left insubstantial traces at most; their presence as a class may be prominent in descriptions of frontier life, but their individual lives slip through the fingers of posterity. One such peddler was Moses Frank, who died in Gallipolis, Ohio, in 1834. His birthplace, birth date, and date of immigration are unknown, and the Gallia County record of his estate lists no heirs. Both his personal effects and his business capital were included in the estate list, an odd assortment of property that included five silver watches, two beaver skins, seven sets of Catholic church ornaments, one buffalo robe, ten old vests, fifteen shirt collars, one gourd, one shotgun, one trunk, and assorted items of personal clothing. These belongings were all sold off to local merchants. Frank also left some cash in silver and gold coins and a $1,000 "draft on the bank of the United States payable in new York to Morris Franck [*sic*]," perhaps a credit issued to him by a New York merchant as an advance for purchasing a stock of merchandise.[20]

Other peddlers were "lost" in a different way. Hyman Lazarus was already forty years old when he emigrated from southern Germany in 1818. Basing himself in the river town of Marietta, Ohio, Lazarus peddled throughout the area before opening a store in the tiny Muskingum River town of Malta, where he married a Christian woman, raised Christian children, and was eventually buried in a Christian cemetery.[21]

As was the case for other modes of commerce, the Ohio River and its tributaries were the lifeline of Jewish peddling, providing easy transportation of goods; in turn, the peddlers' business infused energy into the river towns. Peddlers were always looking for new sites, hoping to be the first to establish a fixed store in a location. As populations grew and concentrated, many Jewish peddlers decided that they might as well be that first storekeeper, or among the first. At least two Jewish families were in Evansville, Indiana, in the late 1830s, and at least two Jewish men lived in Owensboro, Kentucky, by the 1840s. Wheeling, Virginia, had a Jewish population of several dozen before 1850. In the 1850s, Jewish merchants appeared in Lawrenceburg, Aurora, New Albany, and Mount Vernon, Indiana; Ironton, Marietta, Bellaire, and Steubenville, Ohio; Paducah, Kentucky; Parkersburg, Virginia; and several towns in southern Illinois, including Cairo, Golconda, and Metropolis. In many cases, the evidence for these "firsts" is also the evidence of their concern to maintain Jewish connections, by subscribing to Jewish newspapers such as the *Israelite*, published in Cincinnati.[22]

For some up-and-coming peddlers, the small river towns were stepping-stones to careers in the cities. This was the case with Jacob Elsas, whose rise to wealth and reputation in Cincinnati contrasts markedly with Moses Frank's lonely ending in Gallipolis. Elsas was born near Stuttgart, Germany, in 1818 and came to the United States at the age of twenty. Setting out from Philadelphia, he peddled throughout Pennsylvania, Virginia, Kentucky, and Ohio before opening a dry goods store in Portsmouth, Ohio, in 1842. Elsas's business success was substantially aided by his marriage into the Fechheimer family, originally from Mitwitz, Bavaria. Either in Philadelphia or Cincinnati, Elsas met the Fechheimer brothers ("a distinguished group of peddlers," in the description of one historian), and in 1845, he married their niece Jeannette. In 1848, Elsas closed his Portsmouth store to merge his business with that of his wife's family in Cincinnati, where he became a successful merchant and an important leader in both the Jewish and general communities. Numbers of other men later quite prominent in Cincinnati's Jewish community followed the same path, including Henry Mack and Jacob Seasongood.[23]

As exemplified by the career of Jacob Elsas, a critically important factor in Jewish economic success in the nineteenth-century United States was the structure of mutual supports created by the conjunction of economic and family relations. Regional networks of Jewish peddlers were protocommunities; both in cities and towns, obtaining credit and accumulating supplies and stock, and on the road, the activities of peddling created connections between and among individuals and groups. They might meet at regional supply houses or hotels, preferably those run by Jewish merchants, such as Dryfuss' Commercial Exchange and Eating Saloon in Portsmouth, Ohio. As the peddlers created a close-knit group through business and marriage partnerships, the groundwork was laid for organized Jewish communal life. These networks of kinship and business helped populate the Ohio River Valley with Jews while linking them to a regional community.

Especially in the early years of community formation, it was not unusual to find in specific American towns concentrations of landsleit (Jewish individuals originating from the same place). Significant examples of landsleit from a specific German town are found in Cincinnati, which absorbed most of the young Jews of Demmelsdorf, Bavaria, and in Cleveland, the destination for most migrants from Unsleben, Bavaria. In both these cases, the migrant groups were composed of several core families. In the more expansive usage of "landsman" (the singular form of "landsleit"), to cover regions with many Jewish towns, or even entire provinces, the concentrations were even more noticeable. Before the Civil War, more than half of Cincinnati's Jews were from Bavaria, and half of these—or more than one-quarter of all Cincinnati Jews, including the Fechheimers—were from the Oberfranken (Upper Franconia) province. Through use of communal supports, the Oberfrankener Jews became the most successful and stable businesspeople in the city.[24]

Among the small towns on the Ohio River, Gallipolis, Ohio, stands out as a remarkable example of the landsman phenomenon. As the name—"city of the Gauls"—suggests, the town was founded on French immigration: a short-lived settlement of refugees from the French Revolution organized, under dubious pretenses, by the Scioto Company in 1790. Though the original core of settlers dispersed, the town continued to attract French immigrants, and the first Jews in Gallipolis were also French, grouped around several Alsatian families: the Mochs, the Franks, and the Emsheimers.

Though one Abraham Moch was the patriarch of one of the wealthiest Jewish families in eighteenth-century Alsace, the Ohio family seems not to have been related. The Ohio Moch family's home was the village of Schwindratzheim, between Strasbourg and Hagenau. Three brothers, Moses, Elias, and Leopold, arrived in the United States as teenagers in the late 1840s, first settling in Cincinnati, then coming to Gallipolis in the early 1850s. Sadly, young Leopold drowned in the Ohio River there in June 1854. Elias and Moses were soon joined in Gallipolis by their first cousins, Emma and Abraham Moch, who grew up in the Alsatian village of Uhlwiller, a few miles north of Schwindratzheim. Emma and Elias were soon married. In 1862, Abraham married Rosa Baer of Cincinnati; soon after Rosa's death in 1876, Abraham, left with five children ages six through thirteen, married Amelia Blatt, who was also from Uhlwiller via Cincinnati.[25]

The five Frank siblings, a sister and four brothers, were all born near Strasbourg in the 1810s and 1820s. (It is not evident if they were related to peddler Moses Frank, who died in Gallipolis in 1834; Frank was a common Jewish last name.) The eldest brother, Henry, led the way, immigrating in the early 1840s. One Frank brother and one Moch brother ran a clothing store together in Gallipolis in the late 1860s; continuing a traditional Alsatian Jewish trade, Leopold Frank supplemented this business with cattle dealing. In the late 1850s, the Franks and Mochs were joined in Gallipolis by the four Emsheimer brothers—John, Michael, Jacob, and Joseph—who came via Cincinnati. The Emsheimers hailed from the village of Soultz-sous-Forêts, less than twenty miles from the Mochs' village.[26]

Other Jews from Soultz-sous-Forêts settled in the Ohio Valley, including Samuel Klein and Stephanie Heymann Klein of Wheeling. Another group of

Alsatian landsleit settled in Portsmouth. Louis Levi and Gottfried Mayer, partners in clothier Levi and Mayer, and other Mayer relatives, Henry and Isaac, were all from the town of Niederseebach, only a few miles from the Emsheimers' hometown. Still another group of Alsatians settled downriver from Cincinnati in Madison, Indiana. In 1850, the Jewish population there was almost all from southern Germany and Bohemia. By 1860, more than a third were Alsatian. The Sulzer and Ach families, as well as the Geismars and Wormsers, were from one village, Grussenheim; other members of the Ach family had lived in nearby Mackenheim. These families had not only Jewish but also Catholic landsleit, and Raphael Sulzer even sponsored one young Catholic man for immigration to America.[27]

The small Ohio River towns are remarkable for this concentration of Alsatian Jews. Particularly noteworthy is that in mid-nineteenth-century Cincinnati, Alsatian Jews were only about 5 percent of the total Jewish population. In some of the smaller places, such as Gallipolis and Madison, the percentage was much higher.

If Alsatian Jews were overrepresented in the small Ohio River towns, those from Poznań were underrepresented. Between 1816 and 1870, about 11 percent of the Jewish population of Cincinnati was Posener, but only a few Poseners were in the small river towns. Two of those few were men who came to Henderson, Kentucky: Herman Schlesinger, from Breslau (now Wroclaw, Poland), and Morris Metz, from Lissa (now Leszno, Poland).[28]

The reason for the overrepresentation of Alsatians and the underrepresentation of Poseners may lie in their differing European experiences. Jews in Alsace were, even more than Bavarians, used to living in village settings as a small minority surrounded by Gentiles. Poseners, on the other hand, tended to be from more urban settings where they were a larger percentage of the population. It is also the case that in many American Jewish communities, imported cultural differences created effective barriers between Germans (mainly Bavarians) and Poles (mainly Poseners). In many American cities, each group had its own congregation and charitable and social organizations. Perhaps Poznań Jews, feeling Bavarian Jews' condescension, simply chose not to try small towns, where Bavarians predominated so much more than in the cities.[29]

Although the Alsatians were most conspicuous, there were throughout the Ohio River Valley groups of landsleit from German regions as well. Many Jews around Paducah, Kentucky, in the lower Ohio Valley, were related, part of a large network of Dreyfusses, Weils, and Cohns. These families came from villages in the German state of Baden-Württemberg, on the east bank of the Rhein River, less than ten miles from the border with Alsace. Samuel Dreyfuss left for America in 1850; his six younger siblings—three sisters and three brothers, some of whom were quite young when Samuel left home—followed him to Kentucky. Numerous cousins and their spouses lived throughout the lower Ohio River Valley. As with the Mochs, first-cousin marriages reinforced family ties.[30]

The European origins of Jews in the small river communities (at least those for whom information is available) were rather more diverse than those of Jews in Cincinnati. However, though there was not a huge representation from a single province, the plurality—perhaps even majority—do seem to have been Bavarians. Sharing a common culture brought from the Jewish villages of southern Germany and Alsace, Jews in the small Ohio River towns created community among themselves and with the community of Cincinnati.

As the de facto Jewish capital of the antebellum trans-Appalachian West, Cincinnati was thus also the hub of new networks created by contacts within the city, between the city and small towns, and among the small towns. For example, commercial connections between Cincinnati and Portsmouth were close, and several Portsmouth stores were essentially branches of city firms. Isaac Freiberg operated two stores in Portsmouth in the late 1850s, one for "Staple & Fancy Dry Goods, Cloaks, &c" and another for "wh[olesale] Liquors, Wines, &c.," but he went back to Cincinnati by 1860. Clothier Levi and Company was owned by Louis Levi of Portsmouth and Lazarus Bloch of Cincinnati. Similarly, with the firm of Friedman and Eisman ("Wholesale & Retail Clothing, Dry Goods, Boots, Shoes, Hats & Caps &c"), Morris Friedman resided in Cincinnati, while partner Leopold Eisman lived in Portsmouth and ran the store there. The latter firm used the urban connection as a marketing tool, advertising in the *Portsmouth Times* that "being in immediate connection with our extensive establishment at 72 Pearl street, Cincinnati, we are enabled to sell at much lower rates."[31]

Some of the family groups that were the core of small-town communities coalesced after immigration, in the flux of Cincinnati's large and fluid German Jewish immigrant community. This seems to have been the case with an extended family group that settled in Pomeroy, Ohio, in the late 1850s. Bernhardt (Bennett) Baer and Sophia Mayer married in Cincinnati in 1857 before coming to Pomeroy; since he was from Württemberg and she from Hesse, they probably met in the city. So too, most probably, did August Mayer (Sophia's brother) and Mina Herzog, also a Bavarian. The nuclear families augmented themselves with other relatives: Sophia and August's brother Daniel came along to Pomeroy, as did Mina's brother Max.[32]

Intermarriage with Christians was not uncommon in the early years of the central European Jewish immigration, as we saw with Hyman Lazarus in the 1820s, when young men frequently found themselves adrift in America without extended family or Jewish communal supports. As the immigration increased in both size and demographic diversity, there were more Jews with whom to build families and communities. The connections with Cincinnati were particularly critical for single men who were living in small towns with few or no Jews, because the city provided social contacts that could turn into marriage prospects. There were numerous examples of marriages between small-town men and city women: Harry Frank of Gallipolis and Fanny Silverman of Cincinnati in 1851; Aaron Cahn of Gallipolis and Carlina Hellman of Cincinnati in 1854; John Emsheimer of Gallipolis and Rachel Gotz of Cincinnati in 1861; Joseph Kaufman of Vevay, Indiana, and Bertha Fickert of Cincinnati in 1864; Joseph Klaus of Cairo, Illinois, and Fanny Lauer of Cincinnati in 1865; Abraham Stern of Parkersburg, West Virginia, and Rachel Liebschutz of Cincinnati, also in 1865.[33]

The shift from peddling to storekeeping aided Jewish family and community stability. Family formation laid the foundation for the formation of Jewish communities in the small river towns, as marriages and the birth of children increased small-town Jewish populations and created more social stability. In Gallipolis, for example, the Emsheimer family expanded rapidly. Michael Emsheimer married Esther Weikersheimer in New York City in 1863; their son Henry was born in Gallipolis in 1868. In 1864, Esther's sister Fanny came from New York to marry Michael's brother Jacob. Brother Joseph and wife Fannie Siegel had a daughter, Jeanette, in Gallipolis in 1859. In February of the following year, John and Rachel Emsheimer also had a daughter, Belle. Samuel and Caroline Silverman, who moved to Pomeroy by the mid-1850s, quickly populated Pomeroy with their eight children born between 1854 and 1867; Samuel's brother Simon and sister-in-law Esther added three children.[34]

The examples of spouses and siblings who moved to small towns highlight the fact that village-to-city was not a one-way street. But equally important was the emerging network among the small towns. Dispersed along the Ohio River, immigrants created new connections that extended and strengthened the support systems provided by the urban Jewish infrastructure.

Business and family could connect Ohio River Valley Jews to more than one small town, and some Jews moved frequently from town to town. Samuel and Benjamin Wise maintained stores in both Parkersburg and Ironton in the 1850s. Joseph and Fannie Emsheimer lived in Wheeling, West Virginia, in 1862, then in Gallipolis until about 1875, and then again in Wheeling from at least 1876 on. Sometime in the late 1860s, Michael and Esther Emsheimer also moved to Wheeling, where at least one other family from their hometown of Soultz-sous-Forêts lived. Harry Frank originally settled in Ironton, then had businesses in Gallipolis, Cincinnati, and again in Gallipolis. In the late 1870s, Simon and Esther Silverman moved to Gallipolis—the home of his sister Fanny Silverman Frank—but a grown son remained in Pomeroy.[35]

Though secondary to Cincinnati, Louisville was important to Jews in the small river towns in the same ways that the larger Ohio city was. It was a local destination when leaving a small town, as for the Brandeis brothers when they left Madison, Indiana, in the early 1850s. The city provided business connections, for example, to Isaac Mayer, who maintained businesses both in Louisville and in Portsmouth, Ohio. It also served as a social resource for small-town Jews, for example, for Henry Baldauf, a Bavarian immigrant living in Henderson, Kentucky, who married Louisville native Josephine Dinkelspiel in the 1870s. Some of these social resources were provided by family connections. Members of the Dinkelspiel family had been among the earliest Jewish settlers in Louisville and also in Madison, Indiana. Eventually, many more family members settled in Louisville. The peripatetic Joseph Dinkelspiel was there around 1840; he even served as the first regular "minister" of the congregation there. But he was also at various times in Madison, in Marietta and Steubenville, Ohio, and perhaps in Metropolis, Illinois.[36]

Jewish immigrants increasingly found it congenial to stay permanently in smaller towns. In the late 1850s, after something under ten years in Gallipolis, Elias and Emma Moch moved to Cincinnati, where Elias became an important businessman in the pioneering Jewish retail clothing firm of Heidelbach and Seasongood and a leader in the Jewish community. But Elias's brother Moses and cousin Abraham remained in Gallipolis. Twenty years after Jacob Elsas began his business in Portsmouth, brothers Leopold and John Eisman chose the town, already home to a dozen Jewish families, to develop theirs. The Eismans were Bavarians, born in Forchheim, in the Oberfranken province, Leopold in 1834 and John in 1839. Leopold came to the United States in 1860 at age twenty-six and brought his younger brother a year later. For two years, they peddled from different home bases—New York City, then New Brunswick, New Jersey, and Parkersburg, (West) Virginia. In 1863, Leopold opened a men's clothing store in Portsmouth in partnership with Morris Friedman of Cincinnati; John came into the business a few years later. Within a few years, both brothers were married to local Jewish women: Leopold to Fannie Ronsheim (whose family, like the Fechheimers, was from Mitwitz) and John to Fannie Meyer and, after her early death, to Eliza Dryfuss. The families lived out their lives in Portsmouth, active in the Jewish community; Leopold died in 1886, Eliza in 1892, and John in 1913.[37]

Henry Baldauf, born in 1839 in rural Bavaria, came to the United States at the age of fourteen and peddled his way to the Ohio River town of Brandenburg, Kentucky, where his older brother Morris had settled in the late 1840s or early 1850s. After some time peddling in the river towns, the Baldauf brothers opened a store together in Brandenburg, followed by one downriver in Cloverport. They soon found themselves farther downriver in Henderson, where they settled permanently.[38]

In the second half of the nineteenth century, as Jews in small towns built community, the web of regional connections continued to be important. A historian of Jewish Cincinnati relates Jewish identity and regional identity in a summary comment: "To be a Jew in Cincinnati meant not only that one might pray in a different place than non-Jews, or belong to a separate set of organizations. Rather, one's Jewishness was also an important factor in how one happened to have settled in Cincinnati and how long one remained, of where one resided and worked within the city, and how one made a living."[39] A similar dynamic prevailed in the small river towns: Jewishness was an important factor in why and how one came to the town, how one made a living, and how long one stayed.

Old World landsman loyalties were superseded by Jews' new identities as residents and boosters of their towns. As Jews in the small towns created their own institutions and were incorporated into small-town American culture, their relationship to the cities changed. To some extent, the Jews in the small river towns would always be the "country cousins." But increasingly, they identified as Jews of (for instance) Portsmouth, rather than Jews of Cincinnati residing in Portsmouth.

The shift from peddling to shopkeeping was critical to the transformation of European Jewish immigrants into an American middle class. In Europe, Jews, forced into trade, suffered from Christianity's traditional bias against commerce. In antebellum America, by contrast, commerce was not simply tolerated but honored. In one historian's trenchant formulation, "The very economic behavior that had made [Jews] pariahs in Alsace, Bavaria, Posen, and Bohemia made them solid, respectable citizens in an America that admired the self-made businessman."[40] Being a businessman in a small river town could provide security for an immigrant German Jewish man, and this security nurtured a bourgeois identity for German Jewish families. Former peddlers were the core of the commercial middle class throughout the Ohio River Valley.

Even as small-town Jews worked hard to become middle-class Americans, their historical experience of separateness and the reality of their difference continued to bind them together as Jews. If their small Ohio River towns were not as thickly Jewish as their European homes, the Ohio River Valley as a region still provided a supportive context for the growth of Jewish families and the development of Jewish communities, whose institutions could sustain Jews on their frontier of new encounters with a rapidly changing American society.

CHAPTER 3

Finding and Founding Communities

During the first half of the nineteenth century, the Ohio River Valley experienced rapid population and economic growth. With Cincinnati at its hub, the area from Marietta, Ohio, downriver to Evansville, Indiana, grew especially rapidly. Between 1830 and 1860, the populations of river counties on this stretch of the Ohio, both north and south of the river, grew by triple-digit percentages—in some cases more than 300 percent.

Governments fostered this growth with public works development. In 1811, the federal government began construction of the National Road to connect the populous East Coast with the emerging trans-Appalachian West. The road began in Cumberland, in Maryland's western panhandle, and was linked on the east by existing toll roads to Baltimore and by the Potomac River to the newly built federal capital at Washington DC. The entry point to the west was the Ohio River, which the road reached in 1818. Many states in the 1820s and 1830s created artificial waterways to augment the system of natural streams, following the example of New York and its famous Erie Canal. Ohio River cities and towns were linked by canals with interior markets, creating an infrastructure that laid the basis for the later development of railroads.[1]

And Americans' embrace of rail technology was remarkable. After early experiments in the 1820s, entrepreneurs laid track with alacrity: By 1840, the United States had almost three thousand miles of rail, by 1850 about nine thousand, and by 1860 about thirty thousand. In Ohio, between 1841 and 1850 alone, the state chartered seventy-six railroad companies. By the 1850s, all of the major Ohio River ports had direct rail connections with all major markets; the rails operated in synergy with the rivers and canals that continued to transport a considerable share of the region's goods.[2]

The three decades before the Civil War were critical for the development of the towns and cities on the banks of the Ohio River. Moving from farming to agricultural processing and manufacturing, the region on both sides of the river experienced the ups and downs of the volatile antebellum economy. In this dynamic setting, the Ohio River Valley offered ample opportunities for persistent and lucky entrepreneurs.

One of the most appealing tales of nineteenth-century American Jewish history is that of the simple immigrant peddler from a German-speaking land who rises to great fame and fortune as a department store magnate. The sheer magnitude of the success of such men as Adam Gimbel, Edward Filene, Lazarus Straus, and Jacob Kaufmann gives their stories a special salience in the narrative of American Jewry. These men are extreme examples of a phenomenon that shaped not only the economic standing of American Jews in the nineteenth century but their social and cultural profile as well.

Throughout the United States, thousands of young immigrant Jewish men rose to financial success and civic prominence through careers in retailing. The American society that they encountered was transitioning to a market economy, experiencing, in fact, a "market revolution."[3] These immigrants found themselves in the right place at the right time with the right skills. Starting with extremely modest resources, they negotiated the intricacies of the American market economy with imagination, flexibility, and persistence. Within a generation, many were exemplars of the American ideal of the self-made man.

Geographic mobility was the rule rather than the exception among antebellum immigrants; most left their port-of-entry cities within a few weeks of arriving. They often made several stops before settling down permanently, as they learned to match their skills with the opportunities available in various local economies. Sample contemporary local records provide some insight into the shape and extent of Jewish economic mobility in the Ohio River Valley. Between mid-1840 and the end of 1853, some 440 individuals and partnerships registered for peddling licenses at the Jefferson County courthouse in Steubenville, Ohio. About 30 percent of these were Jews, obviously far out of proportion to their numbers in the general population. With these data, it is possible to track the rise of representative men from pack peddling in the countryside to store ownership in the city, investigate their economic strategies, and learn something about the centrality of Jewishness in their creation of a new life in America.[4]

The profile of the Jewish peddlers in Jefferson County was distinctly different from that of the non-Jewish peddlers, most of whom were English and Irish immigrants. Of the Jewish peddlers licensed in this period, three-fourths were pack peddlers; that is, they walked their routes carrying their goods in a backpack. The remaining one-quarter had a horse (or, less frequently, two horses) and a wagon, equipment that stepped them up to the next level in the peddling hierarchy. Of the non-Jews, a majority—though a smaller one, somewhat over half—peddled on foot, and about one-quarter by horse and wagon. The rest, about one-sixth of all non-Jewish peddlers, sold from flatboats on the Ohio River and its tributaries. There were apparently no Jews who had boat stores.

Part of the reason for the lack of Jewish participation in the water-borne trade was no doubt the higher cost of such an enterprise. First, of course, was the investment in the boat itself; keeping it licensed cost a good deal more. In the 1840s and 1850s, a three-month license to peddle by foot in Jefferson County cost from $2.50 to $3.00. If one had a one-horse wagon, it was $5.00; with two horses, $7.00 to $7.50. A boat license for the same time period, however, was $15.00. One had to be sure of a higher profit margin to make the investment in a boat store a wise one.

There were also strategic marketing considerations. Jewish pack peddlers of course traveled by boat throughout the Ohio River Valley. But when they disembarked, they had far more flexibility than they would have had with a boat store in creating their market area; they could go almost anywhere on foot. With a horse and wagon, a peddler could carry even more goods and still retain the ability to touch base in the river ports.

In addition, the rough-and-tumble culture of the river flatboaters (characters like Mike Fink) and later of riverboaters (for instance, Mark Twain) was probably not very appealing to most young immigrant Jewish men. Their orientation was always toward the goal of a more stable life; they aspired to leave the "adventure" of the road for a position as a clerk or manager, and ultimately owner, of a store in town.

With the greater carrying capacity of a wagon and with an urban base, peddlers could sell ready-made clothes, not just materials for their construction, providing isolated families the convenience and prestige of participation in this modern way of clothing oneself. Jewish peddlers bought their supplies from Jewish clothing wholesalers, some of whom—as in Cincinnati—were also manufacturers. So although the peddling life meant young Jewish men were often isolated on the road for weeks at a time, the overall structure of the trade kept them closely connected to the regional urban Jewish businesses that supplied their goods and credit and to the Jewish communities growing in the towns. Economic life and social life were intertwined. One can see this phenomenon in the careers of individual peddlers in the upper Ohio River Valley: the transition from pack peddling to horse and cart to store, and the importance of family and communal ties in the transition.

A good example is the Ballenberg brothers. In January 1841, Julius Ballenberg registered as a pack peddler in Jefferson County, Ohio, probably working for Marx Graf, a Jewish merchant in nearby Wheeling, Virginia. A few years later, Julius and his brother Adolph opened their own dry goods store in Wheeling, which they maintained into the mid-1850s. In 1850, Julius showed up again on the list of peddlers granted licenses in Jefferson County, but this time he had a one-horse wagon and, soon after, a two-horse wagon. Recognizing the advantages of having a traveling salesman, the Ballenberg brothers combined two modes of marketing to extend the reach of their business.[5]

The combination of peddling and storekeeping was also a means of self-help for members of the Heyman family. Alexander Heyman was one of the first Jews in Wheeling, where he moved from Pittsburgh in 1841. That same year, Meyer Heyman (probably a cousin) acquired a peddling license in Jefferson County, probably working out of Alexander's store. Meyer's career progressed slowly but steadily: In 1853, he was still peddling, at least part-time, but by 1857 he had established a fairly substantial dry goods business in Wheeling. By 1864, the year he bought out cousin Alexander, he was even "considered well-off" by observers of local business. Meyer also provided a safety net to his brother Wolff, who was described by a credit evaluator in 1857 as "emphatically 'a poor devil.'" Wolff had a dry goods business in Wheeling that collapsed; after several years obtaining release from his remaining debts, he was back to peddling and clerking, apparently for Meyer.[6]

Wolff Heyman's case was not unique. It was not at all unusual for striving entrepreneurs to experience repeated business failures; there was no road to success that didn't have potholes. Solomon Bloch peddled in Jefferson County from 1848 through 1852, traveling by foot until he could work his way up to afford a wagon. The going was tough. After starting out on foot in March 1848, he was able to register a one-horse wagon in September, but in January 1849 he was back on foot. In another three months, he had a wagon again—and in yet another three months was again without it. This happened one more time before he had an entire year's work from a one-horse wagon. Finally, sometime between 1852 and 1860, Bloch was able to establish himself in Wheeling, where he stayed until his death in 1865.[7]

Through the travails of his work life, Bloch had the lifeline of the Jewish community in Wheeling. Jewish peddlers seem to have felt the need to make firm communal connections, despite—or rather because of—the peripatetic nature of their work. The network of peddlers in the upper Ohio Valley formed the nucleus of the Jewish community of Wheeling. In fact, the list of Jefferson County peddling licenses for 1840 through 1853 includes the names of at least eight men who were then or would later be residents of that Ohio River city. The choice to settle in Wheeling reflected an assessment of the city's promise as a powerful regional center in the antebellum era. In 1811, the city was chosen as the Ohio River terminus of the National Road, and when the road was completed to that point in 1818, tons of merchandise and hordes of travelers began to flow through its wagon terminals, connecting with downriver boats to Cincinnati and Louisville.

The Jefferson County records show that Jews rose more quickly than non-Jews in the local peddling hierarchy. They were more likely to move sooner from pack peddling to horse and wagon than were non-Jews. Jews also more quickly moved out of peddling altogether and into fixed store locations. The locations chosen for fixed stores were often on river routes. "The Shylocks prefer to be on the navigable streams," grumbled one midcentury merchant of his Jewish competitors.[8]

Elements in Wheeling's further growth confirmed the wisdom of Jewish peddlers in locating on rivers but eschewing direct involvement with river transport operation. Starting in the 1850s, America's railroads began to gain ascendancy over watercraft in commercial transportation. The early railroads owed their growth to the river, but by the same token a railroad connection was now necessary for a river town to thrive. In 1852, the Baltimore and Ohio Railroad completed its track to Wheeling; it connected the town via other lines to Cincinnati by 1857, confirming Wheeling's position as a link in the east-west chain. Between 1830 and 1860, the population of Wheeling's surrounding Ohio County grew at three times the rate of nearby Jefferson County, Ohio.

Though the city was a Jewish anchor for many young peddlers in the region, their constant mobility delayed the formation of formal institutions. As early as 1846, the *Occident*, a Philadelphia Jewish newspaper edited by writer and communal leader Isaac Leeser, reported that there was in Wheeling "a sufficient number of Jews to form a small congregation, and we believe likewise that they have met for prayers."[9] Organization of a cemetery association and protocongregation actually took place in 1849; among the founders were three peddlers from the Jefferson County list, Julius Ballenberg, Solomon Bloch, and Seligman Oppenheimer. Bloch, Ballenberg, and Meyer Heyman all served as officers in the 1850s. Passing through Wheeling in 1855, Rabbi Isaac Mayer Wise, the founding father of American Reform Judaism, groused a bit about the disorganized state of Jewish affairs there. But as more Jews settled down, the informal bonds—likely quite satisfactory to the peddler group, if not to Wise—became the foundation of a thriving congregation with the mellifluous name Leshem Shomayim (For the Sake of Heaven).[10]

Meyer Heyman remained in Wheeling, operating a clothing business and staying active in the congregation until his death in the late 1880s. Solomon Bloch's sons Samuel and Aaron (who anglicized their name) owned and operated Block Brothers Tobacco Manufacturers; Samuel died in Wheeling in 1937. A member of the Heyman family was still in the clothing business as late as the 1890s, as were descendants of yet another midcentury peddler, Emanuel Reis.[11]

Wheeling provided a secure context for personal Jewish mobility and communal development. In other Ohio River towns in the mid-nineteenth century, economic and cultural factors created different configurations of Jewish residence and community. The stories of Marietta, Ohio, and Madison, Indiana, exemplify this.

From their town's inception, Mariettans understood it to be something more than an ordinary frontier town. They took pride in its status as the first permanent organized settlement under the Northwest Ordinance and in its cultural inheritance of New England federalism and congregationalism. In the 1830s and 1840s, when the central European Jewish immigration was beginning to swell, Marietta's economy began to move after several decades of stagnation. Population grew accordingly: in 1820, it was only 1,300, but by 1850, it was more than 3,100.[12]

Among those who swelled the ranks were Prussian-born Charles Coblenz and Baden-born Joseph Dinkelspiel, who had both arrived in the Ohio Valley around 1840. They peddled for a while along the river, including in Jefferson County in 1841 and 1842, and registered for naturalization as citizens at the Washington County courthouse in Marietta in 1842. Dinkelspiel kept on moving downriver; he lived in Louisville, Kentucky, from (at a minimum) 1844 until 1846 and was in Madison, Indiana, by 1849. Coblenz, however, stayed in Marietta for some time. Around 1844—or perhaps as early as 1842—he went into business with his brother Samuel, advertising dry goods and groceries as well as ready-made clothing from New York and Philadelphia, all for sale from their location "at the store rooms of Mr. Hill on Greene Street." By 1850, both men had growing families. Charles and his German-born wife, Henrietta, had three children, all born in Ohio. Samuel and his German-born wife, Frances, had a one-year-old daughter.[13]

The brothers had an extended family network. Charles and Henrietta's household in 1850 also included twenty-two-year-old Celena Coblenz, almost certainly a close relative, and eighteen-year-old Bernard Cahn, perhaps a relative, but at least a landsman. Another Coblenz family—Lazarus (who was perhaps an elder brother to Charles and Samuel) and Rebecca and their four children—lived in 1850 in Monroe County, just upriver from Marietta, a few years after their immigration. They were in Marietta soon; in 1854 Lazarus became a citizen there, and his daughter Julia was married there to Jacob Jacobs.[14]

Also living with Lazarus and Rebecca at the time of the census in late 1850 was a young couple, Zachariah Coblenz and Fanny Dinkelspiel Coblenz, who had been married just that summer in her hometown of Madison, Indiana. Zachariah may have been a fourth Coblenz brother, and Fanny was sister to none other than Joseph Dinkelspiel, Charles Coblenz's friend and erstwhile business associate. Yet another related family was that of Joseph Ullman and Sarah Dinkelspiel Ullman. It is not clear whether Sarah was sister or cousin to Joseph and Fanny Dinkelspiel, but she and her husband lived in Marietta from about 1843 until about 1855. Charles and Samuel dissolved their business partnership in 1851. Samuel continued as sole proprietor for another year, perhaps succeeded by Lazarus, but none of the Coblenzes remained in Marietta, or even in Ohio, by 1860.[15]

Had they stayed, they would have found that by the start of the Civil War, Marietta was doing better economically than it had for some decades, thanks to a nascent petroleum industry. But there were countervailing factors. Attempts to link the city into the powerful Baltimore and Ohio rail system via a local line failed for lack of traffic. Compared with other areas of southern Ohio, the land around Marietta was not good enough for truly successful commercial farming—poor soil and hilly topography were problems—and mineral resources were scantier. As historians Andrew Cayton and Paula Riggs put it, "Even with a connection to the outside world, Marietta would not grow . . . [because of] the general economic worthlessness of southeastern Ohio."[16]

In addition, the city was beginning to exhibit some cultural signs that would continue to inhibit growth. Cayton and Riggs note that "visitors in the 1850s admired the beauty and neatness of Marietta. 'The great majority of the dwellings are perfect pictures of comfort,' wrote the correspondent of *The Cincinnati Enquirer* in 1857. But outside observers also continued to detect, amid the small-scale economic upswing, a lack of 'energy.' Marietta 'should be a place of considerable business,' wrote another visitor in 1859. But it seemed that the 'wealthy portion of the community have their capital invested, and are indifferent about the growth of the place. It suits them and they do not want it larger.'"[17]

In the dynamic Ohio River Valley, Marietta's civic leaders looked to their New England past and decided that they would simply opt out of the race. A town with a strong antigrowth mentality was, to say the least, not a major attraction for Jewish immigrants needing opportunity and connection. There continued to be a small German Jewish presence in Marietta throughout the nineteenth century. But only later in the century did a numerically significant community and institutions evolve.

A similar dynamic of local growth and stagnation helped shape the Jewish community in Madison, Indiana. In the spring of 1852, Isaac Leeser wrote in the *Occident* of his travels to Indiana, commenting that though there was but one Jewish family in the capital city of Indianapolis, there were several in Madison, the seat of Jefferson County. Leeser observed hopefully, "Many towns on the Ohio, both above and below Cincinnati, besides Madison, have Jewish inhabitants; and we should not wonder if, should the immigration from Europe continue in the ratio lately prevalent, in the course of ten years twenty new congregations should spring up."[18]

Leeser's optimistic assessment of Ohio River towns certainly seemed justified in the case of Madison. Settled in 1810, the town is at the top of a horseshoe bend in the Ohio River, giving it closer access to Indiana's rich agricultural interior than other Indiana river cities have. Madison is also, as the 1850 *Indiana Gazetteer* noted, "beautifully situated . . . on steep and rugged hills," with most of the city thirty to forty feet above flood level. This advantage made it the largest town in Indiana in 1816, the year of statehood. In 1818, it had more than 800 residents, and in 1830, almost 1,800, placing it second only to New Albany, opposite Louisville. In addition to the dry goods stores, groceries, and taverns that served many river customers, there were several nascent industries, such as a cotton-spinning factory, to serve the local countryside.[19]

The following twenty-five years were a golden era for Madison. Its population quintupled as improved rail lines were opened to Indianapolis and a surface road all the way to Lake Michigan. Madison became Indiana's "Porkopolis": by the mid-1840s, it was the largest pork-packing center in Indiana, and third in the entire Midwest. In contrast to Marietta, Madison was a hothouse of commercial capitalism, with a population of more than eight thousand by the early 1850s and the promise of even greater success.

These boom years also saw the birth of Madison's Jewish community, as the first Jewish settlers, in the late 1840s, were drawn up from the South via the Mississippi and Ohio rivers. Elias and Teresa Hilpp, reportedly the first Jewish family to settle in Madison, in 1846, had earlier sojourned in New Orleans and Louisville. Other early settlers included Aaron Marks, the Kronenberger brothers, and the Hoffstadts. In 1848, Adolph Brandeis came from his hometown of Prague, Bohemia, to Cincinnati, which he used as his base for scouting out a new home in the Ohio River Valley for his extended family. The group of twenty-four comprising the Brandeis-Dembitz-Wehle families arrived in Madison a year later. Whereas most Madison Jews were typical central European Jews, petty merchants from small towns and villages, this clan was urban and professional. Gottlieb Wehle had been a successful merchant in Prague; Samuel Brandeis was a physician; and Lewis Dembitz, who had read law in Cincinnati, practiced in Madison in the early 1850s.[20]

By 1850, there were close to sixty Jews in Madison. Unlike some other Ohio River towns, Madison was home to a diversity of central European Jews: many Germans and Alsatians, but also a representation of Austrians, Poseners, and Bohemians. Most had immigrated in the late 1840s, and Madison was the first town in which they settled. Because many of the families were young and because numerous marriages occurred among Madison Jews, forty-five Jewish children were born in Madison between 1847 and 1860.[21]

In the 1850s, a second wave of Jewish immigrants settled in Madison, some joining family members who had preceded them. Many of the immigrants in this decade were Alsatian landsleit from villages south of Strasbourg. With its numbers growing, the Madison Jewish community began to organize. There were informal meetings for worship probably as early as 1849, followed by the formal organization of Adath Israel and a school in 1853. The congregation purchased land for a cemetery in August 1855 and dedicated a small synagogue the following month.[22]

But the appearance of new settlers in the 1850s was part of a significant turnover in Madison's Jewish population that decade. Numbers had indeed increased, from probably sixty residents in 1850 to eighty or ninety in 1860. The growth was largely natural increase, because families were now larger. The number of families increased somewhat—from fifteen to twenty—but most of these twenty families had not been in Madison ten years previous. Gottlieb Wehle and much of his extended family left for New York City; the families of the Brandeis brothers, Samuel and Adolph, stayed in the Ohio Valley but went to Louisville. Some Jewish population was also drawn off to Indianapolis, as well as to other Indiana towns and to Cincinnati. Scarcely any Jews moved to Madison in the 1860s.[23]

Madison's non-Jewish population was equally fluid in this period, as local economic conditions changed. The railroads, which seemed to promise continued prosperity, turned out to have the opposite effect: Madison discovered, as did many small towns, that railroads not only ran into your town but also ran out of it. With the expansion of the regional railroad system and Chicago's rise to Midwest dominance, Indianapolis's central location became more useful to Indiana business than Madison's door on the river. By 1860, both Indianapolis and Evansville had outstripped Madison in population and importance, and Madison's growth rate subsided. As with Marietta, it was clear that Madison would never be much more than a picturesque small town.

Madison's Jewish community remained small but stable throughout the nineteenth century. In 1868, the congregation moved into its own building, a vacant high school purchased from the city. In 1880, there were thirty-one families, established and affluent; members of many of these families lived in

Madison until well into the twentieth century—one descendant even until 1986.[24]

The seeds of Jewish community planted by the German immigrants often found fertile soil in the small towns of the Ohio River Valley. In 1869, August Mayer wrote proudly to the *Israelite* about his town, Pomeroy, Ohio. In Pomeroy, he reported, "besides salt and coal, we have at present eight Jewish families." It seemed a wealth of resources.[25]

The family was the most basic unit of Jewish community. Largely because they were used to delaying gratification, immigrant Jewish men put off marriage until they felt reasonably secure financially. Since women were expected not to delay marriage if at all possible, wives were usually considerably younger than their husbands. Spouses found each other through several channels. Some couples had made their plans while still in Europe, expecting to marry after emigration. Sometimes men returned to their home village (if they could afford it) or wrote to relatives and friends there to find a bride. Other couples met through their networks of American acquaintances and business contacts; a brother's business partner often turned into a match for a young Jewish woman.

When these families began to have children, they had them often. Studies of central European Jews in American cities, where the size of the community provides a large database, have amply demonstrated this. For instance, in Columbus, Ohio, by 1880, only about one-fourth of Jewish families had fewer than five children. In Cincinnati, the Jewish population more than tripled from 1850 to 1860; even though this was a decade of massive immigration, the percentage of Cincinnati Jews who were American-born grew from one-third to almost half, suggesting an equally astounding contribution from fecundity.[26]

The same pattern is evident in the fragmentary data available from small Ohio River towns. In Madison, Indiana, there were at least twelve Jewish households with children in 1860. These twelve families had a total of thirty-eight children, all of them born in the previous decade. Most of the fathers were in their thirties when their first child was born, four were in their late twenties, and one was in his forties. The mothers were on average a decade younger. Similarly, in Wheeling, in a sample of eight families, most of the men were in their thirties when they became fathers, and most of the women were in their twenties when they became mothers. In both towns, these were mostly young families with an average of three or four children each—which was probably just a start.[27]

Because families were large, widowers often remarried quickly in order to provide care for their children. In Marietta, Ohio, Charles Coblenz's first wife, Henrietta, died in 1862, leaving four children ages eight through seventeen;

within two years, he had married Sallie Wurtzburger and they had had the first of five children together. Simon Gumberts of Evansville, Indiana, was the father of thirteen children with two wives: having been widowed from one Rothchild, he married her sister—with the interesting result that the two sets of children were both half-siblings and first cousins.[28]

The phenomenon of immediate remarriage points to the fact that support from the nuclear as well as the extended family was critical to Jewish immigrants' rise into the middle class. Jewish men had a reputation as good and stable providers, and this was often credited for their rise to the middle class. But the contributions of wives and daughters were also critical to economic mobility, though the institution of marriage and the patriarchal family tended to conceal their roles, both as providers of household service and child care and as workers in family businesses. Women's business activities were often conducted behind business facades bearing men's names. For instance, when Abraham Uri opened a dry goods store in Mount Vernon, Indiana, in the 1870s, his wife, Louisa, supplied millinery services—but her name was not part of the business name and was not mentioned in advertising or publicity.[29]

Generally speaking, the more quickly the family ascended to the middle class, the sooner the women became disengaged from the day-to-day aspects of business. It was a logical consequence of acculturation. In America's colonial era, other merchants were used to Jewish women functioning in trade; after all, at the time, all women, even those of the upper classes, were regularly involved in economic activities. But as manufacturing moved from the home to the factory, the public and private domains were sundered; men were assigned to the (competitive) public sphere and women to the (nurturing) private sphere, creating the so-called cult of domesticity that was an integral part of the rise of the middle class. Jewish immigrants, as much as other immigrants and native-born Americans, aspired to a life in which mother kept house and father brought home the bacon (or its kosher equivalent).[30]

The family was an important site of acculturation, and here women would play a critical role through their adaptation of Jewishness to American domesticity. In their adherence to the American ideal of womanhood, German Jewish women created their own Jewish women's culture and negotiated the adaptation of American middle-class manners and values to the German Jewish milieu. As the community grew and its institutional structure ramified, women helped anchor Jewish culture to American bourgeois mores.

For the most part, the German Jewish immigrants in the American cities of the colonial and revolutionary eras had integrated into the institutions established by the earliest immigrants, who were primarily Sephardim; they adopted Sephardic customs, acknowledged Sephardic authority, and, eventually, intermarried with Sephardim. But the newly arrived village Jews of the mass migration were not always welcome in the synagogues and other institutions of the existing small, affluent, and acculturated American Jewish community in the East Coast cities. In fact, old congregations such as New York's Shearith Israel began to admit members only by secret ballot, with the intended result of excluding those they felt would not fit into their society. The newer immigrants thus founded institutions in which they could feel comfortable and express their specifically German Jewish sensibility. They developed a communal infrastructure adapted to meet their needs as new and upwardly mobile Americans while retaining their link with the Jewish past and Jewish values.[31]

In cities with substantial Jewish populations, institutions rapidly multiplied with the increase in immigration. Ironically, social exclusion on the basis of European regional origin persisted, this time expressed as antipathy between Germans and Poles. Some of this antipathy came from existing prejudices imported from Europe. Some was due to class differences rooted in wealth and acculturation; class differences were, of course, related to length of time in America—with the advantage to the Germans. Poles and Germans also had different religious customs and traditions, for instance, in their pronunciation of Hebrew. Though not substantive, these distinctive practices were meaningful links to the past and thus heightened the barriers between the two groups, resulting in a multiplication of organizations to meet specific needs and desires.

Jews in small towns mostly avoided this duplication of institutions. Two or three Jewish families from Alsace would find their commonalities with two or three families from Bavaria more salient than their differences, given the greater difference between them and the much larger Christian population. This did not mean, however, that Jews in small towns were free from conflict. Rather, the negotiation of differences required cooperation and sometimes grudging concession—it was simply unfeasible for one faction to walk out and set up elsewhere. In Madison, Indiana, for instance, controversy among Jews of different religious inclinations over the proper form of worship in the town's one congregation drove away their rabbi but created space for coexistence until the passage of time muted the sources of difference.[32]

A critical factor in the success of American Jewish communities large and small was the continued support and involvement of the elite. In Germany, many Jews of the economic and intellectual elite converted to Protestantism or otherwise abandoned the Jewish community. In America, however, the elite became important communal leaders and philanthropists. But because there was in the trans-Appalachian West no existing elite of Jewish wealth or culture such as German immigrants encountered in the older East Coast cities, social status, and therefore leadership, was more fluid. This was especially true in the small towns, where, given their concentration in a narrow range of storekeeping activities, the Jewish communities were on average much more homogeneous economically than those in the cities. But they were not oblivious to status differentials. In Madison, for instance, it seemed obvious that Gottlieb Wehle, older, wealthier, and well educated, should be president of the newly formed congregation in 1853. In tiny Pomeroy, August Mayer, a physician, took the leading role.[33]

In one very important respect, the experience of German Jews settling in cities and small towns was the same: they shared a pragmatic, grassroots approach to communal organizing. Two factors shaped this approach. One was structural. Since the European religious elite was less likely to emigrate, migrants in the United States found themselves thrown onto their own resources to create institutions. For Jews from devout but poor and uneducated backgrounds, these resources were primarily the same street smarts that were serving them well in American business. The other factor was psychological. Though they yearned for continuity and comfort, immigrant Jews could not re-create the Jewish institutions of their European homelands. The voluntarism inherent in the United States' separation of church and state left space for individualism in a new way. Responding to social and cultural conditions around them, American Jews created synagogues, charities, and clubs that were, in historian Hasia Diner's words, "mediating structures that organically and creatively, if haphazardly, linked the new with the familiar."[34]

In a pragmatic way, Jewish communities first addressed the most exigent demands of Jewish life; therefore the first institution organized by newcomers was an association to provide Jewish burial. These associations were often dubbed "benevolent societies," a concept that blended the traditional *ḥevra kadisha* (burial society; literally, holy society) with the imperative of *gemilut ḥasadim* ("doing acts of benevolence"; providing burial is, in Jewish tradition, the foremost such act). The benevolent society's roles might also include public worship, religious education, assistance to the poor, and social events, though it was often supplemented or replaced by specialized organizations: synagogue, school, and lodge. The benevolent societies, then, were transitional institutions, creating a site for Jewish association while providing for critically important social needs and laying the groundwork for future institutional development.[35]

This pattern certainly held in the cities of the Ohio River Valley. In Louisville, for instance, the earliest Jewish associations were benevolent societies founded in the 1830s. The first synagogue, Adas Israel, incorporated in 1842 and erected its first building in 1850. Other institutions quickly followed, including a B'nai B'rith lodge in 1852 and a branch of the Young Men's Hebrew Association in 1864. Pittsburgh Jews began in 1846 to discuss organizing; in 1847, they founded the Bes Almon Society to provide cemetery plots and burial rites, and in 1848, the city's first synagogue, Shaare Shomayim.[36]

The benevolent society was the first Jewish institution in many small towns of the Ohio River Valley as well. In many places the benevolent society functioned as the worship community, meeting in members' homes or business buildings; gradually various community functions were coordinated under the aegis of a congregation. In Owensboro, Kentucky, Jews were meeting informally as a community by 1859, and in 1862, eighteen families, under the name of the Hebrew Benefit and Burial Society of Daviess County, purchased a cemetery. This ḥevra kadisha was also the worship community until 1878, when congregation Adath Israel built a permanent synagogue. In Paducah, Kentucky, the ḥevra kadisha, named Chevra Yeshurum, was organized in 1859 and acquired a cemetery property. After the Civil War, Chevra Yeshurum also took on the role of synagogue. In 1868, it sponsored High Holidays services for the first time, meeting in a room above the dry goods store run by Manfred Livingston; in 1871, it reorganized itself as Congregation Bene Yeshurum. Wheeling's Congregation Leshem Shomayim traces its inception to 1849 with the formation of a cemetery association and the purchase of a section of the city's Mount Wood Cemetery. Informal worship may have preceded the organization of Wheeling's benevolent society, but only in the early 1860s did Leshem Shomayim achieve some regularity of meeting schedule and location.[37]

In many other communities there was a period of informal association that preceded the establishment of a congregation, and though these precursors may not have been chartered as benevolent societies or called by that name, they almost certainly functioned as such. In 1855, a Jewish resident of Portsmouth, Ohio, reported to Isaac Leeser of the *Occident* that Jews there had organized a congregation. Three years later, in September 1858, a congregation of a dozen families formally constituted itself as Kal a Kodesh Beneh Abraham. Similarly, in January 1859, the *Israelite* reported that the Jews in Pomeroy, Ohio, had formed a congregation. Not until February 1868 were incorporation papers filed for what the county clerk entered in the record books as "Ohave Scholom Church." Jews in Cairo, Illinois, made provisions for Jewish burial as early as 1853; a congregation was organized a decade later. In Evansville, Indiana, informal worship began about 1850; Congregation B'nai Israel was formalized in 1857.[38]

The ad hoc nature of communal organization meant, of course, that not all communities fit the pattern of ḥevra kadisha–to–congregation. Not only was a burial society not invariably the first step, but some small communities skipped that step altogether. In 1864, the Frank and Emsheimer families took the lead in organizing a congregation in Gallipolis, Ohio. But the congregation never had its own cemetery in town. Some of the town's Jews were buried in Cincinnati, others in nearby Portsmouth. One might infer that the failure to provide a cemetery expressed some lingering sense of being temporary in town, yet among those buried in Cincinnati were members of the Moch and Frank families, who remained in Gallipolis for a long time. In the same year that they organized their own group, Gallipolis Jews also contributed to the building of the synagogue in Portsmouth. The Jewish infrastructure was built over space as well as over time.[39]

Often there was a parallel organization to the benevolent society specifically for women; not infrequently the women's group antedated the men's society or the congregation. But it is difficult in many cases to date the inception of women's organizations, for they tended to operate informally before incorporating or taking other steps. In 1865, two dozen women in Wheeling organized the Ladies' Hebrew Benevolent Society to provide social welfare and educational services and to raise money for the congregation. In Pomeroy, Ohio, the women's auxiliary filed incorporation papers a few months after the congregation was formed in 1868, though it is probable that they had already been meeting.[40]

In mid-nineteenth-century America, Jewish women could not be official members of their congregations unless they were widows of members; their organizations were often called auxiliaries, although they performed basic tasks of general welfare work and, quite often, fund-raising for the synagogue. The separate-but-equal status of women's organizations is evident from the fact that leaders were often spouses of male congregational leaders. In Pomeroy, for instance, founding officers of the Hebrew Ladies' Benevolent Association included Caroline Silverman, Sophia Baer, Esther Silverman, and Mina Mayer; their husbands—Samuel, Bennett, Simon, and August—were incorporating officers of the congregation. As with men, women were linked by membership in a local organization to the larger Jewish community, for instance, when the women of the Portsmouth Ladies' Hebrew Benevolent Society contributed to a fund-raising drive organized by Cincinnatians for a home for widows and orphans in the Midwest.[41]

For some Jewish immigrants, religion remained a distinctly secondary concern; they preferred new, American forms of Jewish organization that expressed a secular identity. Of all the nonreligious Jewish organizations, the fraternal order B'nai B'rith (Sons of the Covenant) was the first and without a doubt the most important in the nineteenth century. With its reach extending to small communities across the United States, B'nai B'rith was in the nineteenth century the only effective, truly national American Jewish organization.[42]

B'nai B'rith was founded in 1843 in New York City by a group of young immigrant German Jewish men who initially had come together on a purely social basis: to drink together at Sinsenheimer's saloon on Essex Street. Some of the men were already members of fraternal orders such as the Masons and the Odd Fellows. But they also desired an organized fellowship with other Jews, though it would be a fellowship outside the synagogue, in order to avoid contentious religious questions.

B'nai B'rith's founders reconceptualized Jewish community, inspired by the general fraternal orders that were so important to nineteenth-century American social life. They constructed a model for a new, voluntary form of association, one that might be more appropriate to the New World than inherited forms of Jewish association. The new order of B'nai B'rith was modeled on the Masons, with such trappings as secret greetings, insignia, and regalia, but with reference to specifically Jewish symbolism. For instance, the president was called the Grand Nasi (Prince), which was the title in talmudic times for the head of the highest Jewish court.

B'nai B'rith thus amalgamated Jewishness and Americanness to create a secular alternative for immigrant Jewish men. Practically speaking, in the highly mobile society of antebellum America, it provided a network of contacts for Jewish young men on the make; being a member of B'nai B'rith provided instant recognition among Jews around the country. In a society without governmental social services or a fully developed insurance industry, B'nai B'rith provided valuable disability and death benefits and, eventually, a network of homes for the elderly, orphanages, and hospitals open to all Jews. As a parallel to general fraternal orders, it also provided additional legitimacy and validation to Jewish identity in the eyes of non-Jews. Soon it became involved in the defense of Jewish interests at home and abroad.

By the 1860s, there were lodges across the entire country, in large and small cities and towns. Cincinnati's first lodge was founded in 1849, Louisville's in 1852, and Pittsburgh's in 1862. Lodges were founded in Evansville, Indiana, in 1860; Madison, Indiana, in the 1860s; Cairo, Illinois, in 1867; Paducah, Kentucky, in the 1870s; and Owensboro, Kentucky, in 1874. In the cities, B'nai B'rith's innovation and importance were in providing a neutral ethnic turf for Jewish fraternization. This was no doubt part of the appeal in small towns as well. But probably even more important for small-town Jews was that affiliation with a national organization provided a window onto the larger Jewish world and an opportunity to participate in national Jewish affairs.[43]

As a determinedly secular organization, B'nai B'rith had a complex attitude about involvement in Jewish cultural and, especially, religious activity. Many local lodges sponsored programs of Jewish education for adults and children, Jewish libraries, and lectures on Jewish topics, and some lodges even sponsored religious observances, in spite of the initial goal of transcending that. In Paducah, Kentucky, for instance, it was the B'nai B'rith lodge that spawned the men's and women's committees that reorganized the ḥevra kadisha into a full-scale congregation. In Cairo, Illinois, B'nai B'rith managed the Jewish cemetery.[44]

Though aimed at a different demographic group, the Young Men's Hebrew Association (YMHA) was, like B'nai B'rith, primarily socially and culturally Jewish rather than religious. Based on the model of the Young Men's Christian Association, which endeavored to protect young men from the evil influences of the big city, the YMHA movement was instigated in the 1850s to provide a Jewish setting for young men's leisure activities. In larger cities such as New York and Philadelphia, the YMHA had an expansive mission to provide opportunities for education, socialization, and physical fitness; branches in smaller cities and towns usually served primarily as social clubs. In Parkersburg, West Virginia, the YMHA was founded in 1869 as an ethnic social and educational club and aid society for "thoroughfaring co-religionists." Again like B'nai B'rith, some YMHAs sponsored Jewish education and religious observances, even including synagogue worship; the Parkersburg group offered its club space for religious services to any who desired to organize them.[45]

There is no evidence that anyone took it up on its offer. In the Parkersburg Jewish community, numbering at least fifteen families, ethnic identity and secular affiliation were apparently more compelling than religion. The YMHA led to the organization of the Hebrew Society in 1875, but the founders made it clear that this was not, strictly speaking, an exclusively Jewish benevolent society. As reported in the *Parkersburg State Journal*, the society intended to raise and distribute funds for general community charity "without regard to sect or nationality." Whether under the auspices of the Hebrew Society or not, Parkersburg Jews did, by the 1880s, meet in private homes for High Holidays services, but there was no formal congregation until 1909.[46]

For many immigrant Jews in America, either B'nai B'rith or a benevolent society was their primary Jewish affiliation, replacing the synagogue. But the extreme appearance of this phenomenon in Parkersburg provides the exception that proves the rule with respect to small towns. Some small portion of a town's Jewish community might choose to affiliate only with nonsynagogal organizations, but in small towns the congregation was the center of Jewish life. Aside from the need to avoid duplication of effort, other factors were at work. In the social structure of small-town America, it was the synagogue, as a parallel to Protestant churches, that best expressed and legitimated Jewish identity in America, in the eyes of both Jews and Gentiles.

In the vast majority of the Ohio River Valley's small towns, the dominant Jewish institution was the congregation, and local recognition among fellow Jews was a function of congregational leadership. Specialized organizations for men, women, or young people were de facto adjuncts to the central focal point of the synagogue. And the congregations themselves were more than just religious institutions, with their activities including mutual aid, philanthropy, Jewish education, and social events. The congregation was the central address of the Jewish community in the small town, regardless of the individual Jew's level of religious observance; it provided a place to feel secure with other Jews and to express one's group identity.

The earliest informal networks of self-help, such as those constructed by peddlers, adumbrated the construction of formal social and cultural institutions. As noted, in not all locations on this Jewish frontier did Jewish institutions take root and thrive; variables of place and persons affected permanence. But up and down the river, Jews in small towns built lives based on close family relations, on the communal ties of benevolent societies and fraternities, and—perhaps paramount—on a new understanding of Jewish religious life. Their experiences were similar in some ways to those of fellow immigrants who had settled in Cincinnati and other large American cities, but they differed in other respects. By the same token, as the years passed, small-town Jews came to share many characteristics of their non-Jewish neighbors while retaining a sense of separateness and specialness.

Religion became a major marker both of this separateness and of this sameness. Jews were immigrants and non-Christians, but they understood Judaism as essentially compatible with American life and undertook to nurture both. New expressions of Judaism grew from a strong inheritance of traditional culture and faith and the welcome promise of integration into America in the crucible of intracommunal conflict and in conversation with Christian America.

CHAPTER 4

Religious Conflicts and Congruity

For three months in early 1860, Rabbi Max Del Banco of Evansville, Indiana, had a running feud in the Jewish press with a congregant who detested the rabbi's liberal religious ideas. The *Occident*, a defender of traditional belief and practice, had reported on the Evansville community, touting its orthodoxy, based on the report of a local correspondent. Del Banco fired back in the pages of the moderately reformist *Israelite*. The community was by no means "orthodox," he wrote; "all [of the approximately forty members] follow and admire the principles of reform, except one or two." It was one of those putative exceptions—"somewhat the only Orthodox here," in Del Banco's opinion—who had written to the *Occident*. Unfortunately, the *Occident*'s dissenting correspondent was also the congregation's secretary.[1]

The exchange of letters was only one battle of an ongoing war. From a Sephardic family, Del Banco was born in 1825 in Hamburg, one of the earliest centers of Jewish religious reform,[2] and it is probable that he acquired his convictions there. In his *Israelite* letter, Del Banco charged that "orthodoxy despises any thing that relates to common sense, but admires only blind belief in outworn ceremonies and hereditary laws and customs." The secretary, the pseudonymous "Judah," in turn accused the rabbi of "vanity" in promoting an agenda shared by no one else; he also commented sarcastically on "how fond Mr. D. is of delivering his reform sermons, which, as he boasted, every body admires, and all of which may be read first in the [radical Reform journal] *Sinai*." The secretary added darkly that despite his pseudonym, he suspected that Del Banco knew exactly who he was.

"As long as I will be preacher and teacher here," Del Banco pledged, "orthodoxy will have little to boast upon." In spite of his bravado, though, he had to admit that "at present . . . our service is conducted according to old custom, but this, I hope, will alter soon." What altered soon was his employment; he left Evansville probably that same year.[3]

Many communities in the mid-nineteenth century roiled with debates over the direction of American Judaism. These debates reflected the internal struggle to respond to modernity that had engaged Jews in the Western world for about a century, a struggle that was particularly sharpened by the unprecedented conditions of Jewish life in America. Jews in the Ohio River Valley, in large and small towns, were in the eye of the storm. They played a critical role in formulating the response that became institutionalized in American Reform Judaism.

The beginnings of the Reform movement in Judaism are found in German Jews' experience of emancipation in the early nineteenth century. Increasingly exposed to non-Jewish life, Jews gradually became comfortable with ways of thinking and behaving that seemed to conflict with inherited Jewish patterns. Soon some Jews were proposing deliberate changes to these inherited patterns, both in doctrine and in practice. But Reform Judaism was not an assault launched by heedless assimilationists against a solid and faithful traditionalism; religious change was inextricably entangled with the promises, imperatives, and perils of civil emancipation and social integration.

As emancipation slowly and fitfully reached the Jews of western and central Europe, traditional Jewish communal authority broke down, leaving individuals less dependent on the community. Simultaneously, under the influence of Enlightenment humanism, Gentile intellectual and cultural progressives were increasingly open to contacts with Jews. Initially, as in the case of Berlin's nascent Jewish upper class of the 1790s, this created a severe identity crisis for the urban Jewish elites who first negotiated these new relationships. Many became alienated from the Jewish community, and many even defected, converting to Christianity. In the face of this, some Jewish leaders became convinced that the new conditions of life called for new attitudes and actions. On the one hand, as Jews came closer to civil and social equality, it was imperative to validate Judaism to Christians, to prove Jews' ability to be fellow citizens and comrades. On the other hand, it was also imperative to validate Judaism to Jews, to provide an option so that the choice between modernity and Jewish allegiance was not so stark. In large part, religious reform was driven by a concern to keep Jews Jewish.[4]

Under the influence of contemporary philosophy, German Jewish intellectuals of the early nineteenth century reconceived Judaism as a creation of history, as an ongoing process through which essential, universal truth would be revealed. They became convinced that Judaism's natural development had been unnaturally inhibited by the persecutions of unenlightened medieval

Christianity. The essential spirit of Judaism had been suffocated for these many years, and now it was possible to release it. Judaism thus had a great and glorious future as a beacon to all mankind, a prospect that they linked to the biblical concept of the people of Israel as *ohr la-goyim*, "a light to the nations."

In this broader view, traditional Jewish concepts were revised to emphasize universal values rather than particularistic Jewish interests and self-understandings. Hopes for the return to Zion and the reestablishment of temple sacrifices were seen as an outdated reaction to historical conditions that no longer prevailed; the biblical messianic hope was reinterpreted as a human goal, Judaism's mission to redeem the world. This transformation accomplished several things. First, it validated Jews as acceptable citizens of the nation-state: German Jews (for example) were indisputably Germans, with no expectation of a literal return to Zion or the reestablishment of Jewish sovereignty there. Second, the new universalism staked a claim for the relevance of Judaism to contemporary society. The essence of religious faith, the early Reform thinkers agreed, was morality, and nowhere were moral truths better expressed in Jewish terms than in the writings of the biblical prophets. From the prophets, they excavated a perspective that emphasized universal religious truths and moral teachings and located religious authority in reason and conscience rather than in law.

This new (for Judaism) conception of religion focused on the personal subjective religious consciousness, so the task of organized religion was *Erbauung*, the "uplift" of the individual consciousness. The traditional style of worship was textually rigid (the liturgy was entirely in Hebrew) and highly participatory, with a complex structure not evident to the uninitiated. It proceeded at a generally fast (but not fixed) tempo in a manner that outsiders often perceived as chaotic. With the breakdown of communal authority, traditional Jewish learning had weakened; now congregations began to pray, and rabbis to deliver sermons, in German, the community's new primary language. Sometimes organs and choral music were introduced to create an atmosphere of devotion; worship services were shortened. Especially in the cities, home to a growing Jewish bourgeoisie, these new practices coincided with an overall change of manners that subtly shifted Jewish preferences to a more subdued religious style. For both ideological and practical reasons, the watchword of the era was "decorum."

By the 1840s, the intellectual project of reform in Germany was coalescing into a movement. It was a widely diverse movement, ranging from radical antirabbinism to moderate change based on *halakhah*, traditional Jewish law as interpreted by rabbis over the centuries. But as the nineteenth century progressed, the contours of a mainstream reform were beginning to emerge: use of the vernacular and of organ and choir music in liturgy; disuse of traditional male head coverings; a lenient attitude toward the dietary laws; affirmation of core practices such as circumcision; the abolition of the second day of holidays, except for Rosh Hashanah (the New Year festival)[5]; and rejection of the most radical proposals, such as those to make Judaism conform to modernity by observing Shabbat on Sunday. One could find rabbis and laypeople across the spectrum of opinion.

In addition, of course, there was always a third voice in the conversation: the German state governments, determining what they would or would not permit. In Germany, Jewish religious decisions and development remained constrained by Gentile politics.[6] But this was not the case in the United States, which would turn out to be, in the phrase of Michael Meyer, the movement's historian, "the Reform movement's land of promise." Like the biblical Israelites' entry into their promised land, however, it was not to be a smooth journey.[7]

Reform Judaism in the United States has often been misinterpreted as entirely a German import because of the emphasis that historians placed, until the mid-1970s, on the activities of rabbis, most of whom were immigrants from German-speaking countries. In this view, the social conditions of American Jewry simply provided the soil in which the rabbis planted ideas of reform. After the mid-1970s, however, historians began to look at what actually went on in nineteenth-century American synagogues, among average American Jews. One such important historian, Leon Jick, argues that changes in religious practice were created by immigrants' own pragmatic responses to specific American social and economic conditions, rather than by their acceptance of any ideological program propounded by rabbis. Religious reform in America was the German Jewish immigrants' attempt to reshape their beliefs, their ideas, and their community in a way that enabled them to participate fully in American society while retaining links with the Jewish past. Jewish immigrants took the initiative to create a modern religion to fit their new, modern self-understanding and their new economic and social status.[8]

The project was not completely without precedent in the United States. An abortive attempt at religious reform was made in 1825 by a young, Americanized faction within Beth Elohim of Charleston, South Carolina, a bastion of Sephardic-rite traditionalism founded in 1750. The manifesto of the renegade Reformed Society of Israelites bore some resemblance to principles of German Reform philosophy. But the independent driving force was the desires of a younger constituency: mostly native born; intellectuals, professionals, and civil servants as well as merchants; active in politics and civic affairs. Although the separate organization soon withered, the experimenters became part of a faction that led Beth Elohim in the 1840s to pioneer more sweeping changes. Even without providing a direct model, the religious changes made by the members of the Reformed Society of Israelites in response to their perception of the conditions of American freedom adumbrated the changes that immigrant German Jews eventually made as well.

But while these Jews were prepared to consider various reforms to their practice, they did not initially see this as part of—or even precursor to—any sort of organized movement. Laypeople were comfortable with making changes that seemed appropriate to their circumstances, but until the late nineteenth century, they had no desire to institutionalize this process into an ideological movement. It was the rabbis who created the institutional structures of American Reform and who translated the philosophical ideas of the German reformers into an American idiom. So the synthesis of American and Jewish identities was the democratic creation of both a pragmatic laity and philosophically oriented rabbis. The Ohio River Valley would be an important site of this activity, becoming a vital center of institutional Reform Judaism.

In the early years of the central European immigration, the desire for religious change was not strong. The immigrants had already changed their homes, their language, their surroundings; they wanted their synagogues to be anchors of the old, familiar, comforting tradition in this sea of change. Private practice, however, was much more flexible; subject to pressures of economic necessity and social convenience, Jewish men and women in America chose their private practice based mainly on pragmatic criteria. Some fundamental practices, especially circumcision, were followed almost universally. Enough families still observed the dietary laws that many communities retained a shoḥet to provide kosher meat. A number of communities in the mid-nineteenth century even maintained mikvaot, ritual baths that are necessary for observing the laws of marital sexual relations.[9]

Observance of Shabbat posed a particularly difficult problem, since merchants were under competitive pressure to open their stores. But this may not have been an unprecedented challenge. Contrary to stereotypes, in many German villages it was not the poorer, less educated Jews who were the most traditionally observant. Rather, strict observance tended to be the prerogative of the wealthy, who could afford to take the time away from work for regular prayer and study and who could engage Hebrew teachers for their children.[10] In America, a democratic attitude and pragmatic compromise could bridge the observance gap: rather than seeing Shabbat observance as an all-or-nothing proposition, Jews in America chose to do what they could and what they wanted to. They might meet very early to pray, and then open their stores. But even if—or maybe especially because—their personal observance waned, they clung to traditional liturgy, language, and behaviors in the synagogue.

Their communal life was rather chaotic. Unable to attract rabbis from Europe, most American communities had to rely for quite some time on non-ordained functionaries, men whose reputations and level of Jewish learning varied considerably—though generally both were very low. They were jacks-of-all-trades Jewish professionals—shoḥet, ḥazan (cantor), and often mohel (circumciser) rolled into one. Most did not—and could not—provide strong guidance, and laymen continually challenged their authority. A notable exception to the poor quality of these professionals was Isaac Leeser. Born and educated in Germany, Leeser immigrated in 1824 to join a family business and soon found his talents used as ḥazan of Philadelphia's Mickveh Israel, an old Sephardic-rite congregation. Stepping in to fill other voids in American Jewish life, Leeser was an astoundingly active writer, publisher, educator, translator, and organizer—a seemingly bottomless well of resources for the struggling American Jewish community of the antebellum era.[11]

But even many of the attempts by the indefatigable Leeser to arouse interest in Jewish culture and education were, though accepted in his Sephardic community, rejected by the more recent immigrant Germans as *ḥukkat ha-goyim*, forbidden imitations of non-Jewish practice. Ordained rabbis fared no better. The first two to appear in the United States, in the early 1840s, Abraham Rice and Leo Merzbacher, were frustrated with their low status and inability to influence their congregations: Rice quit his Baltimore pulpit after nine years and opened a grocery business; Merzbacher suffered an early death.[12]

The 1850s were a critical decade for American Judaism. It was a period of tremendous population growth, partly from natural increase but even more from a wave of immigration in the wake of Europe's revolutionary disturbances in 1848. Among these immigrants were rabbis who hoped to transform American Judaism. Communities were changing rapidly in thriving regions like the Ohio River Valley, and intracommunal conflict was inevitable. Because of their particular approaches, grassroots institutions such as benevolent societies and B'nai B'rith were somewhat immunized against internal conflict. But religion was another story. Some historians have seen these conflicts as clashes between an intellectual elite that wanted a thoughtful and consistent response to the challenges of modernity and a pragmatic laity that just wanted a Judaism that worked. But pragmatism was not the only issue. The resistance of some ordinary Jews to reformist pressure came also from deep-seated religious emotions and the desire to retain traditions in a new and rapidly changing environment. The stage was set for battle.

Madison, Indiana, was one such field of battle. Madison's Jews, who had been meeting informally for worship probably as early as 1849, organized

Adath Israel and an affiliated school in 1853. They dedicated a small synagogue in September 1855. Initially, the congregation was a do-it-yourself proposition: Joseph Dinkelspiel (late of Louisville and Marietta) served as ḥazan and sḥohet for a time, as did A. M. Hoffstadt, whose store building hosted the synagogue on its second floor. Then, in January 1856, the congregation advertised in *Die Deborah*, Cincinnati's German-language Jewish newspaper, for a full-time, all-purpose Jewish functionary: a ḥazan and sḥchet also able to teach children Hebrew, German, religion, and biblical history. Thirty-four-year-old Bernhard Felsenthal was soon engaged.[13]

Felsenthal's appearance in Madison was fortuitous. When he immigrated in 1854, he headed for Louisville, where his brothers were already living. Trained as a teacher in Germany, Felsenthal first moved to Lawrenceburg, Indiana, upriver nearer Cincinnati, to serve as tutor to the children of the Adler family. From Lawrenceburg, he left for Madison in March 1856. By then, the community had about fifteen families. The men—that is, those who were eligible, and therefore likely, members of the congregation—were mostly in their mid-thirties; almost all had emigrated from German states or Alsace in the late 1840s and early 1850s.[14]

Felsenthal had had both a traditional Jewish education in his Rheinland hometown and secular (though not university) training. As a student and later a teacher in a small-town Jewish school and as an avid reader, he was exposed to the ideas of religious reform percolating throughout German Jewish society. Upon arriving in the United States, Felsenthal attached himself publicly to the cause of reform. He polished his English-language skills and began to publish his views, religious and political, in the Jewish and secular presses, in both English and German. Felsenthal's intellectual role model was Rabbi David Einhorn, a radical Reform rabbi in Baltimore known for his uncompromising stances; while in Madison, Felsenthal started writing for Einhorn's journal *Sinai*. In March 1857, also from Madison, Felsenthal published a three-part series on Reform in *Die Deborah*, which gives insight into the nature of Jewish religious discourse in mid-nineteenth-century America. The clash between the rabbi and his congregants was part of the process of the creation of new models of American Jewish leadership and of a democratic American Jewish laity.[15]

Felsenthal's *Die Deborah* articles purported to be a transcript of congregational debates on his suggestions for liturgical reform in Madison. The first article started by portraying a small but feisty community. The congregation was "among the smallest in the western United States," but it held regular services and children's classes. There were monthly congregational meetings, with many "fruitful discussions." At one such meeting, on February 1, 1857,

Felsenthal (by his report) took the floor to propose changes to the young congregation's mode of worship. Noting that in recent months, services had occasionally been cancelled for lack of attendance, he promoted the worthwhile aims of regular worship: not just community continuity but personal edification and uplift.[16]

Felsenthal thought he had a solution to the problem of apathy: a program of thoroughgoing religious reform. "One could," he explained, "raise an objection to me: 'You speak of edification, instruction, and improvement through worship. But our customary worship doesn't edify or instruct or improve me. Its language is foreign, its form is repulsive and tasteless, the eternal repetitions [of prayers] are tiresome, [and] its excessive length enervates the spirit rather than elevating it. Moreover, it is in large part based on opinions and convictions that our contemporaries no longer believe. What should I do in such a worship service?' Gentlemen, to the one who confronts me with such a comment, I must [say] without embarrassment that you're right." Felsenthal was convinced that the lack of interest in religious services was attributable to a sort of liturgical arteriosclerosis. The language must be changed: Jews no longer understood Hebrew and did not know the meaning of the prayers, making true devotion impossible. Likewise, the length of the traditional service should be curtailed to promote "devotion and solemnity"; a long service presses people to hurry through their prayers "like a high wind." A shorter service would also permit time for a sermon, which Felsenthal considered "an essential part of divine service."

The form of the liturgy was not the only issue Felsenthal raised; content concerned him as well. Modern Jews should drop all "notions, views, hopes [and] wishes" that were not part of modern belief, such as the desire for the restoration of temple sacrifices. If a remodeled form would increase devotion, he believed, a philosophically consistent content would reveal the truth of "our lofty Israelite religion, the most beautiful on the whole wide earth." By emphasizing the "eternal teaching" of "virtue and morality," Jews would demonstrate their standing "as members of an eminent people before other religious societies."

Felsenthal was careful to base his arguments on precedent. He invoked not only traditional rabbinic sources but all the sages of the Bible and Talmud: "Neither *Avraham Avinu* [Abraham our father] nor *Mosheh Rabbenu* [Moses our teacher], neither *Shlomo ha-Melekh* [King Solomon] nor *Eliyahu ha-Navi* [Elijah the prophet] ever said a single passage of our entire *Tefilah* [prayer] . . . and I think all of you would agree that *Mosheh Rabbenu* was a good *Yehudi* [Jew]." Abraham never davened Shacharit (prayed the morning service),

Felsenthal continued, and Rabbis Akiva and Meir never said all the piyyutim (religious poems) contemporary Jews did.[17]

But Jewish tradition was not his only point of reference. The context of modern life was equally important. From its early days in Germany, Felsenthal averred, religious reform had a proud history in some of "the greatest and most cultivated European congregations," and "the greatest Rabbis" now supported it. In the United States, there were a "respectable number" of reforming congregations in cities such as New York, Philadelphia, Albany, Baltimore, and Charleston. "Wherever thinking and enlightened Israelites live together," Felsenthal proclaimed, "they take into account the progress of the time in religion." He urged his congregation to "show the world that we here in Madison are, though few in number, great in our intentions and full of holy zeal for our divine Judaism, that also thinking and enlightened Jews live [here]."

Finally, Felsenthal made his suggestions for the specifics of the Shabbat service. It would follow the outline of the traditional service but with a few omissions, some sections read in German, additional responsive readings, and a half-hour sermon. Felsenthal wanted women as well as men counted to the minyan.

The reaction to his proposals was immediate and, predictably, divided. One member—disguised for the article as Mr. X—immediately expressed his horror at Felsenthal's ideas. "Should someone like this be teaching Yiddishkeit [Judaism] to our children?!" Mr. X exclaimed, branding all reformers "goyim." Mr. Y then spoke up in Felsenthal's defense. The report of the remainder of the debate so thoroughly covers the exposition of the traditional position and so elegantly delineates the Reform refutation that one is tempted to attribute a fair amount of editing to Felsenthal. Yet though his words may be in the mouths of his defenders, the narrative retains a sense of personalities that seems true to life.[18]

Mr. A, a "radical," took Felsenthal's logic to its extreme, proposing the abolition of Hebrew entirely, even for the Torah reading. This extremist statement permitted Felsenthal to emphasize his reverence for tradition, how he "deliberately" retained some Hebrew for its emotionally uplifting, even mystical, power. Others expressed additional reasons: to protect the integrity and authenticity of the Torah, to retain a bond with Jewish communities around the world. When Mr. A suggested that "Hebrew is indeed one of Jewry's embracing bonds, but the weakest of all"—superseded by a common monotheistic faith—"the zealous [Mr.] X" went ballistic.

But we must pray only in Hebrew, Mr. X insisted, for "whole worlds depend on a single letter." After all, doesn't the tradition require one to correct a scribal error in a Sefer Torah (Torah scroll) immediately? Against this mystical understanding, Mr. Z made the rationalist's argument that the scribal practice is simply for the sake of ensuring accuracy. This drove Mr. X to further paroxysms: "The existence of whole worlds is conditional on each vowel, the angels of Heaven employ each little stroke. . . . Get me away from your newfangled things—they are all sins!" On the issue of counting women to the minyan, Mr. X was, of course, opposed. Everyone knows this idea is wrong, he asserted. "Didn't you read this just a few days ago in the *Deborah*?"

At this point the article became uncomfortably personal. Mr. X's assertion was greeted with laughter and snide comments. Mr. Y, "who attended a Latin school for two years as a youngster, said, '*O sancta simplicitas!* [Oh simple faith!]'" Retorted X, "Mr. Upsilon, you have offended me. What are you doing, rebuking me in Latin? You said yesterday that I was an old blockhead [*Ochs*, in German]—a decent man would say 'orthodox'—*you* are a blockhead." Here Felsenthal permitted himself a sarcastic aside on the intellectual quality of the opponents of Reform: they made arguments from tradition "of which the Poskim [rabbinic legal authorities] had never in the least dreamed. Perhaps we should publish the insights of our learned theologians, never before heard in front of a large audience." One can easily imagine the smirk on his face.

The remainder of the debate was similarly unproductive. Felsenthal even admitted that many in attendance were bored by the proceedings, accusing them of insensitivity to anything except "bread and amusements." During the course of the conversation, Mr. E had made it clear that he would rather be playing cards than discussing religion. It seems that for many of these men, high-flown philosophical talk was at least a waste of time, and perhaps silly. They knew what it was to be Jewish; why change? They might often ignore it, but it was there for them.

Though Felsenthal reported at the end of his third article that the congregation called an additional meeting for further discussion, no account of that meeting (if indeed it was held) appeared. Despite Felsenthal's portrayals of support, his arguments were ultimately unpersuasive. Frustrated, he left Madison in 1858 for the greener pastures of Chicago, where he forged a remarkable and long career as a Reform rabbi (despite his lack of formal ordination) and early American Zionist.

The Madisonians were used to Felsenthal attracting controversy. Six months before the debate over reform, in the fall of 1856, he had ruffled the feathers of his congregants with his public advocacy of John Frémont's presidential candidacy on the ticket of the new Republican Party. The *Madison Daily Evening Courier* reported the dispute and commented that "freedom of speech and Mr. Felsenthal were sustained." Sympathetic, like-minded rabbinic colleagues encouraged Felsenthal's assertiveness. The recalcitrance of the Madison congregation was only temporary, an East Coast friend advised him; just as the sun traveled from east to west, Reform would inevitably progress across the country.[19]

Without other evidence, it is impossible to determine exactly who in the Madison congregation supported Felsenthal and who opposed him. One of Felsenthal's partisans was almost certainly Michael Frank, at whose home the rabbi boarded. Felsenthal lost a probable supporter within a few months of his arrival in Madison when Gottlieb Wehle, the titular and de facto head of the community, moved to New York City. Wehle seems to have been able to act as a peacekeeper in the Madison community. Indeed, the congregation's resolution of tribute, published in the *Israelite* upon Wehle's move in April 1856, credited him with dispelling "the former disunion and discord" in the community—perhaps the flap over Felsenthal's politics.[20]

Wehle and his extended family had added a unique element to the Madison Jewish scene; their background was far different from that of other Madison Jews. The Wehles were not village Germans but a wealthy, even aristocratic old Jewish family from Prague. In addition, they were Frankists, remnants of a mystical eighteenth-century Jewish sect that followed the charismatic and bizarre Jacob Frank. Frank saw himself as the inheritor of the messianic soul of the eccentric Shabbetai Tzvi, the famous false messiah who caused massive spiritual and social unrest in seventeenth-century Jewish Europe and the Mediterranean with his visions of imminent redemption.[21]

Though the early Frankists had engaged in some rather dubious esoteric practices, by the nineteenth century what remained in their heirs' minds was a theology of rebellion, a sense of being engaged in protest against the intellectual and spiritual constraints of orthodox law. This rebellion clearly had implications for the ongoing response to modernity. As Gottlieb Wehle's son wrote in the late nineteenth century, his forebears had found in Frankism "a tonic influence, a refreshing impetus in a system of mystic idealism that opened an almost boundless prospect of intellectual and moral expansion. To break with Judaism was impossible, to give it a higher and broader significance was the only way open to them."[22] Thus the Frankists were intrinsically inclined to support the Reform movement. This tendency never had a chance to play out in Madison, however. By 1856, having decided that the town was not living up to their expectations, Wehle and his extended family left. Some members of the family went back to Europe; others dispersed to American cities, including Louisville.

In numbers and wealth, the Wehle-Brandeis family may have had a high profile in Madison, but the rest of the Jewish community was more conventional. Of the seventeen men who were likely to have been the nucleus of the congregation, eight were Alsatians and four were Germans. Four were variously described as Prussian, Polish, or both (they were probably from Poznań), and one (Gottlieb Wehle) was from Bohemia. The background of most of them was probably rather conservative. But though several had been in the United States for only two or three years, eight of them had been in the country for at least seven years. Most of these men were in their mid- to late thirties and early forties; most were married (the women of the community had a similar range of geographic origins) and had at least a few children. They earned their livings largely as peddlers, tailors, and clothing dealers.[23]

What this profile suggests is that most Madison Jews were still in transition, working their way up the economic ladder and building families. In this respect, Felsenthal's comment about "bread and amusements" is most telling. Felsenthal was an intellectual. The men to whom he was speaking were immigrants who worked hard and, no doubt, relished their opportunities for relaxation while wishing to fulfill their Jewish obligations. Moreover, maintaining the status quo was a safe course for a community too small to support more than one congregation. The sort of religious reform that would eventually appeal to most immigrant German Jews was not based on lofty philosophy. It was an Americanized Judaism that took its cues from the realities of the immigrants' lives, responding to their new sensibilities as they entered America's middle class.

The sort of radical reform that Bernhard Felsenthal unsuccessfully marketed in Madison did, however, find a home in another Ohio River Valley city. In Wheeling, Virginia (later West Virginia), physical, social, and political geographies converged to make the town into an early stronghold of radical Reform Judaism under the influence of Rabbi David Einhorn and his Baltimore congregation, Har Sinai.

The physical link between the cities of Wheeling and Baltimore was forged by the National Road in the first third of the nineteenth century and strengthened by the Baltimore and Ohio Railroad in the middle third of the century. In the 1820s, use of the National Road momentarily pushed Baltimore ahead of Philadelphia as the second-largest city in the United States. The road also put Wheeling on the map both literally and metaphorically. Livestock, coal, and other commodities flowed to and through Baltimore and Wheeling in impressive quantities, as did human traffic. Many European immigrants heading for the West chose to enter the United States at Baltimore to take advantage of access to the National Road. With the immigrants and migrants, writes the foremost authority on the road, "came ideas and institutions that they would employ to fashion a new human geography on the trans-Appalachian landscape."[24]

One feature of this new human geography, of course, was the Jewish settlement on the Ohio River. By the mid-nineteenth century, there were close to twenty Jewish families in Wheeling.[25] The viability of Wheeling's Jewish community depended on the commercial viability of the city, which in turn depended on remaining in the transportation loop as railroads supplemented (and then replaced) the National Road. The connections between the physical geography of the Ohio River and the built geography of the National Road and then the Baltimore and Ohio Railroad closely determined the cultural geography of Jews in this corner of Virginia.

The business and personal connections between Jews in Wheeling and Jews in Baltimore were strong. Many Wheeling Jews had entered the country at Baltimore and stayed there for some time. There was a branch in Wheeling of Baltimore's Wiesenfeld and Company department store, operated by a member of the family. Abraham Sonneborn, an 1846 immigrant who moved to Wheeling in 1860, was older half-brother to Henry Sonneborn, who became extremely wealthy in clothing manufacture in Baltimore during and after the Civil War. (Before the war, Henry had a clothing store in Fairmont, Virginia, now West Virginia.) The communities were linked not only by family and business connections but also by what in the nineteenth century might have been called a harmony of sentiments. Among the cultural influences traveling the Baltimore-Wheeling route was the radical Reform Judaism associated with Rabbi David Einhorn. Wheeling Jews adopted ideas from Baltimore's Jewish cultural milieu, choosing a model of Americanization that fit hand-in-glove with the ideological life of their new city.[26]

Einhorn came to the United States in 1855 to be rabbi of Baltimore's Congregation Har Sinai. Forty-six years old then, and already an experienced rabbi and scholar, Einhorn was a meticulous, uncompromising, take-no-prisoners intellectual. He exalted the universalism of the essential idea of Judaism—ethical monotheism—and emphasized the Jewish mission to carry this message to the world. Revelation, Einhorn taught, is progressive; therefore the revelations articulated through the Talmud and rabbinic law in their specific times and places are no longer binding. Jews should pray only those words and practice only those customs that they completely and rationally believe; emotions and affection for tradition are not sufficient criteria. He also argued that American Jews should retain a strong attachment to the German language, not for its own sake but as the spiritual language of progressive religion.[27]

This ideology was something of a specialty item, and Einhorn's direct influence in America was rather limited: Har Sinai had only about seventy member families while he was rabbi there, from a total Jewish population in Baltimore of about seven thousand. His indirect influence was mediated largely through the careers of his close rabbinical colleagues and disciples and his lay supporters in Baltimore and beyond.[28] Wheeling's connections with and similarities to Baltimore promoted Einhorn's influence in the Ohio River Valley.

One critical commonality was a sense of "borderness." Baltimore's location oriented it economically to North, South, and—via the railroads—West; politically as well as economically, the city's face turned in many directions. Maryland was deeply split by the slavery crisis into an antislavery west and a proslavery east and south. Baltimore, in the middle geographically, was influenced by both positions. In 1861 the secession crisis threw the city into chaos; it was symptomatic that the first bloodshed of the Civil War occurred during riots against federal troops there in April 1861.[29]

The debate raged as well in Baltimore's synagogues. Rabbi Bernard Illoway, of the traditionalist Baltimore Hebrew Congregation, was a significant national Jewish voice in favor of slavery and secession. At the moderately traditional Oheb Shalom, Rabbi Benjamin Szold (who had himself arrived in the United States only in 1859) went to great—even extreme—lengths to preserve Jewish neutrality on the sectional dispute. At Har Sinai, and in the pages of *Sinai*, Einhorn vociferously preached a gospel of abolitionism and unionism.[30]

Einhorn's outspoken views gained both strong adherents and equally strong enemies. Many Jewish immigrants were not yet quite comfortable enough in America to feel that their safety as Jews could never be in jeopardy if they were deemed a social irritant; as a result, Jews as a community attempted to maintain a scrupulous political neutrality. Politics was deemed a purely individual pursuit; anything that hinted at a group position, such as formal pronouncements from rabbis, was anathema.

Within Har Sinai, devotion to Einhorn's principles was strong, but even the rabbi's most ardent supporters were wary of being too demonstrative to the outside world about their opinions. Einhorn was impervious to these worries. In 1861, as riots ripped Baltimore, he fled to Philadelphia under threats from antiabolitionist agitators. Deeply frightened, his congregation refused to consider his return unless he adhered to their policy of public silence on political matters. Einhorn of course refused. Outraged at what he perceived as Jewish cowardice and abandonment of Judaism's moral mission, he was proud to have been forced out of Baltimore.[31]

Einhorn's ideas, though controversial in Baltimore, fit well into the social-political-cultural matrix that Jews occupied in Wheeling. In January 1859,

Augustus Pollack addressed an adulatory letter from Wheeling to *Sinai*, announcing that the Hebrew Benevolent Society of Wheeling had elected Einhorn to honorary membership. This almost certainly reflects continuing close connections between Wheeling's Jewish community and Congregation Har Sinai. Although no records from Har Sinai are extant from before 1854, records from the 1850s and 1860s include family names that also appear on the rolls of Wheeling's congregation Leshem Shomayim in those same decades.[32]

The personal connections reinforced ideological connections. Wheeling Jews shared the unionism that was implicit in Einhorn's messianic theology of America. They shared his dislike of slavery, though for them this translated into support of the Republican Party and its free-soil platform rather than into Einhorn's perfectionist abolitionism. Both unionism and antislavery were also embedded in the politics of their German cultural milieu, a German culture that Einhorn exalted as the wellspring of Reform. In the immediate pre–Civil War decades, the same mechanics of geography—roads across the mountains—that exposed Wheeling Jews to Einhorn's ideology of American Reform also created the cultural and political conditions that made their choice of that ideology compelling.

Although Wheeling was, by the eve of the Civil War, the second-largest city in Virginia, it had always been an anomaly within the state, located as it is in a panhandle squeezed between Pennsylvania and Ohio. Like Baltimore, Wheeling felt its in-betweenness. Politically located in the South, it was in all other ways part of the North: commercial and industrial rather than agricultural, supporting protective tariffs and government-funded internal improvements. Railroad politics was a significant component of northwest Virginia's growing dissatisfaction with state government throughout the antebellum era; those who supported northwest Virginia separatism understood the relationship among economics, transportation, and ideology. No north-south roads or rails linked northwest Virginia to the Deep South or even to southern Virginia. In 1827, the Virginia General Assembly had vetoed the Baltimore and Ohio's original plan for a southern Virginia route because it would make western Virginia "the backyard to Baltimore," to the disadvantage of Richmond. However, northwest Virginia, particularly Wheeling, was perfectly willing to be Baltimore's backyard and one of the Midwest's front doors.[33]

Additionally, northwest Virginia was demographically and culturally more typical of the North than the South, with migrants from New England and Pennsylvania and the highest percentage of European immigrants in the state. Probably half of Wheeling's immigrants, including, of course, virtually all its immigrant Jews, were German born. Although, as in Maryland, there were significant political rifts in northwest Virginia, antislavery and unionism were deeply rooted. The area's unionist strongholds were the "rising towns" along the Ohio River and the Baltimore and Ohio line. "Union men," a contemporary observer noted, "are the middle classes," and that was especially true of Wheeling's commercial and industrial elite. In the 1860 election, virtually all of Lincoln's Virginia support came from the northwest, especially Wheeling.[34]

Reflecting the unique geopolitics of Virginia, these cultural and political differences were both the cause and the effect of serious sectional tensions within the state. In the long run, the cultural geography configured by these tensions was mapped onto the political geography of the United States in the separation of western Virginia and the creation of West Virginia. In 1861, Wheeling quickly took the lead in the fight against Virginia's vote for secession from the Union, and then in the northwest's movement for secession from Virginia. Wheeling was the provisional state capital from 1863 to 1869.

Wheeling's Jews shared the cultural and political proclivities of their city and welcomed opportunities to develop commercial interests at the nexus between South and West. They were urban dwellers, middle-class (or aspiring middle-class) businesspeople, and immigrant Germans—and therefore unionists and Republicans. By 1860, Jews in the North were almost all Republicans; a German Jew was editor of Wheeling's German-language paper, the Republican *Der Patriot*. Those Jews from West Virginia who fought as soldiers during the Civil War were all in the Union army.[35]

The story of the aforementioned Augustus Pollack illustrates this typical convergence of ethnic, geographical, political, and religious factors. Born in 1830 in the Rheinland, where his family traded livestock, Pollack left Germany in the late 1840s. After arriving at Baltimore, he clerked for a few years in a non-Jewish dry goods firm there. In 1852, he went out on his own, and in 1854, he moved the business to Wheeling, as he was quoted in an 1890 biography, "upon the solicitations of friends." He married Rosalie Weinberg, also a German-born Baltimorean, in 1855.[36]

During the Civil War, Pollack was in the Home Guard and helped to organize a German company of Wheeling volunteers for the Union army. He was a financial backer of *Der Patriot*, among other involvements in German cultural and expatriate political affairs. Although he did not himself run for office (since, his biography demurred, he was "in no sense a politician"), he was active in local Republican politics. He invested in local railroads and gave speeches in favor of tariff legislation.[37]

Although Pollack left Baltimore before Einhorn arrived, it is clear that he was a moving force in the Wheeling community's turn toward Einhorn's reform. In addition to writing the first communication to *Sinai* in 1859, he may well have been the correspondent who reported about Leshem Shomayim in several subsequent issues. In the fall of 1862, the congregation reported on the introduction of liturgical reforms during the High Holidays. "Things are moving valiantly," read the report. "A new spirit reigns. . . . From all sides resounds the cry: Forward!"[38] The congregation confirmed its loyalty to Einhorn's radical reform in 1869 by adopting his heavily edited prayer book, *Olat Tamid*, one of only a few very small congregations to do so. The congregation also remained aloof from plans for a union of congregations proposed by Einhorn's ideological and personal foe, Isaac Mayer Wise.

Wheeling's experience was an exceptionally stark example of the border nature of the nineteenth-century Ohio River Valley, its ties with Baltimore reflecting the valley's southernness and its unionism reflecting its northernness. Coinciding with Wheeling Jews' unique experience of Americanization, Einhorn's Reform Judaism provided them a mode of expression most appropriate to their unique local setting. But for the most part, American Jews would follow the lead of the moderate reformer Rabbi Isaac Mayer Wise of Cincinnati. It was no coincidence that Wise's national Jewish leadership emanated from the Ohio River Valley.

CHAPTER 5

A Judaism for the Middle Class

In December 1858, Rabbi Isaac Mayer Wise of Cincinnati attended the dedication of a temporary synagogue in Portsmouth, Ohio, set up in rented space in the Masonic building at Third and Washington streets. Wise gave several talks during his stay in Portsmouth, propounding to a receptive audience of Jews and Gentiles his developing vision of a new American Judaism. Writing in the *Israelite* just before his visit, Wise averred that it was in the small towns like Portsmouth, those unique repositories of American values, where Jews were not "too much absorbed in business and pleasure pursuits," that American Judaism would flourish. In the small towns, he declared in charmingly colloquial English, American Jews were truly "wide awake for their religion."[1]

The centrality of the Reform synagogue in small-town Jewish life represented the culmination of a multifaceted process of economic, social, cultural, and religious change experienced by mid-nineteenth-century Jewish immigrants. Americanization was a group experience as well as an individual one, involving both ideas and behaviors. Situated in the cradle of American Reform Judaism, and representing the Jewish achievement of American respectability, the small Jewish communities of the Ohio River Valley were at the center of these changes.

One catalyst for the spread of moderate religious reform was Jews' search for a place in middle-class American society. Economic success, which many were achieving, was only one component of middle-class status. At least as important—and even more elusive—was a certain set of refined manners appropriate to respectable people, a pattern of genteel behaviors that demonstrated to society one's understanding and appreciation of the finer things in life.[2]

By the 1850s, these new cultural norms had diffused from large cities to provincial centers and even to country villages; they had spread from the East

Coast to the West, even in some of the earliest stages of settlement. (Not so coincidentally, of course, Jews as merchants were central to the spread of these norms as expressed in material culture.) With access to this class status available to almost anyone who would play by the rules, the creation of middle-class respectability was a triumph of social democratization. Twenty-first-century Americans, accustomed to an informal social and cultural style, often disdain the notion of "respectability," equating it with craven conformity. But the term has a very basic sense: being worthy of others' respect. The opportunity to be respectable was particularly—and poignantly—important to Jewish immigrants who still remembered the disrespect and indignities Jews experienced in Europe.

Seizing this opportunity required the internalization of new norms. For Protestant Americans, this cultural development took place over the course of more than a century, starting in the early 1700s, so respectability was a natural part of their middle-class life by the time most central European Jews arrived in the United States. Immigrants, then, were to an extent playing catch-up. Likewise, American Protestant religious practice had already come to terms with the new values. In the early eighteenth century, New England Puritans began learning to sing hymns in unison, rather than letting each person sing as he or she pleased while chanting psalms. At the end of the century, Congregational churches, heirs to the Puritan heritage, began to install organs and ornate decoration, inspired by the aesthetic of Anglicanism, the colonial gentry's denomination of choice. Already by the mid-nineteenth century, some Protestants waxed nostalgic for the old, simpler style, without elaborate pews and windows, choirs, or organs, for a time when people dressed plainly and preachers were more passionate than elegant. In 1856, one observer regretted that "as in every other denomination, Methodist churches came to be made up of well-dressed worshippers, sitting in beautiful structures, listening to educated ministers."[3]

The trajectory of nineteenth-century American Judaism is thus not surprising: the synagogue changed to reflect Jews' new self-understanding, in the same way that churches had changed to reflect Protestants' new self-understanding. But Jews were operating under unique pressures. In an atmosphere of freedom unprecedented in recent Jewish history, Jews in nineteenth-century America, paradoxically, felt a great need to prove themselves to non-Jews. No doubt they also felt at least as great a need to prove themselves to themselves.

As the central institution in the Jewish community and as the aspect of Jewish life most publicly visible to non-Jews, the synagogue was the forum for the construction and presentation of Jewish respectability. The buildings themselves were one aspect of this: in many cities Jews built large and impressive synagogues that could rival any church. Among the earliest popular liturgical reforms were the introduction of the English-language sermon, to demonstrate, through linguistic competence, that Jews were not foreigners, and organ music, to demonstrate their cultivation of finer aesthetic sensibilities.[4]

Of great importance was individual behavior within the synagogue. The traditional Jewish public prayer style of lightly controlled chaos, spontaneity, and physical movement was often seen as embarrassingly similar to the camp-meeting revivalism of lower-class American Protestants, a style that refined Protestants had abandoned. Therefore, Jewish congregations enacted rules against talking during prayers and used choirs and organ music to direct and enforce musical conformity. The eventual abandonment of male head coverings—by 1880 "the hallmark of reform"—also reflected the internalization of American manners; after all, gentlemen knew to remove their hats indoors. Careful attention to principles of decorum, order, and thoughtful devotion would prove to middle-class American Protestant society that Jews could adopt genteel modern values as well.[5]

The culture of respectability was strong throughout the Ohio River Valley, as it shared in the bourgeois regional culture of the trans-Appalachian West. And certainly, not only Jews in the larger cities demonstrated a concern for respectability. In fact, it might have been even more compelling for Jews in small towns. After all, as historian Robert Wiebe comments, "small-town life was America's norm" until the early twentieth century; in an atmosphere of overall homogeneity, "people of very different backgrounds accommodated themselves to this Protestant code which had become so thoroughly identified with respectability, and the keepers of the national conscience applied its rules with slight margin for the deviant."[6]

Because Americans saw religion as a powerful engine of morality and orderly behavior, social acceptance and respectability could be achieved through affiliation with these institutions of social order. Thus the formal congregations could do double duty for American Jews: serving their adaptation to American society while providing Jewish fellowship and connection with tradition. In the smaller towns as much as in the cities, Jews had to find a way to accomplish both of these things, to strike a balance of their various goals and needs. It was not entirely comfortable: experiencing a sort of cognitive dissonance, immigrant Jews, especially in the 1850s, often vacillated between the demands of tradition and the demands of their new lifestyle.[7] Valuing both Judaism and Americanism, they searched for a way to be proud, modern Jews and Americans.

If one individual could be considered responsible for the resolution of the immigrants' cognitive dissonance, it would be Isaac Mayer Wise. "Wise was known everywhere in American Jewry," notes Michael Meyer, "a powerful force that moved sometimes in this direction, sometimes in that, but was always driving toward some goal." Wise's goal, in the broadest sense, was the naturalization of Judaism to Americanism. He was the major figure in translating ad hoc pragmatic reforms, a jumble of ideas and practices, into an organized Reform movement.[8]

Wise was born in Bohemia in 1819; although he had a smattering of both yeshiva and university education, he was largely self-educated and almost certainly not formally ordained. With his wife and young daughter, he arrived in the United States in 1846 and immediately immersed himself in the chaotic life of the American Jewish community. On one notable occasion, this active engagement was literally enacted: during his first rabbinate in Albany, New York, conflicts with the congregational president over their respective prerogatives led to a free-for-all fistfight in the synagogue on Rosh Hashanah.

Aggressive, entrepreneurial, and pragmatic (even perhaps sometimes opportunistic), Wise thrived in the free market of religion. He did not start with a rigid agenda of religious reform: on some matters he was traditional, and on some progressive, depending on how they served his larger purposes. Not an intellectual, he was nevertheless a quick study and prolific communicator. With seemingly limitless energy, he organized and proselytized; he was an entrepreneur, a salesman. Institutions more than ideas were his unique contribution. For almost fifty years, he was rabbi of Cincinnati's Bene Yeshurun congregation, definitely the right man in the right place at the right time. When Wise arrived in Cincinnati in 1854, it had the third-largest Jewish community in the United States (after New York's and Philadelphia's) and the largest in the West. Within the up-and-coming bourgeois German Jewish culture epitomized by mid-nineteenth-century Cincinnati, Wise molded a new American Judaism and, through a network of publications and organizations, spread the word across the United States.

Wise had a missionary's zeal for his dream of an American Judaism. He saw a population divided by its European origins, following the different customs of Spain, Germany, Poland—*minhag Sefarad*, *minhag Ashkenaz*, *minhag Polen*. What he wanted, and what seemed to him the obvious next step in the historical progress of Judaism, was a *minhag Amerika*, an American custom. It was critical, in Wise's mind, that American Jews follow one practice. And unlike the older practices, this new practice could express and affirm the essential compatibility of Jewishness and Americanness. Wise was concerned both with Jewish unity and with developing an American-Jewish synthesis, for these goals were really one. The sad state of immigrant Jews in America was the heritage of their experience in Europe; with "no self-respect, no price left," he argued, they were easily drawn into "a wretched imitation of Christian customs." "The Jew must be Americanized," Wise exhorted, "for every German word reminds him of the old disgrace. . . . The Jew must become an American in order to gain the proud self-consciousness of the free-born man." Jews would finally be respected and would respect themselves. With this new consciousness, with a "Jewish patriotism," American Jews would be the first in modern times truly free to release Judaism's powerfully redemptive universal message into the world.[9]

Within a decade of arriving in Cincinnati, Wise had an impressive list of accomplishments. In his first year, he founded a newspaper, the *Israelite*, to further his goals of unity and reform. The *Israelite* carried news of Jewish communities from all over the United States and its territories, from communities of all sizes, no matter how remote their location. Through the *Israelite*'s national circulation, Wise linked American Jews by drawing them into a sense of shared destiny and shared values and subtly directed them toward religious reform; he also established himself as the leader of this drive for unification and reform.

There were numerous important specific projects and causes. Wise campaigned relentlessly against Christian missions to American Jews and cultivated the goodwill of numerous Christian clergymen and local and national politicians. In 1857, he published the first version of *Minhag Amerika*, as he titled his edition of the prayer book. Mostly in Hebrew, with a lightly modified text, *Minhag Amerika* quickly became the most widely used prayer book in the United States. Some of Wise's ambitions were not immediately realized, including, in the 1850s, plans for a union of congregations and for a seminary. But he triumphed years later with the establishment of the Union of American Hebrew Congregations in 1873 and the Hebrew Union College in 1875.

An emphasis on the influence of gentility and respectability in American Jews' adoption of Reform Judaism overlooks the fact that Wise, as reform's cheerleader, was hardly genteel. Rather, he was naturally comfortable with the combative strain in nineteenth-century American society. In the pages of the *Israelite*, he spared no abuse of the opponents of reform, whom he characterized (in only one example, from March 1860) as agents of "the blindfolded ghost of superstition [and] the masked moloch of hypocrisy and bigotry."[10] In some respects, Wise's aggressiveness was viewed positively by the American Jewish community—here was someone who could play by the rough-and-tumble rules of American public life. Wise certainly used the rhetoric of respectability in appropriate forums, linking it to ideas of democracy and progress and therefore making that progress available to his immigrant constituents.

But respectability was something one had to fight for—and no false gentility kept Wise from asserting what he thought was right.

By the 1870s, through their own experience and the prodding of leaders like Wise, American Jewry had matured decisively. Its frontier days long past, Cincinnati was now a capital of middle America and of Jewish America, a city where middle-class respectability and a reformed Judaism coexisted happily. In fact, Ohio historian Henry Howe, writing in the 1870s, even pronounced the city "a sort of paradise for the Hebrews."[11] The elements of this post–Civil War vision of paradise included the convictions that Jews could succeed economically in America, that they could interact freely and equally with non-Jews, that working for civic betterment was their obligation as both citizens and Jews, and that they were the vanguard of a new, and specifically American, Judaism.

From his Cincinnati base, Wise spread this vision to Jewish communities across the United States. Wise's personal presence was enormously important to his project of unity and reform. In addition to writing, he traveled widely and frequently throughout the country, enlisting allies from both the rabbinate and the laity, promoting the formation of congregations, and exhorting Jews on their duties and potentials as Americans. Since, as a newspaper editor, Wise could travel by rail for free (a usual perk in this era), his two modes of outreach—the newspaper and "circuit riding"—were mutually reinforcing. In 1855, he started his first journey back east on an Ohio River steamboat, stopping to visit the Jewish communities at Louisville and Wheeling. Jewish merchants and other visitors from out of town also often visited his Cincinnati synagogue and carried reports back home. Linked by geographic proximity and ties of work and family to the Jewish culture of Cincinnati, Jews in the small Ohio River towns were the perfect audience for Wise's message.

Portsmouth, Ohio, was precisely the sort of town in which the conditions existed for the development of the new conception of American Judaism. The town offered both ample economic opportunities to Jewish merchants and social opportunities to Jewish citizens.

Portsmouth's prosperity was founded on Ohio River commerce, and it grew quickly after the arrival of the first steamboat there in 1811. In 1829, the local newspaper listed no fewer than 911 steamboat dockings for the year, almost 3 per day.[12] The town was given a significant boost by the completion in 1832 of the Ohio and Erie Canal, which connected it with Lake Erie at Cleveland via Columbus. Drawing on regional agricultural resources, Portsmouth specialized in shipping corn and pork products to the American South. By the 1860s, railroad connections augmented the network of inexpensive transportation, boosting industrial growth in the production of iron, clay, and sandstone. In that decade, Portsmouth was the only town with a population over ten thousand in the entire mineral region of southern Ohio, from Washington through Scioto counties.[13]

The group that organized Portsmouth's Congregation Beneh Abraham in the fall of 1858 numbered about two dozen men, of all ages and marital statuses. All of them were merchants or clerks; most sold clothing and dry goods, and several sold cigars or liquor. Their businesses were clustered in a six-square-block area of town at the confluence of the Ohio and Scioto rivers. Though some lived five or six blocks away from the business district, many lived at or very near their places of employment. Some of them, those who were proprietors of their own establishments, could probably be considered already middle class; others, especially the clerks, were still on the lower rungs of the ladder. A few months after the congregation was organized, the Jews of Portsmouth set up a synagogue on one floor of a downtown building owned by the Masons, not far from the business district.

As he did with many new congregations, Isaac Mayer Wise attended the dedication of the synagogue in December 1858. For the congregation, it was an opportunity to have an important figure—a rabbi from the big city where many had family and business connections—validate their presence and their project. They no doubt realized that, because they were the religious anomaly in town, it behooved them to make their Judaism accessible and comprehensible to non-Jews; dedication ceremonies were the perfect opportunity to open the synagogue doors and thereby dispel some of the mystery. For Wise, the event was an opportunity to present the values of the new American Judaism to Jews, with the hope of attaching them to his goals, and to Gentiles, with the hope of enhancing the reputation of Jews and Judaism.

The weekend of the dedication was filled with events. On Friday evening, at synagogue services, Wise's oration was directed to the Jews of Portsmouth. As reported in the *Israelite*, he urged the community to fulfill its mission: "To preserve and promulgate principles and doctrines of which the prophets tell us, that they are intended by Providence to redeem and unite humanity in light, truth, justice and freedom." On Sunday evening, he addressed a general audience on "the influence of the dispersed Israel on the progress of civilization."[14] These small congregations, in the small towns of the American heartland, were for Wise the pioneers of his new American Judaism. Through integration into these typical American communities, they would re-create the image of the Jew: they would win acceptance from Gentiles as being demonstrably integral to the American scene and would cultivate pride in the Jewish contribution to America. Wise's assessment that in small towns Jews were not "too much absorbed in business and pleasure pursuits" may have reflected a romantic mythology rather than a reality. But he was correct that, in their own fashion, small-town Jews were indeed "wide awake for their religion."

It was significant that Beneh Abraham rented space from the Masonic order, of which many of the Jewish men were members. In the mid-nineteenth century, fraternal orders (among other voluntary associations) had a special and critical role in American society. Though segregated by social class, fraternities were often well integrated in terms of cultural backgrounds. Often in small towns, almost all Jewish men belonged to lodges such as the Masons.[15]

As an institution, Masonry, which originated in England, had a checkered past in the United States.[16] In the colonial and early national eras, it was an important part of elite American culture, and many leading colonial Jewish—as well as non-Jewish—merchants were Masons. Seriously damaged by political opposition to its elitism (and secrecy) in the 1830s, the fraternity was revived in the 1840s and 1850s on more democratic lines, and it was this more middle-class organization that attracted up-and-coming Jewish immigrant men. In fact, the Masons, among all fraternal orders, were a bastion of bourgeois values, a place for immigrant men to refine their business contacts and their professional and social manners. The culture of Masonry was accessible to Jews: it was based on the Enlightenment principles of universalism and tolerance and even used some Jewish (that is, biblical) language and iconography in its rites and symbols. It was a powerfully meaningful system. Some nineteenth-century American Jews even blended Masonic ritual and Jewish ritual, especially in the conduct of funerals, and many fledgling synagogues rented space in Masonic buildings.

Because of the Masons' importance to the Portsmouth congregation, Wise took the opportunity of his visit also to address the members of the lodge. By praising Jews' involvement in American fraternalism, he could cultivate the bond of Jewish and American values so necessary to Jews' Americanization. Wise had once asserted that "Masonry is a Jewish institution whose history, degrees, charges, passwords and explanations are Jewish from the beginning to the end." In Portsmouth, he reiterated this notion, declaring that the "leading principles of Masonry are so much our own"—a fine note of encouragement to both Jews and Gentiles.[17]

It is clear from reports of the Portsmouth event that the Jews there were already beginning to absorb genteel American aesthetic preferences. Wise noted approvingly that the prayers for Friday evening and Saturday morning services were chanted "in a harmonious and simple-sublime manner." The old style of prayer was on the way out, but other traditions remained, particularly separate seating for men and women. More thoroughgoing changes would evolve over the next few years.

The importance of Masonic membership for Jewish men illustrates how the concern for respectability was often expressed in gendered terms. By the mid-nineteenth century, American Jews' notions of appropriate male and female behavior were diverging considerably from traditional norms. Note two historians of American Jewish women, "Though foreign to traditional Judaism, the notion of women as men's moral superiors had penetrated American Jewry" by that time.[18] This moral superiority was expressed in part by greater religiosity. The bourgeois expression of American feminine religiosity through church attendance was at odds with traditional female Jewish religiosity, which was based in the home, but now Jewish women were the majority in attendance at synagogues, as Protestant women were in churches.

Similarly, for acculturating American Jews, the traditional separation of men and women in public worship (usually by placing women in a balcony) was increasingly seen as an implicit denigration of women's spirituality. The practice was criticized for highlighting, rather than diminishing, attention to sex and for its foreignness—it reeked of the "Oriental" exoticism of the seraglio. American congregations increasingly adopted mixed seating. Often, the logistics of converting a recently purchased church into a synagogue provided the necessary excuse, or at least backdrop. But elsewhere, as in Portsmouth, there were no such logistical concerns. When Beneh Abraham in 1864 bought a portion of the Masonic building in which they had been renting, their new permanent space featured mixed seating where before there had been separation. This so-called family seating signified Jewish acceptance of the nineteenth-century American conception of the family as a spiritual refuge from the harsh, competitive world.[19]

The acceptance of American gender norms created a space for Jewish women to have a significant impact on acculturation. Jewish women adopted the regnant ideology of domestic feminism, in which the woman's nurturing role in the home validated her charitable and religious volunteer work outside the home. Through benevolent societies, synagogue sisterhoods, and Sunday schools, Jewish women modeled American female values in their Jewish world. They were good American women, but on specifically Jewish terms—adopting some Protestant values while rejecting their necessary connection to Protestantism alone. Jewish commitments molded their notion of American womanhood.

Likewise, American commitments molded their notion of Jewish womanhood. Through their activism, American Jewish women asserted that they could be good Jews, if on terms that implicitly defied traditional Jewish mores. In the past, such important communal tasks as education and fund-raising were never delegated to women. These were tasks of the kehillah, run by the men. Adopting the values of American domestic feminism validated Jewish women's claim to these important roles. Women's organizations "became an influential force in Jewish communities across the country, as well as in American society at large."[20]

This twofold adaptation was a critical component in Jews' acceptance into the middle class. Piety and charity were considered hallmarks of respectable womanhood, and so Jewish women's involvement in public religious and charitable activities staked a claim for respectability on behalf of the Jewish community. Through Jewish women's organizations, individual Jewish women acculturated to America at the same time that they helped create an American Judaism that was appropriate for a genteel, bourgeois people. In 1861, Portsmouth's Reverend Isaac Strouse applauded this new role of women in Judaism: through the Ladies' Hebrew Benevolent Society, "the good ladies of this place . . . have done so much toward the prosperity of this Congregation. They have fitted up the synagogue in a very nice and becoming manner; they are always first in attendance at the synagogue; in short they are always foremost in every noble and generous undertaking. . . . [S]hould I sometimes get weary or tired, if I should meet with no support, I shall think of the good ladies of Portsmouth, and I know—all will be right."[21]

An important development in a congregation's life was the hiring of a rabbi. The Portsmouth congregation's first Jewish professional, in 1858, was Abraham Lasker, who acted as ḥazan. In 1860, Isaac Strouse arrived, having served the previous year in the congregation in the upriver city of Wheeling.[22] Functionaries such as Lasker and Strouse were commonly referred to as "reverends" or "ministers," on the one hand to distinguish them from ordained rabbis and on the other hand to make their role transparent to the communities' Protestant neighbors. The Protestant terminology certainly sounded more "respectable" than the Hebrew *shamash*, which can be translated as the rather old-fashioned "beadle" but is also "attendant," "servant," or even "janitor." In German, the position was often designated by the more dignified *Lehrer und Prediger*, "teacher and preacher," and American congregations sometimes used this term.

In mid-1861, the congregation hired Judah Wechsler, a trained rabbi with some experience in America. He had some familiarity with the Ohio River Valley: he had lived in Bellaire, Ohio, in the mid-1850s, during which time he was married to Jeannette Rosenbach from Cumberland, Maryland (the town on the eastern terminus of the National Road). The wedding was performed, coincidentally, by Isaac Strouse, who then lived in Wheeling.[23] The Bavarian-born Wechsler had both a traditional yeshiva education and secular university training and was a moderate reformer like Wise. At the High Holidays in the fall of 1861, there were, in Wechsler's words to the *Israelite*, "many improvements in the [Portsmouth] synagogue. Many prayers are abolished, the Haftorah is read either in English or German, the Thorah is read by me in a plain, and not in singing manner, and not the least of all, there is a choir established. . . . I shall very shortly recommend other reforms to the Congregation, and have the utmost confidence, that they all will be adopted."[24]

Indeed, within a month, Wechsler reported to the *Israelite* that he had convinced the congregation almost unanimously to adopt *Minhag Amerika* and to shorten the weekly Torah reading to a triennial cycle. The net result, he announced proudly, was that the service was very much like that of Wise's congregation. As with Felsenthal in Madison, Wechsler's first burst of enthusiasm was apparently a bit premature. The next spring, in May 1862, in another letter to the *Israelite* praising the progress of reform in Portsmouth, Wechsler admitted that though *Minhag Amerika* had been approved, it was being introduced only gradually.[25]

Wechsler also spent time with the Jews in nearby Gallipolis, who maintained a connection with the larger Portsmouth community. In September 1864, he officiated there at the wedding of Jacob Emsheimer and Fanny Weikersheimer and, as he reported in the *Israelite*, "in a very short time afterwards another union was accomplished in the formation of a congregation" called B'nai Israel. Henry Frank was appointed temporary president and Michael Emsheimer temporary secretary; Leopold Frank offered his "elegant hall" as a temporary synagogue.[26]

Wechsler was very pleased with the proceedings and with the Jews of Gallipolis. The city, he noted, "was formerly a place of no significance, but since the last three years in consequence of its situation became a place of considerable importance. . . . Our brethren are also doing well, and although but 12 families are residing there, I predict for Judaism a glorious future in this city, because the proper spirit is manifested." Wechsler was generally optimistic about the future of Judaism in the small towns of America. "I have never [had] more pleasing experience than here," he effused. "I satisfied myself more than ever, that Judaism exercises too profoundly an influence upon every Israelite as to remain long indifferent." Again, Wechsler may have spoken prematurely, but in 1869, the *Israelite* reported that "our friend Emsheimer" confirmed the successful establishment of the congregation, "Minhag America of course."[27]

When he came to Portsmouth, Wechsler had grandly announced in the *Israelite* that "notwithstanding all obstacles which would come in my way, I would advocate every measure which I consider just and right. . . . [I] promised that I would ever be guided by the words: 'Let there be light.'" Eventually, he became frustrated by what he perceived as the slow pace of change and by the small size of the congregation, and he left in 1864 for a congregation in Indianapolis. But the late 1860s and 1870s saw much movement toward reform in American Judaism—if at a slower pace than some rabbinic leaders desired—and a reformed Judaism was gaining an accepted place in the public religious landscapes of small towns.[28]

The synergy of Jewish civic respectability and religious reform was evident in Madison, Indiana. In 1868, Adath Israel moved into its own building, a vacant high school purchased from the city. The *Israelite* reported that local Christians—in an apparent fit of boosterism—had "prompted" the Jews to make this move so that all religious denominations would be appropriately represented in Madison. Indeed, Protestants and Catholics alike "liberally subscribed" to the building fund. Wise's colleague Rabbi Max Lilienthal (who had visited Madison occasionally in the early 1850s) came from Cincinnati for the dedication. In 1869, the congregation formally adopted *Minhag Amerika*, and in 1873, it installed an organ in the synagogue.[29]

Likewise, in September 1871, the Jews in Paducah, Kentucky, held a public dedication for a small synagogue to house Bene Yeshurum. As Isaac Bernheim, a Paducah Jew who was later prominent in Louisville, noted in his memoirs, "A Synagogue was a novelty and attracted a large number of people who up to that time had never seen such a house of worship and had but a faint idea of Judaism, its principles and ideals." Within a few years, the congregation had abandoned the orthodoxy that many (including Bernheim) felt separated them from the "progressive" thrust of American ideals.[30]

In Evansville, where Max Del Banco had skirmished with "Judah" over reform in 1860, both reform and respectability seemed to be triumphing by the end of that decade. In 1864, Congregation B'nai Israel laid the cornerstone for a permanent synagogue building at Sixth and Division streets; in 1865, the temple, in so-called Moorish-Saracenic style, was completed and dedicated, with Isaac Mayer Wise in attendance. Simultaneously, the congregation opened a day school, at which their "reverend," Simon Hecht, taught religion, Bible, Hebrew, and German.[31]

The Evansville synagogue was a grand statement of the Jewish community's aspirations: reportedly it cost $45,000 to build and could seat six hundred, though a decade later the community still numbered far fewer than that. One can speculate that the model was the elaborate Moorish-style building then being erected by Wise's Cincinnati congregation. That project, which began in 1863, was completed in 1866 at a cost of more than $250,000. The cost of

Evansville's project, however, was greater than the numbers alone would indicate. The controversy over reform seems to have split the community, for Orthodox Congregation B'nai Moshe made its appearance by 1870.[32]

Other communities with smaller numbers would also tread cautiously along the path of reform, but the path was still clear. In Mount Vernon, Indiana, in 1873, after some years of makeshift High Holidays services in various locations in town, seventeen men from among the twenty or so families organized Congregation Ansche Israel and bought an abandoned schoolhouse to use as a synagogue. Writing to the *Israelite*, a local correspondent admitted frankly of "want of unity and cooperation among the members." Trying to include people of "widely divergent" Jewish backgrounds and preferences into a cohesive small group was hindering development. Those offended by certain decisions were threatening to quit, which would endanger the very existence of the congregation. "Thus we are prevented from acting with much independence," he noted, "but must attempt to please everybody." By the early 1880s, the congregation was using the former Christian Church building as a synagogue, and by the early twentieth century, the congregation was unambiguously Reform.[33]

Judaism was indeed becoming respectable—as in the rest of America, so too in the Ohio River Valley. One community was somewhat suspect, however, for neither lay initiative nor rabbinic prodding created a congregation. In comparison with Jews in other river towns, Jews in Parkersburg, West Virginia, were notably unenergetic about organized religion. In April 1875, Isaac Mayer Wise came to town to perform the wedding of Charles and Rowena Rauch's daughter, Lilly, to Morris Cohn. Wise reported in the *American Israelite* that Parkersburg was "a nice, clean, busy little city" with about fifteen Jewish families, one of whom, the Pragers, owned the most prominent dry goods store in town. "All of Parkersburg" was at the wedding—which was actually a double wedding, since Wise also oversaw the conversion to Judaism of the bride's mother (by means of a declaration in front of an open Torah ark) and the remarriage by Jewish tradition of the bride's parents.[34]

Wise found this Jewish community sadly lacking in certain aspects of respectability. The women knew how to conduct themselves as proper Americans: "The ladies of Parkersburg [who had organized a benevolent society] are all very affable and kind." But he commented contemptuously, "The gentlemen are all sinners and publicans, for they can not afford to support a Hebrew congregation."[35] Wise's choice of insults cannot have been arbitrary; he probably used the New Testament cadence (one thinks of "Pharisees and hypocrites") to emphasize that refusing to participate in public religious life could delegitimize Jews in Christians' eyes. Not that Wise was any admirer of Christianity—quite the contrary. But properly Americanized Jews were not sinful and materialistic; they were virtuous and generous, and their institutions announced this to the ambient society.

As Jews became Americans personally (in terms of their own identity) and locally (in their local institutions), broader trends in American life also affected Jews nationally. In the antebellum era, the organization of like-minded local churches into national denominations had provided Protestantism with a portable religious identity, a reliable ministry, educational resources, and support in outreach to the unchurched. By 1840, being part of a national religious union was a hallmark of a church's seriousness and institutional respectability.

In 1873, a union of American Jewish congregations—long a goal of Wise, Leeser, and other rabbis—was finally born, with its institutional and demographic center in the Ohio River Valley. Ironically, the project of creating a union succeeded precisely when Wise was able to let go and leave it to lay initiative—while, as one might expect, still campaigning vociferously for it. Several national rabbinical conferences, held between 1855 and 1871, had produced only ideological dissension; the bottom-up approach succeeded because the laity could more easily set aside ideological disagreements to work on practical matters. The organizing conference created a structure of denominational supports to, in its words, "establish, sustain and govern a seat of learning for Jewish religion and literature; to provide for and advance the standards of Sabbath Schools; and to aid and encourage young congregations."[36] The new Jewish denomination, calling itself the Union of American Hebrew Congregations (UAHC), was not specifically intended to promote reform, though that seemed to be—at least in its moderate version—where most congregations were moving in any event.

Leadership of the UAHC was taken by the large Cincinnati congregations, but the small communities of the Midwest were its backbone. Close to three-quarters of all midwestern congregations in existence in 1877 were members of the union at some point in the nineteenth century, as were two-thirds of all those in the South—and only one-fourth of those in the Northeast. In addition to five congregations from Cincinnati and two from Louisville, several Ohio River towns sent delegates to the 1873 organizing convention, including Evansville (both B'nai Israel and B'nai Moshe, with eighty-two and twenty-seven members, respectively), Portsmouth (reporting twenty-one members), and Madison (reporting twenty-two). Owensboro, Kentucky's congregation joined in 1874.[37]

The connections fostered by Wise over the years paid off in the response to the UAHC. Wise and his colleague Rabbi Max Lilienthal had aided Beneh Abraham's fund-raising by giving several lectures at the Portsmouth Opera

House in March 1870. When the call for the union organizing convention went out, the congregation responded with alacrity. Mayer Eichelstein and Leopold Wise volunteered to attend at their own expense, and when Portsmouth finalized its membership in the UAHC, it was by unanimous approval of the congregational board.[38]

Representatives of the small communities took active roles in building the UAHC. Samuel Meyer of Evansville served on the first executive board. The bulk of the initial funding—$10,000—for the new rabbinical school, to be called the Hebrew Union College, was provided by Henry Adler of the small Ohio River town of Lawrenceburg, Indiana. (Adler was a friend of Wise, who, of course, became first president of the college.) Additional contributions came in from Lawrenceburg and from Paducah, Pomeroy, Portsmouth, and even Parkersburg. Joining the UAHC gave congregations in small towns a formal link to the larger Jewish world, important both for their own development and for presenting their religion to non-Jews.[39]

Some modern writers have judged America's nineteenth-century German Jews very harshly, denigrating their concern for respectability as craven assimilationism. Arthur Hertzberg declares that the German Jewish immigrants, who were "willing to travel as light as possible" on the road to economic success "by abandoning much or even all of their religious and cultural distinctiveness," were primarily interested in "refurbishing their synagogues so that they would be acceptable to the Gentile majority." Essentially, Hertzberg implies, their only principles were money and Gentile approval. Henry Feingold claims that the nineteenth-century reformers "had thrown out the baby with the bath water.... [casting] out much that made Judaism distinctive," and that "in many cases the acceptance of Reform became merely a *rite de passage* for transferring one's loyalty to one of the less Christologized Protestant sects, such as Unitarianism."[40]

Hasia Diner admits to having come to her study of America's German Jews with a similar prejudice: that they were "stiff and formal, afraid to assert their ethnic identity, and their primary goal, apart from achieving economic wealth, was to be accepted and to blend into America." Her research made her far more sympathetic to the immigrants' balancing act of respectability and acculturation with tradition. She argues that despite substantial changes to practice, the sheer number and variety of Jewish institutions, in all parts of the United States, in small towns as well as cities, proves that "American Jews demonstrated a deep wish to live as Jews" and that, in a climate of religious pluralism, "Jews suffered little for their distinctiveness," which they actively celebrated. After all, American Jews "could celebrate holidays when no one else did, they could emblazon their buildings with Hebrew letters and Jewish symbols, and they could boldly state [particularly in debates on the role of religion in the public sphere] that the Christianity of the majority was not theirs."[41]

This "deep wish to live as Jews" was quite evident in the small towns of the Ohio River Valley in the post–Civil War era. Jews continued to move to small towns from cities and from town to town along the river, starting new businesses. They continued to develop Jewish institutional life. In 1874, a nucleus of related families in Ironton, Ohio, who had formerly belonged to Beneh Abraham in Portsmouth organized their own congregation. In the 1880s, the hundred or so Jews in Henderson, Kentucky, organized a congregation, a women's auxiliary, a cemetery, and a school. Even the tiny group in Gallipolis employed a "teacher and preacher."[42]

In the optimistic 1870s, it seemed to many American Jews that they had created a synthesis of Americanism and Judaism that would mutually reinforce the messianic goals of both. At an increasing pace, the rhetoric of respectability modulated into the rhetoric of ideology. Jews could attach a systematic Reform ideology to their middle-class American values because they validated many of the same concepts: individualism, voluntarism, and mission. Mixed seating was increasingly identified with women's emancipation, and separation seen as necessarily discriminatory; order and decorum became supporting evidence for the essential rationality of Judaism. American Jews had developed their synthesis before developing a systematic explication thereof, so that pragmatic reforms served ideology as much as vice versa. A fully articulated institutional ideology would emerge in the Reform movement in the 1880s.[43]

Like other Jews in America, Ohio River Valley Jews pursued religious reform as part of their project of becoming Americans. Their particular location in the region helped shape that pursuit. Also like other Jews in America, those in the Ohio River Valley found resistance to their inclusion, and here, too, their experience was shaped by their region.

CHAPTER 6

The Community within a Community

On December 17, 1862, the following order came across the desk of Captain L. J. Wardell, provost marshal of the Union army forces in Paducah, Kentucky, a town of about five thousand on the Ohio River. The order was wired from the Holly Springs, Mississippi, headquarters of the Union's Department of the Tennessee, which was under the command of General Ulysses S. Grant.

> The Jews, as a class violating every regulation of trade established by the Treasury Department, and also [military] department orders, are hereby expelled from the department within twenty-four hours from the receipt of this order.
>
> Post Commanders will see that all of this class of people are furnished passes and required to leave, and any one returning after such notification will be arrested and held in confinement until an opportunity occurs of sending them out as prisoners, unless furnished with permit from these headquarters.
>
> No passes will be given these people to visit headquarters for the purpose of making personal application for trade permits.

It was signed by Assistant Adjutant General Jonathan A. Rawlins "by order" of Major General U. S. Grant.[1]

This was the infamous General Orders No. 11. Though rightly described by historian Bertram Korn as "the most sweeping anti-Jewish regulation in all American history," the order was almost completely disregarded outside the immediate area of Holly Springs.[2] The exception was Paducah, with a Jewish population of about thirty families. Following orders, Captain Wardell hurried all Paducah Jews, except two sick old women, onto a boat heading upriver to Cincinnati.

There were very specific reasons that this incident occurred in the Ohio River Valley. The Civil War was a trying time for Jews in the valley. As we have seen, the Ohio River functioned as both border and seam; in the antebellum years, it divided slaveholding and free states while uniting northern and southern banks around the use of the river. The sectional conflict heightened this duality. The Ohio River did not divide the Union from the Confederacy; slaveholding Kentucky never seceded, and western Virginia renounced secession. But the river straddled the Union and the Confederacy politically and culturally. Jews in the Ohio River Valley experienced new challenges as sectional political tensions churned up a free-floating antisemitism that was mutually reinforcing with war-induced stresses.

The Paducah incident had its roots in a larger issue in the war's western theater. The outbreak of the war had constricted the export of southern cotton but had not lessened the demand in the northern states and in Europe. To meet this demand, the U.S. Treasury Department decided to permit a limited cotton trade within those areas of the Confederacy under Union control. The Mississippi River, part of Grant's area of command, was the main avenue of shipment. Not surprisingly, this lucrative trade could not be effectively controlled by the license requirements and other regulations that the Treasury attempted to impose. Cotton trading quickly became the province of speculators and was rife with corruption. Administering regulations was the army's responsibility, and it infuriated Grant and his staff to be distracted from military activities to administer this game of greed and private enrichment. Grant would have preferred to stop the cotton trade in his department entirely, but that was clearly not acceptable to the Treasury. Frustrated, Grant lit on one group he thought he might be able to control.[3]

War-induced suspicions dogged Jews throughout the Ohio River Valley. Jews were accused of war profiteering in both South and North, but as a border area, the Ohio River Valley was particularly fertile ground for accusations of Jewish disloyalty to the Union, especially by illicit trade with the Confederacy. Early in the war, these accusations surfaced in newspaper articles in Covington, Louisville, and Cincinnati. In particular, Cincinnati Jewish textile and clothing merchants were accused of war profiteering, since they met much of the Union army's massive requirements for clothing and blankets. "The terms Jew and trader were in fact often used synonymously [in v]irtually every diatribe delivered against the speculators by army officers or others in the Mississippi Valley in 1862," historian Stephen Ash discovered. "Sherman habitually denounced

'Jews and speculators' in the same breath and Grant ordered officers dealing with traders to take special precautions with the 'Isrealites' [*sic*]."[4]

This general scapegoating of Jews legitimated the scapegoating of the Jews in Paducah specifically, because that city was experiencing unusual economic and social tensions. Because Kentucky, as a border state, was critical to the Union, control of Paducah, only fifty miles up the Ohio from the Mississippi, was vital to Union strength in the region. But the residents of Paducah were deeply divided in their loyalties. Before the war, Paducah had been an important point for trade between South and North. Southern markets were now cut off. To parcel out the remaining commercial power and keep tabs on possible furtive southern connections, the Treasury Department gave control of Paducah's commercial life to a hand-picked pro-Union board of trade. This board issued the permits necessary to do business in town.

Trouble was inevitable, and soon army officers, government officials, and local merchants were all accusing one another of corruption. In this atmosphere of suspicion, local Jews—mostly established residents and none involved in the cotton trade—were singled out in the minds of many Gentile citizens the way they had been in the mind of Ulysses Grant. No Jews were on the board of trade, and none were issued business permits by the board; they were bereft of political protection, and their expulsion was a satisfying diversion. It was also a logical consequence of antisemitism embroiled in nasty wartime politics.[5]

The Jewish reaction to the expulsion has gone down in the annals of American Jewish history as proof of America's exceptionalism in the face of what would have been in Europe unexceptional antisemitism. Jews not only felt free to protest to the government but expected—and demanded—that their grievances be remedied. With respect to this response, too, the Ohio River Valley setting was important. Paducah Jewish leaders, including the Kaskel and Wolff brothers, immediately sent telegrams of protest directly to President Lincoln and appealed to other Jewish communities in the region for help. Within a few days, Jews all along the Ohio River, especially in the large communities of Cincinnati and Louisville, were assisting the protest. In January 1863, Cesar Kaskel, accompanied by Congressman John A. Gurley of Cincinnati, met with Lincoln, who ordered General in Chief Henry Halleck to countermand Grant's order. Lincoln also met with a Jewish delegation from Louisville and Cincinnati and expressed his regret at the incident.[6]

The disarray caused by the expulsion set the Paducah Jewish community back only temporarily. Many were back in town within a few years, and by 1866, there were again about thirty Jewish families in town. Grant later admitted to having acted hastily and thoughtlessly: "During war times these nice distinctions [of rights] were disregarded. . . . We had had no time to handle things with kid gloves." He did not address the underlying prejudices, and in the long term, evaluations of the incident and assessments of blame reflected general pro- or anti-Lincoln sentiment generally, rather than attitudes about Jewish issues or civil rights. When Grant ran for president in 1868, Democrats publicized the incident more to embarrass Grant than to defend principle. "The most sweeping anti-Jewish regulation in all American history" had virtually no practical effect on the lives of Jews in America.[7]

The challenges of the Civil War, however, did provide a quick course in Americanization for Jewish immigrants; the war accelerated their social acculturation and raised their political awareness and participation. It also required a fine-tuning of the balance between Jewish loyalties and self-defense on the one hand and the exercise of American political rights and personal political preferences on the other hand. Overall, American Jews were just as divided on the sectional conflict as other Americans. Opinions ranged from strenuous abolitionism to rabid "fire-eating" (the period's colorful term for Confederate nationalism), though there were relatively fewer Jews at either extreme and more in the large middle ground. Generally speaking, Jews' positions were informed by the regnant ideology of the part of the country in which they lived. Southern Jews supported slavery and fought for the Confederacy; northern Jews supported free labor and fought for the Union.[8]

Ambiguity thus characterized the position of Jews in the Ohio River Valley (especially the lower valley), in the maelstrom of overlapping political and cultural influences. In Kentucky, a Union state with strong Confederate sympathies, some Jews served in the Union army and some in the Confederate forces, as did other Kentuckians.[9] In 1856, Rabbi Bernhard Felsenthal had upset his Madison, Indiana, congregation with his outspoken support of the new Republican Party. And in Cincinnati, a controversy between Isaac Mayer Wise and his congregation revealed some of the political tensions endemic to the Ohio Valley as a whole.

In responding to the sectional crisis, Wise placed his understanding of the needs of the Jewish community above all other considerations. He was ambivalent about slavery, but to him that was not the paramount issue. Wise believed wholeheartedly that American freedom was the only hope for the true flourishing and progress of Judaism, and he feared that the breakup of the Union would threaten this freedom. To Wise, the continued denial of freedom to black slaves was a small price to pay for Jewish security. Similarly, in his mind, abolitionism did not advance the cause of freedom but was in fact a threat to it: hypocritically demanding the freedom of some people (the slaves), the abolitionists, he believed, simultaneously threatened other people's freedoms with a Protestant "Christian America" agenda, indifference to Jewish rights, and hostility to immigrants generally. In an *Israelite* editorial after South Carolina's secession in December 1860, Wise blamed "red Republicans and habitual revolutionists . . . German atheism and American puritanism who know no limits to their fanaticism . . . [and] wicked preachers" for "breaking down the fortress of liberty, the great bulwark of our best hopes."[10]

When the Union actually split, however, Wise considered it a greater threat to freedom to ignore states' rights and try to force the southerners back into the Union than to let them go and maintain peace in the remaining sections. Therefore, he refused to speak out either in favor of the Union or in support of the war effort. But while asserting neutrality, he blamed the Republicans for the breakup of the Union and was in fact an active member of the peace faction of the Ohio Democratic Party, the so-called Copperheads. In 1863, when the arch-Copperhead Clement Vallandigham was the Democrats' nominee for the Ohio governorship, Wise was nominated for state senator on that ticket.[11]

Though much of the evidence was covered up, it is clear that this nomination set off a major crisis in Wise's relationship with his congregation. The congregational board, though acknowledging that they felt "honored by this demonstration of confidence bestowed upon [him]," passed a resolution "politely, but most emphatically" requesting that he decline the nomination. Ostensibly, the board was concerned that political activities would interfere with Wise's congregational responsibilities. Yet they had never before objected to his many outside activities and frequent travels. "Politics, especially in time of war," Wise's biographer observes, "was something on which they [Wise's congregants] had opinions of their own," and Cincinnati Jews were mostly Republicans.[12]

In a bizarre juxtaposition of antisemitic rhetoric and support of an individual Jew, the Democratic *Cincinnati Daily Enquirer* lambasted "the Shoddy contractors"—that is, leaders of the Cincinnati Jewish community, many of them clothing manufacturers—for inhibiting Wise only because he was a Democrat and not, like them, Republican.[13] Ironically, much of Wise's support of Vallandigham stemmed from a concern with Jewish equality and interests: Vallandigham had helped American Jews protest antisemitism abroad and had in 1861 opposed a military chaplaincy bill that provided only for Christian chaplains.

Rabbi Judah Wechsler of Portsmouth, who shared Wise's views, also found that his Jewish and political loyalties were intertwined. Wechsler detested abolitionists, especially those in the pulpit, whom he held responsible for the war. In 1864, he lashed out at the local Republican newspaper in the pages of the Democratic *Portsmouth Times*. Wechsler angrily defended the patriotism of American Jews:

> I notice in the last number of the *Tribune*, a wrong and false statement, republished, which is, I believe, taken from the Chicago *Tribune*. . . . The extract, as published, reads thus: "Will we have an [*sic*] dishonorable peace in order to enrich BELMONT, the ROTHCHILDS [*sic*], and the whole tribe of Jews who have bought up Confederate bonds, or an honorable peace won by GRANT and SHERMAN at the cannon's mouth." There is not a word of truth in the whole statement. BELMONT is no Jew. ROTHCHILDS never bought any Confederate bonds, and is not interested at all in this war. The Jews are as honest, as loyal and patriotic as any other class of men. . . . You must let the Jews alone; they love this Union better than you do, and their moral character can favorably be compared with yours. . . . I can only hope that the Editor of the *Tribune* did not closely examine the paragraph above, or he would not have published it.[14]

Ohio Valley Jews were caught between a rock and a hard place; Democratic papers criticized them for supporting the Republicans, while Republican papers repeated allegations of Jews' "offensive conduct" in being "the most adroit smugglers."[15] Any partisan political position required a balancing of Jewish and other interests, but in an America that had only begun to wrestle with racial prejudice, all Jewish political participation required self-defense as a vital component of social integration.

Although regional factors explain why the expulsion of Jews from Paducah during the Civil War happened in its particular place and time, the incident also illustrates some generalizations about antisemitism in the United States. There are many reasons why American antisemitism differs from the classic European version. Jews as a group in America never experienced the strains of emancipation that European Jews (or, for that matter, American blacks) did; because the United States was always modern, there was no real backlash against Jews as representatives of modernity. Consensus politics has kept antisemitism and, usually, other extremisms out of mainstream political life. The practical demands of American capitalism, the political ideals of American individualism and egalitarianism, the social fluidity of a mobile society, and the realities of cultural pluralism and religious voluntarism have always acted as a restraint on the oppression of Jews and other white minorities. At various times, there has been more religious persecution of Baptists, Quakers, Catholics, and Mormons than of Jews. Even in the worst days of nativism, Jews suffered far less than Catholic or Asian immigrants. And antisemitism was never politically institutionalized, as were the two most intractable American racisms, against blacks and Native Americans.[16]

What does account for American antisemitism? Some historians emphasize social and economic competitiveness—antisemitism as a weapon in the battle for prestige and status in American society. Other historians put more emphasis on developments in American Christianity, blaming ascendant Protestantism for creating and spreading anti-Jewish animus. Both are right, for American antisemitism is built on a substratum of ancient prejudices deep in European culture. These negative stereotypes, ultimately rooted in the early Christian conflict with Judaism, do not create acts of antisemitism but do make them possible. Under specific circumstances—social and economic competition, or religious fanaticism, or nativism—the antagonisms latent in negative stereotypes of Jews can be activated into overt antisemitism.[17]

But in the American Protestant mind, negative stereotypes of Jews coexisted with positive ones in an elaborate and inconsistent way. American Gentile attitudes emerged in a distinctive pattern: in the Protestant mind, Jews evoked an "ambivalent image," compounded from inherited attitudes about the "mythical Jew" and new experiences with the "Jew next door." Most salient in antebellum and Gilded Age America were the religious and economic images. On the one hand, Jews were admired as descendants of the Old Testament people; on the other hand, they were suspected as dangerous to the Christian society that many Protestants assumed America was. On the one hand, the Jewish businessman was admired for his success, as an exemplar of the Horatio Alger ideal of the self-made man; on the other hand, this same businessman was suspected of sharp practice, since he was, after all, the descendant of the crafty and unscrupulous Shylock.[18]

Over the course of the nineteenth century, as the Jewish population in the United States increased and dispersed, more and more non-Jews came face to face with the Jewish Other. American Protestants' inherited ambivalence was disrupted by personal contacts with real Jews; they experienced a disconnect between the "mythical Jew" of their imaginations and the "Jew next door" who seemed to contradict the myths. Individuals came to terms with this cognitive dissonance in different ways. Some simply ignored the contradictions or rationalized that *their* "Jew next door" was the exception to the rule—perhaps by attributing the positive aspects of this Jewish man or woman's character to an inner, latent, Christian essence.[19]

Others engaged in what historian Jonathan Sarna has called a process of reconceptualization; that is, they began to reconsider the received wisdom and to change the paradigm, to accept individual Jews on their own merits. This was a complex and subtle process, and Jews remained highly aware of and sensitive to Gentile opinion. But the emphasis on the changes in non-Jews' minds can obscure the extent to which reconceptualization was a two-way street. American Jews were participants in the process, both consciously, through their self-presentation, and unconsciously, through their ordinary daily activities as citizens and neighbors. In fact, concern with non-Jewish opinion encouraged Jewish self-defense, tied up as it was with the maintenance of one's reputation—an important facet of life, especially in a small town.[20]

Jewish participation in the ordinary daily life of the small town reinforced the shared interests of Jews and non-Jews. A positive attitude about Jews as successful merchants and as fine bourgeois citizens often appeared in local newspaper reports of Jewish social and organizational life in the Ohio River Valley's small towns. Jewish social events were reported with the same boosterish enthusiasm applied to non-Jewish news. For example, the Portsmouth paper reported that Jennie Herzog, "a Portsmouth belle," had attended a "Jewish ball" in Ironton, and that the wedding of Mose Wise and Clara Lehmann was attended by "the elite of our Jewish society with a fair sprinkling of favored Gentiles."[21] The prosperity and public leadership position of the Rosenbaum family meant the local paper in Mount Vernon, Indiana, kept up with their activities: Daniel Rosenbaum bought both a farm property and a lot in town, with the intention of opening a dairy business in the country and erecting a $25,000 residence in the city; Daniel and his brother Moses opened a retail store; and Moses's twenty-three-year-old son Jacob had "the finest buggy and horse in the city"—all this in 1881 alone. In 1882, the paper proudly reported the "profitable visit" to town of a relative of Manuel and Jacob Cronbach; when the relative "was told that our town is not improving as fast as it should be [his] confidence in the future of Mount Vernon thereupon moved him to purchase $2,000 of this city's bonds."[22]

As evidenced by the Civil War experience, local politics was an important arena for forging a new Jewish-Gentile relationship. Early in America's history, local political power had passed from religious and intellectual elites to the mercantile classes; this concentration of political power perforce involved Jewish merchants and their interests, creating opportunities for integration and self-defense. There are many examples of Jews' local political activity in the small towns of the Ohio River Valley. Meyer Weil, who peddled in western Kentucky before the Civil War, went into business in Paducah as a tobacco trader. A unionist and Democrat (and described by a contemporary as "a distinguished looking man and fearless to the point of recklessness"), Weil was elected mayor of Paducah for three terms between 1871 and 1881. He also spent two terms in the state legislature. In Portsmouth, Ohio, in the 1870s, Isaac Mayer was active in local Democratic politics; he held city office and was, according to the Democratic paper, "pretty good on the run." Bernard Kahn, who lived intermittently in both Ironton and nearby Jackson, Ohio, for almost twenty years, was a member of the state legislature from Jackson County before moving to Cincinnati in 1878. In Henderson, Kentucky, Morris Baldauf served in city government in the late nineteenth century, as did Al Zilenziger in Parkersburg, West Virginia.[23]

Involvement with the public schools also served Jewish interests while helping create a positive image. Another Parkersburg Jew, Solomon Prager, demonstrated his civic commitment by providing in his will for the establishment of an academic prize for boys ages nine through fifteen in the city's public schools. Like other clergymen, rabbis were involved with the schools, as evidenced by this item from a local newspaper in 1873: "The Portsmouth High School Alumni have our thanks for a choice selection of sweet things, by the hand of Rabbi [Simon] Gerstmann. A splendid repast was served the graduates by Misses Jennie and Hattie Fisher [apparently non-Jews], at their residence, on Friday evening of last week." Through such activity, Jews could assert their interests in the face of Christian cultural dominance. In Cincinnati, where school politics played out on a larger stage, Jews even allied with Catholics in 1869 to keep Protestant religious instruction out of the public schools.[24]

The Ohio River Valley was home to a great many German Christian immigrants, both Catholic and Protestant, a fact that complicated relationships between Jews and non-Jews. In the 1870s, Germans constituted almost half of all foreign-born residents of Ohio; in Scioto County, site of Portsmouth, it was more than half. In some respects, the presence of non-Jewish Germans provided a cushion to absorb culture shock. In their language, Jews and Gentiles shared one aspect of outsider status, which might render the Jew less conspicuous. They were also used to each other in certain economic roles, so Jews could feel more comfortable about German Christians as customers of their businesses. Both read the German-language press, which reflected these imported cultural traits. In Marietta, Ohio, for instance, the English-language press refused to take ads for liquor stores and bars, so *Die Zeitung* was the only print advertising outlet for Jewish and other, mostly German, liquor merchants. Among political activists and intellectuals—those with a German university education—there were considerable convergences of sentiment. Rabbis Bernhard Felsenthal and David Einhorn, for example, felt that German culture was intrinsic to their spiritual and intellectual lives. Many middle-class Jews participated in German cultural activities such as music festivals.[25]

But the sense of Jewish-Gentile difference was also imported from Germany, and as in Germany, social relations were fraught with ambivalence.

Social interaction between the two groups was limited in many cities, including Cincinnati. There are indications that relations were easier, if not intimate, in smaller towns; this seems to have been the case in many Ohio River Valley towns. Over the long term, however, Jews found that as they became more American, they had more in common with other Jews—even from different countries—than with Gentiles from the same country.

In addition, despite an apparent mutuality of interests in civic order generally shared by Jewish and Gentile merchants, economic competition complicated their relationships. Non-Jews often made recourse to negative stereotypes of their Jewish competitors. There is abundant documentation of this in the reports of one of the nineteenth century's leading national credit-reporting bureaus, R. G. Dun and Company, predecessor to Dun and Bradstreet. One of the earliest such organizations, founded in 1841, the firm used branch offices and local correspondents—businessmen, lawyers, and bankers—to collect information about merchants who were applying for credit from wholesalers. Occasionally the reports included hard data on a business's finances, but more often they were simply evaluations based on subjective impressions, local reputations, and, occasionally, deliberate malice.

In the small towns of the Ohio River Valley, as elsewhere, local agents often mentioned a subject's Jewishness in their reports regardless of whether they gave a good or bad credit rating. An evaluation of Joseph Emsheimer of Portsmouth—"A Jew. . . . Small but regular business"—is typical. The reporters and their clients shared a stereotype so pervasive that a Wheeling reporter could expect his reader to understand when he described Julius Ballenberg in 1845 simply as "same as all Jews."[26]

Often the reports contained blatant contradictions between the Jewish stereotype and the individual's reputation. The "Jew next door" challenged the "mythical Jew." Simon Moses was, the Madison, Indiana, reporter noted, "a Jew & we would say not v[er]y reliable, but has here to fore had the reputation of being prompt in meeting demands vs. him." The same reporter noted of Ascher Hoffstadt that "there is a suspicion that he will fail but still we see no outside reasons why he should." George Newberger of Ironton was "a Jew, but has the reputation of being hon[est]," and Marx Graff of Wheeling was "a Jew, the best of his race whom we have known." In Gallipolis, Moses Frank was rated "good, although a Jew," and his brother Harry "good as the best tho[ugh] a Jew."[27]

Part of the problem was that non-Jews misunderstood (and often put the worst construction on) aspects of Jewish economic behavior that differed culturally from "American" norms. Historically, the pressures of earning a living in Europe had encouraged Jews to be as flexible as possible in business. For instance, many Jews' instinct was to rely on each other rather than outsiders.

In order to protect themselves, Jews went to great lengths to keep their businesses within the family, or at least within the "tribe." But American credit reporters were suspicious of such practices as shared legal titles and elaborate—and changeable—partnership arrangements. In Ironton, during the depression of the 1870s, reports made sure to note that the Weilers, Newbergers, and Newmans all transferred ownership of family assets to the wives' names to protect credit under the husbands' names.[28]

Jews were less likely to own real estate, preferring to keep their capital liquid, also an ingrained habit. To a people who had been forbidden to own land in most of Europe, this seemed a reasonable strategy for maintaining flexibility. But the credit evaluators were suspicious that this suggested a lack of commitment to the community and a predisposition to unhealthy speculation. For instance, Meyer Heyman of Wheeling was described thus: "Is as good as a Jew can be without owning R[eal] E[state]; consid[ere]d very well off by the [local] merchants."[29]

Jewish businesses also generally took greater risks for business expansion, and there were, to be sure, many business failures. Operating with the full repertoire of antisemitic stereotypes, Dun's reporters often put a negative spin on this fact. As one historian points out, "Differences were interpreted and embellished so that they became evidence of defects. Hence the failure of Jewish businesses provided evidence not for ineptitude or foolhardy risk-taking, but of deception."[30] Noting that the Emsheimer brothers had failed once in another town, a reporter in Gallipolis in 1865 claimed that they "have done pretty well in [their] present location and will go along and pay up as long as it answers to do so. When it pays better to 'sell out' they will play the old game over again." When a relative took over Abraham Moch's assets, the reporter commented, "Some parties here think it was a sham sale."[31]

But between the lines, there is sometimes a hint that a Gentile reconceptualization of Jews was underway. In the reports from several towns (Gallipolis, Ironton, and Marietta, for example), comments about a subject's Jewishness are far more common in the 1850s and 1860s than they are in the 1870s and 1880s. Comments in the later years tend to be about Jews who are new in town. Over the course of time, it seems, a Jewish merchant could prove himself. The credit history for Simon Horkheimer of Wheeling provides a good example. In 1860, the reporter notes, "We suppose [Horkheimer and his partner] to be good but [they] own no R[eal] E[state]. They are Jews and you know how far to trust them." By 1867, Horkheimer is "one of the few good Jews we have in the city." Just over a decade later, references to Horkheimer's Jewishness have disappeared. His credit rating is always "very good"—he is even "one of our leading men"—a city councilman, director of a local bank and an insurance company, owning "fine R[eal] E[state]." Through his business success and civic activities, Horkheimer the Jew has become Horkheimer the respectable.[32]

The relatively neutral ground of civic and business activities thus provided important opportunities for Jews to cultivate their reputations as they affirmed the notions of "progress" so central to small-town boosterism. And through a careful presentation of their updated, reformed Judaism, Jews could share with Gentiles their new understanding of Judaism as an American religion. Presenting Jews and Judaism as a natural part of America's public religious life, small-town Jews emphasized the similarity of their and other Americans' values and interests. Yet they did not disguise Judaism's uniqueness. As American society groped toward a workable pluralism, Jews saw themselves—and were seen—as simultaneously similar and different, as both Americans and Jews.

Much of small-town life revolved around religious institutions, and local newspapers often reported on Jewish communal activities, such as the installation of a new rabbi, the dedication of a synagogue, or the election of congregational officers. The papers noted the dates of the High Holidays for practical reasons—Jewish stores would then be closed. Other Jewish holidays were occasionally acknowledged, even if misunderstood, as in an 1875 *Portsmouth Times* article about Passover that mistakenly informed readers, "During this time nothing but unleavened bread will be used for food by the members of the Jewish synagogue." The Portsmouth public learned in 1871 that Beneh Abraham's new rabbi gave his inaugural sermon in English rather than in German—a significant statement about acculturation in a town with a number of German immigrants.[33]

Synagogue building was a prime opportunity for staking out Jewish difference within sameness. By inviting the non-Jewish public to participate in this and other Jewish communal activities, small-town Jews claimed for their religion a place in public life as legitimate as Christianity's, and by assuming Protestants' agreement with that legitimacy, they secured it. Placing the synagogue in the foreground of American Jewish life, Jews could not only contribute to their own survival but also, by marking their place on the small town's social map, aid and abet the process of Gentile reconceptualization.

Through the building of synagogues, Jews contributed, in the non-Jewish mind, to the moral stability of society represented by houses of worship. Writing about the new Adath Israel building in Owensboro, Kentucky, in 1877, the local newspaper commented, "Very general credit will be accorded the plucky congregation, who, right in the thickest of the political and financial troubles of the country, have succeeded in building in our midst a house of divine worship hardly second to any in the city." Religious respectability was explicitly linked to economic bona fides; the story continued, "The city owes much of its commercial reputation to the vim and enterprise of this class of people."[34]

The architecture of the Owensboro synagogue was itself a significant statement of American Jewish identity. In its overall plan, and with its Gothic stained-glass windows, the building resembled local churches, suggesting at least an aesthetic harmony of religious persuasions. But like the more famous Plum Street Temple in Cincinnati, home to Isaac Mayer Wise's congregation, the building also announced Jewish uniqueness: the fanciful miniature Moorish domes atop the Owensboro temple's facade deliberately suggested—through artistic reference to the "Oriental" origin of Judaism and, particularly, to the "golden age" of Jews in medieval Muslim Spain—Jewish distinctiveness and even a taste of high-class exoticism. Owensboro's Jews used this architectural language in the same way that those of Wise's congregation did when they constructed their elaborate temple, an icon of the Moorish style.[35]

The Jewish community of Portsmouth, Ohio, deliberately positioned itself in the mainstream of the town's life. As early as 1863, five years after its founding, the congregation was regularly listed in the local church directory on the front page of the *Portsmouth Times*. The dedication of the congregation's new meeting place, in 1864, was designed to emphasize this integration. Bespeaking the town's prosperity and the Jewish community's stability, it was the first permanent synagogue owned by an Ohio congregation outside a major city. (The others were in Cincinnati, Cleveland, and Dayton.)[36]

The new synagogue was actually the old Masonic hall in which the congregation had originally rented space. They now purchased two-thirds of the building, with the Masons retaining the third floor. The first floor housed a schoolroom and social hall, and the second floor the sanctuary, which now featured mixed, or family, seating. At the dedication ceremonies, a crowd joined the procession that carried the Torah scrolls from the Ronsheim home, which had served as the temporary meeting place during building renovation. Rabbi Judah Wechsler described the event in the *Israelite*: "A fine band of music at the front of the procession, four girls dressed in white, carrying the rods of a splendid kind of curtain [a chuppah], under which the law was carried by the two oldest members of the congregation, then again four girls dressed in red, white and blue, and a large number of Israelites, as well [as] a great many Christains [*sic*] proceeded then to the synagogue." Whether or not there were in fact more than five hundred people involved (as Wechsler claimed), it was a large crowd. The curiosity of many had no doubt been piqued by the notice placed by the congregation in the *Portsmouth Times*, inviting "all the ministry and their congregations, the court, council, press, and the citizens generally" to the festivities.[37]

The Presbyterian church choir provided the music, though some felt the desired interfaith atmosphere was not entirely achieved. Despite the invitation to the local Christian clergy, grumbled Wechsler, "whether they thought it was unbecoming to their dignity, or whatever may have been the cause, but few were present. The catholic [*sic*] priest of the German church seemed even offended that he was invited to attend the dedication of a Jewish synagogue." The events confirmed Wechsler's conviction that the Christian clergy generally—"these fanatic priests"—were a "drag-chain" on the laity's natural movement toward "progress and enlightenment."[38]

But on the lay level, social integration and religious culture seemed to reinforce each other. Christians donated to the Portsmouth congregation's building fund in 1864, as Jews donated to church building funds. These donations expressed the importance of cultivating a generally religious American culture as much as the importance of cultivating good neighborly relations. Publicly thanking the Presbyterians for their participation in the dedication, the Portsmouth congregation declared, "We hail with joy and gladness the liberal and enlightened spirit manifested by these ladies and gentlemen, and hope the time is not far distant when we will all meet as brothers and sisters in one Great God, who has created us all."[39]

In Gallipolis, too, Gentile support was part of the process of Jewish community building. To raise funds for a synagogue, the nascent congregation gave "public entertainments" such as the one announced in the *Gallipolis Dispatch* in March 1869, held at Frank's Hall and "enlivened with music and dancing." Later that spring, their fund-raisers evidently successful, the congregation opened a small synagogue on the upper floor of a downtown building. The local newspapers carried stories of the Friday evening dedication ceremonies, at which Mr. Strauss, the ḥazan, officiated as the Sefer Torah was placed in the ark. The prayers were in Hebrew, with the exception of a special dedicatory prayer in German; Torah commentary was also delivered in German. "The whole was impressive," wrote one reporter solemnly, "inspiring even the Gentile visitor with a sense of the purity and holiness of sacred things, and a reverence for the Glory of the Ancient Church." Commented another, "While listening to the pleasant harmony of the (to us) unknown tongue, we wandered back to the days of David, of Abraham and of Moses; in the far off ages of the past, when the forms and ceremonies, that we then beheld, were a part of the daily life of the pious, God-fearing Israelites of old."[40]

Though Judaism's past was its most immediately appealing aspect to many Gentiles, the Jewish community made sure to emphasize its contemporary relevance. Gallipolis's newspaper reported on other events in the Jewish community, for the development of religious institutions, even non-Christian, was "one of the evidences of progress in our midst." A few months before the synagogue dedication, a reporter attended a public examination in the Hebrew school run by Strauss. The exercises included Hebrew and German reading and translation. "Mr. Joseph Emsheimer then spoke in terms of warm approbation of the progress of the pupils and predicted that a new era was about to dawn upon the Jewish denomination in this city," the story continued. "After he had concluded, a very elegant pyramid cake was cut and distributed among the children and all present."[41]

The ramifications of this transparency of synagogue life are evident in the phenomenon of conversions to Judaism, which were increasingly acceptable by the mid-nineteenth century. It was becoming clear that intermarriages could bring non-Jews into the Jewish people as well as draw Jews away. For instance, in 1869, the wife of Abraham Nathan, a grocer in Portsmouth, converted to Judaism. The couple had lived in town for about a year, during which time Mrs. Nathan reportedly attended synagogue faithfully every Shabbat.[42]

Another case from Portsmouth was reported to the *Israelite* in 1864 by Judah Wechsler. The candidate was the fiancée of Dr. Daniel Mayer, an immigrant who had served as a Union army surgeon in the Civil War. "An accomplished lady of Western Virginia, whose name was Ada Walker, renounced by her own free will, Christianity, and was for some time instructed in the principles of Judaism by me," Wechsler wrote. He marveled that "time has changed. While in former centuries there were recorded many conversions from Judaism to Christianity . . . we are now enabled to record quite the contrary. Hardly a week passes off without any conversions to Judaism." After Walker's conversion ceremony, Wechsler performed her wedding to Mayer. As a token of her appreciation, Walker presented the rabbi with an unusual present—a handkerchief on which she had embroidered the Hebrew words of the Sh'ma.[43]

This public presentation of Jews and Judaism worked to reinforce both the sameness of and the difference between small-town Jews and their Christian neighbors. It emphasized Jews' bourgeois respectability while exposing non-Jews to new concepts. But at least in the small towns of the Ohio River Valley, the discourse of civic life and local boosterism helped create a sense of civic cohesion and inclusivity.[44]

Negative stereotypes and latent hostilities do not create antisemitic behaviors automatically but operate within the context of the specific time period and social setting. The experience of Jewish-Gentile relations differed for small-town Jews from the experience of those who lived in larger Jewish communities in the cities. Small-town Jewish life was in some ways less visible—there were no ethnic neighborhoods or large, imposing synagogues—but in other ways it was more exposed. Interaction with Gentiles was constant in business, in neighborhoods, on the streets. The one synagogue symbolized the whole Jewish people; in the frequent absence of a rabbi, one or a few individuals represented Jewish interests officially. The impact of each individual Jew was magnified.

America's so-called Gilded Age of the 1870s and 1880s provides an example of the way the social setting can foster or neutralize antisemitism. The extremely competitive—even cutthroat—business climate of postbellum America created a culture of rigorous competition for social status, and the ambivalent image of the economic Jew took on a new salience for those who viewed Jews as a threat to their own ability to gain or retain status. Many Jews from the central European immigration had in fact become quite well-to-do, some acquiring the means for conspicuous consumption before they had fully acquired the niceties of Victorian America's "refined" manners. The result was the flourishing of a stereotype of the aggressive, ignorant, and ill-mannered Jewish parvenu pushing his or her way into proper society. In the upper economic strata—and increasingly in the middle class—social discrimination against Jews, which had been fairly minor before the Civil War, began to increase noticeably across the country. Suddenly, Jews were being turned out of schools, clubs, and other selective venues where they had earlier been welcome.[45]

Social discrimination against Jews based on status competition was not uniform throughout the United States; there were distinct regional and local variations. The evidence, historian John Higham concludes, demonstrates that the phenomenon "generally affected small towns less than cities of perhaps 10,000 population or more; that it influenced the trans-Mississippi West less than the East or older Middle West; and that it touched the South least of all." But specific characteristics of each community were critical, and the paramount factor was the stability or instability of the Jewish population, that is, "the degree to which [its] growth . . . disturbed the existing social structures." Even in large cities, if the Jewish population grew only in proportion to the overall growth of the town, social structures could adapt.[46]

Most small towns of the Ohio River Valley did not attract new Jewish residents in numbers sufficient to upset the status quo. Only the upper Ohio Valley, closer to Pittsburgh, experienced a large increase in Jewish population in the late nineteenth century, though within the context of a greatly increased total immigrant population. One can also speculate that in the Ohio River Valley, the residue of cultural southernness offset the influence of the older Midwest. For the most part, small towns retained more social openness and were less competitive. The social discriminations that assaulted the moneyed Jewish aristocracy of the cities—restricted luxury hotels, restricted clubs, restricted elite private schools—were ones that would not often have been relevant to small-town Jewish families. In a society where non-Jews could easily have face-to-face interactions with Jews, where social aspirations could be only relatively modest, and where a reformed and respectable Judaism was part of the local landscape, the malevolent antisemitism of the Gilded Age less often reared its head.

Of course, this does not mean that the people of the small towns of the Ohio River Valley were free of prejudice, and particular local circumstances could create conditions for its expression. For example, a complex of factors affected events in Marietta, Ohio. Largely as a result of a civic antigrowth attitude, mid-nineteenth-century Marietta was one of the few small river towns of the Ohio Valley that did not have an organized German Jewish community; there were few Jewish residents. From 1869, the Frank family, who also owned businesses in downriver Gallipolis, had a clothing store on lower Front Street. But the three other clothing stores listed in the 1873 city directory, and all of the dry goods stores, were owned by non-Jews; of the six merchant tailors listed, none were Jewish.[47]

In the 1870s and 1880s, a few more German Jewish families settled in Marietta. In 1875, the Hurwitzes came from Cincinnati to open a store selling liquor and cigars and stayed about ten years. In 1882, Morris Luchs was sent to Marietta from Bellaire, Ohio, by his father, Samuel, to set up a branch of the family wholesale liquor business. In 1887, Samuel Sulzbacher came from Chillicothe, Ohio, and opened the Home Clothing House. Both Luchs and Sulzbacher were native-born sons of German immigrants.[48]

Luchs's business was quite successful. Within a few years, the local Dun agency credit reporter affirmed that he was "of good capacity[,] char[acter] & habits"; his references included some of Marietta's leading Protestant businessmen. He was an active member of a local fraternal organization with the politically incorrect name of the Improved Order of Red Men. Over the years, he moved his business twice to better quarters, farther from the seedier part of town near the Ohio River. Despite the morally suspect nature of his trade, Luchs was quite respectable and served, as did all upstanding businessmen, on the committee to organize Marietta's centennial in 1888.[49]

Sulzbacher had opened his store with an advertisement proclaiming, "Why the Home? Because we propose to make our home among you, and make your homes happier by furnishing you good, reliable goods at *fair* prices." He evidently prospered: In early 1888, a credit report noted that he was "doing a good business." An 1891 county history reported that the Home Clothing House's merchant tailoring department ("the crowning glory of this house") employed "fifteen good practical assistants." Sulzbacher threw himself into civic affairs, serving on the finance committee of the centennial committee.

Sam Sulzbacher advertises in the *Marietta (OH) Weekly Leader,* July 17, 1888.

He sponsored a square in the centennial quilt, using the space to advertise his promise of a "square deal."[50]

Sulzbacher and the Luchs brothers came to Marietta at a time of rapid local population growth, spurred by a regional oil boom in western Pennsylvania, southeastern Ohio, and northern West Virginia. Between 1870 and 1900, though Washington County overall experienced less growth than other neighboring counties (19 percent), the city of Marietta experienced a great deal more—a full 156 percent. Growth and urbanization challenged the midcentury cultural status quo, and in this turbulent milieu, antisemitism—reflecting the negative side of the ambivalent Jewish economic image—surfaced. In July 1888, the above advertisement appeared in both the *Marietta Times* and the *Marietta Weekly Leader*.[51]

Since this remarkable advertisement is the only evidence of the event or events, it will probably never be possible to determine exactly what happened. But one might conjecture, based on the timing, that it was linked to Sulzbacher's involvement in controversies surrounding the city centennial celebrations, controversies that were indicative of continuing ambivalence within Marietta about the pace and direction of change. There was friction between those (mostly Anglo-Saxon descendants of early settlers who were the cultural elite) who insisted on a historically oriented celebration on the city's traditional "birthday" of April 7, and others (mostly businessmen) who wanted a larger, more commercialized celebration during the summer months. Some members of the former group were appalled at the notion of changing tradition to accommodate commerce; it was a betrayal of the community's founding values. Others were more conciliatory. Douglas Putnam, from a founding family, suggested that "possibly a large majority of our modern population, either home or foreign born, will not be satisfied with a tame historical celebration. They know little of pioneers, pioneer history and pioneer families. Yet their attention had been called and their aid solicited [by the business group] toward a celebration on a broader scale and of a more spectacular character than is, perhaps, consistent with a 7th of April commemoration. And they have from various motives responded with a liberality and enthusiasm which deserves recognition." Putnam suggested a compromise resolution, so the city ended up with two celebrations, one in July with fireworks and one on April 7 that was, according to a local observer, "no doubt the most intellectual."[52]

In this case, then, where the means of civic boosterism were disputed, perhaps activism exacerbated social conflict and exclusion rather than muting them. It perhaps also made a difference that there was no Jewish institution in Marietta to represent Jewish stability and respectability and that Marietta's merchants had little experience of Jews in their circle of competitors. One thing is clear: Sulzbacher did not fear defending himself. With his sarcastic and humorous advertisement, he took the negative image promoted by the antisemites and turned it into a promotion for the positive image. He must have enjoyed exposing them and then tweaking their noses about his business expertise, saying, in effect, "Not only am I not going to let you call me names, but I am going to show you that I'm a better businessman too!"

Whatever the impetus for Sulzbacher's ad, its very appearance is significant. It demonstrates a fundamental and unique fact of the American Jewish experience: American Jews have, unlike Jewries in other places and times, felt free to defend themselves. The lives of nineteenth-century American Jews involved a certain doubleness. On the one hand, they were anxious to find the security of acceptance in American society; on the other hand, they had a strong sense of Jewish identity and of participating in American society as both Americans and Jews. As Hasia Diner sums up the ethos of the era, "On balance, the tone of nineteenth-century Jewish culture expressed a basic trust in the American system and its people, and took statements about goodwill and tolerance at face value. Because Jews believed in the American creed, they did not hesitate to draw attention to themselves as somehow different, yet at the same time entitled to equal access to the bounties of America."[53] This was certainly true of Sam Sulzbacher.

As they wrestled with their relationship with non-Jews, Jews in the small communities of the Ohio River Valley had other, perhaps even more pressing, concerns in the second half of the nineteenth century. They had to find ways to sustain their communities, to keep their institutions solvent and effective, to secure a pattern of small-town Judaism that could sustain future generations. Local and national developments, in the American economy and in Jewish life, would both challenge and support them.

Portsmouth, Ohio, in 1855, from *Rambles in the Path of the Steam Horse* by Eli Bowen. (Courtesy of the American Jewish Archives, Hebrew Union College Jewish Institute of Religion, Cincinnati, Ohio)

Bernhard Felsenthal (exact date unknown, but probably while he was rabbi of Zion Temple, Chicago, 1864–87). (Courtesy of the American Jewish Archives, Hebrew Union College Jewish Institute of Religion, Cincinnati, Ohio)

Isaac Mayer Wise (exact date unknown, but between 1846 and 1864). (Courtesy of the American Jewish Archives, Hebrew Union College Jewish Institute of Religion, Cincinnati, Ohio)

The Buckeye Block, Gallipolis, Ohio, 1874, with J. Weil's store at left. (Courtesy of Henny Evans, Gallia County Historical and Genealogical Society, Gallipolis, Ohio)

(*Left*) Joseph Dinkelspiel in his later years (probably 1880s). (Courtesy of The Temple: Congregation Adath Israel Brith Shalom Archives, Louisville, Kentucky) (*Below*) Temple Adath Israel, Owensboro, Kentucky. Courtesy of Lee Shai Weissbach

(*Left*) Moses Strouse with his wife's younger siblings Florita and Leslie Eichel, Evansville, Indiana, 1890s. (Courtesy of University of Southern Indiana Special Collections and University Archives Department, Evansville)

ight) Eoff Street Temple (Congrega-on Leshem Shomayim), Wheeling, est Virginia, early 1900s. (Courtesy of e American Jewish Archives, Hebrew nion College Jewish Institute of Reli-on, Cincinnati, Ohio)

(*Above*) The Beren family on their porch, Marietta, Ohio, 1910s. (Courtesy of Slack Research Collections, Dawes Memorial Library, Marietta College, Marietta, Ohio) (*Below*) Marietta Jewish families attend a wedding in Kansas City (probably early 1920s). At far left is Sussman Ruby. On the left, in the third row, are Sarah (Rabinowitz) and Bernard Revel with one of their sons. (Courtesy of Sonia Lebow Goldish)

Breaking the ground for Temple B'nai Israel, East Liverpool, Ohio, 1921. (Courtesy of Herschel Rubin)

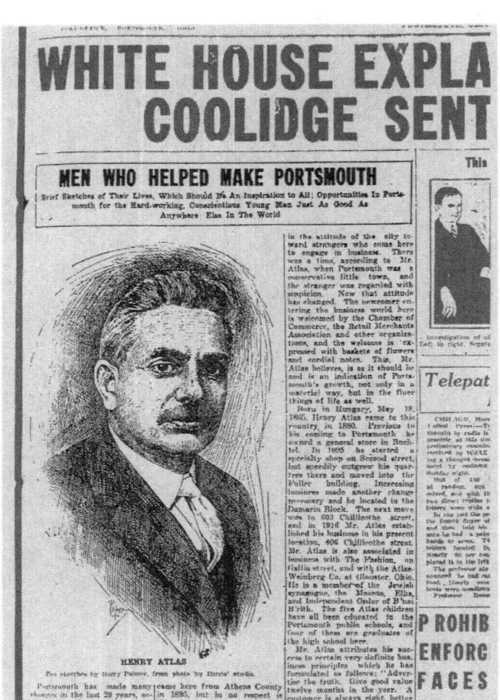

WHITE HOUSE EXPLA
COOLIDGE SENT

MEN WHO HELPED MAKE PORTSMOUTH

Brief Sketches of Their Lives, Which Should Be An Inspiration to All; Opportunities In Portsmouth for the Hard-working, Conscientious Young Man Just As Good As Anywhere Else In The World

HENRY ATLAS

Pen sketches by Harry Palmer, from photo by Harris' studio.

Portsmouth has made many changes in the last 28 years, according to Henry Atlas, who came here from Athens County in 1895, but in no respect is this change more marked than in the attitude of the city toward strangers who come here to engage in business. There was a time, according to Mr. Atlas, when Portsmouth was a conservative little town, and the stranger was regarded with suspicion. Now that attitude has changed. The newcomer entering the business world here is welcomed by the Chamber of Commerce, the Retail Merchants Association and other organizations, and the welcome is expressed with baskets of flowers and cordial notes. This, Mr. Atlas believes, is as it should be and is an indication of Portsmouth's growth, not only in a material way, but in the finer things of life as well.

Born in Hungary, May 18, 1866, Henry Atlas came to this country in 1880. Previous to his coming to Portsmouth he owned a general store in Buchtel. In 1895 he started a specialty shop on Second street, but speedily outgrew his quarters there and moved into the Fuller building. Increasing business made another change necessary and he located in the Damarin Block. The next move was to 603 Chillicothe street, and in 1916 Mr. Atlas established his business in his present location, 406 Chillicothe street. Mr. Atlas is also associated in business with The Fashion, on Gallia street, and with the Atlas-Weinberg Co. at Glouster, Ohio. He is a member of the Jewish synagogue, the Masons, Elks, and Independent Order of B'nai B'rith. The five Atlas children have all been educated in the Portsmouth public schools, and four of them are graduates of the high school here.

Mr. Atlas attributes his success to certain very definite business principles which he has formulated as follows: "Advertise the truth. Give good value twelve months in the year. A customer is always right, better refund money than argue."

This

Telepat

P ROHIB
ENFORC
FACES
DIFFICU

(*Above*) The Sunday school of Congregation Agudath Achim, Aliquippa, Pennsylvania, 1932. One extended family provided one-third of the entire student body, as well as teachers and the principal. (Courtesy of Dr. David Chamovitz) (*Left*) Henry Atlas makes the front page of the *Portsmouth (OH) Daily Times*, March 6, 1924.

(*Above*) "Sam Yablok relaxes in his spacious Pioneer Junk Co. office" was the caption of this photo, which appeared with an article about Yablok's retirement in the *Marietta (OH) Times*, August 16, 1980. (*Below*) East Liverpool, Ohio, 1986, with Temple Beth Shalom on the right. This is the building erected by B'nai Israel in 1921. (Courtesy of the photographer, Andrew Borowiec [from his 2000 book, *Along the Ohio*])

CHAPTER 7

Maintaining Community

The Civil War was a transitional time for the Ohio Valley as the importance of the river to the regional economy declined. Although it did not change fundamental local economic structures, the war exacerbated river communities' prewar tendencies toward growth, stagnation, or decline. In Evansville, Indiana, for instance, industry was given a significant boost that enabled the city to move to the level of a regional center. Other towns experienced wartime booms only to run out of steam by the late nineteenth century. Cairo, Illinois, was unable to overcome its prewar handicaps of a limited industrial base, lack of a productive agricultural hinterland, run-down infrastructure, and susceptibility to frequent and severe flooding.[1]

In the United States as a whole, the post–Civil War expansion of finance capitalism and industrialization notably accelerated urbanization. American cities, on the rise before the Civil War, grew to sizes unheard of in the antebellum era as new technologies and modes of management further centralized both industry and commerce. Populations soared as workers—both rural migrants and foreign immigrants—flocked to centers of employment.

A good number of Jewish businesses in the United States were positioned for growth as a result of wartime and postwar expansion. A prime example was the Jewish-dominated clothing industry: small shops became factories for mass production of army uniforms and, after the war, transferred their capacity to the growing ready-to-wear market. Among the clothing merchants making this transition were the Mack brothers of Cincinnati, who grew their business on the basis of government contracts for Union military uniforms.[2]

By 1880, most of the Ohio River towns that had Jewish communities had total populations of more than five thousand, and a few had at least ten thousand. In late-nineteenth-century terms, these places had moved into the category of small city. In the longer term, the importance of large and medium cities outstripped that of small cities; the economic expansion and concentration that benefited larger urban centers and urban Jews came at the eventual detriment of smaller cities and towns—and, of course, their small Jewish communities. Yet in the short term—through at least the first quarter of the twentieth century—small cities retained a secure niche in regional urban networks, and such towns also remained an important part of the Jewish experience.

Jews have always been a disproportionately urbanized segment of American society, preferring to live with a substantial number of other Jews in a large general population. Based on his analysis of an 1878 survey of the American Jewish population, historian Lee Shai Weissbach demonstrates that American Jews of the postbellum era were "highly concentrated in a relatively limited number of identifiable communities, both large and small." At least 83 percent of American Jews lived in towns and cities with more than 5,000 total residents, whereas only 25 percent of all Americans lived in such comparatively large places. A large general population and a relatively large Jewish population tended to go hand in hand. The two dozen largest American cities—all with total populations over 75,000—all had Jewish populations of 1,000 or more, and 71 percent of American Jews lived in these places. Another 13 percent lived in the 134 cities and towns that had at least 100 but fewer than 1,000 Jewish residents. Despite this concentration, in 1878 there were at least 868 localities in the United States with fewer than 100 Jews.[3]

The Ohio River Valley seems to have been even more concentrated than the national average. More than 80 percent of Jews in the valley were in the three cities with 1,000 or more Jews: Cincinnati (with 8,000), Louisville (with 2,500), and Pittsburgh (with 2,000). Another 10 percent lived in communities of at least 100 but fewer than 1,000 Jews, including Evansville and Madison, Indiana; Owensboro and Paducah, Kentucky; and Wheeling, West Virginia. The remainder were scattered throughout the valley: the 1878 data list thirteen Ohio River towns with fewer than 100 Jews, though there were at least fifteen more such towns.[4]

The increased urban concentration of the late nineteenth and early twentieth centuries had critical ramifications for small Jewish communities. Weissbach notes that most of the places in the United States that had more than 100 but fewer than 1,000 Jews in 1878 failed to grow sufficiently to break into the larger Jewish population category by 1907. On the other hand, the number of towns in the middle range (100–999 Jews) increased to 524 by 1927. Of these, only 15 percent had Jewish communities established before 1878; obviously, small towns continued to be sites of Jewish growth.[5] Weissbach points out that, taking into account the high mobility of Jewish immigrants, it is clear that "far more American Jews had passed through a small Jewish community at some time during their lives than would be assumed from the fact that in any given year only a small percentage of the Jews in the United States lived outside the nation's major Jewish centers."[6]

Beyond mere demographic persistence, the small Jewish communities showed remarkable institutional persistence, holding together to hold on to Jewish life where they were. According to the 1878 survey, at least sixty-six towns with fewer than 100 Jews maintained some sort of Jewish communal organization.[7] Individual Jews might come and go, but in the small towns, Jewish population and a sense of community persisted, often expressed in a small congregation—but also even in the absence of successful communal institutions.

Ironton, Gallipolis, and Pomeroy, Ohio, in the mid–Ohio Valley, are cases in point. Ironton's nascent congregation of 1874 seems to have faded quickly. But Jews continued to move into as well as out of Ironton, and there may even have been a new women's organization around 1900. The Gallipolis congregation was active to some extent for at least two decades, for the local paper reported in 1884 that a student from Hebrew Union College had led an "interesting" Rosh Hashanah service "in the room back of the Council Chambers in the Shober block." Certainly, the congregation was defunct by the turn of the century. But there were still three Jewish-owned clothing stores and about a dozen Jewish families. Lacking railroad connections, the town of Pomeroy declined along with river traffic to become a dirty and depressed coal town, but because it was a regional retail center, there were still Jewish stores into the early twentieth century. And Jews in all these towns continued to make connections with Jewish institutions in Portsmouth, Ohio; Ashland, Kentucky; and Huntington, West Virginia.[8]

Some mid-nineteenth-century Jewish communities created new institutions in the latter part of the century, aligning themselves with the Americanized Reform synthesis that seemed to work well with small-town culture. Around 1880, thirty years after the first Jewish settlers arrived, Jews in Henderson, Kentucky, began to regularize their Jewish life. In 1884, the women organized a Hebrew Ladies' Auxiliary, which obtained a Jewish cemetery and started a school. In the mid-1880s, High Holidays services were held in various locations, and in 1887, Congregation Adas Israel was incorporated. Shabbat services were held in rented rooms until 1891, when Morris and Henry Baldauf donated land for a temple, spurring their fellows to action by specifying in the deed that the building must be completed and paid for within two years. This challenge was meant to secure a permanent place for Judaism in Henderson's social landscape. And Henderson's Jews were well in the mainstream of late-nineteenth-century American classical Reform Judaism. At the cornerstone laying for the new temple in July 1891, they listened approvingly as Rabbi Leo Franklin of Hebrew Union College declared, "The Israelites are not a nation—they are a religious body banned [*sic*] together to promulgate a belief in the Oneness of the Creator."[9]

In Paducah, Kentucky, a new, explicitly Reform congregation was incorporated in 1893 as successor to Bene Yeshurum, which had faltered some years earlier. Paducah's Jewish population by the 1890s was about three hundred individuals, and the temple's membership roster listed ninety heads of families, suggesting that a large majority of the Jewish community affiliated religiously. Most temple members (who were almost all men) were also members of the local B'nai B'rith lodge. The choice of the unimaginative name Temple Israel, easily identified as Jewish, signified an acculturated self-understanding (more easily comprehensible to non-Jews than the more obscure, older Hebrew name); the dedication of a new building on Broadway, Paducah's main thoroughfare, announced the Jews' central place in Paducah's life.[10]

Perhaps inspired by Paducah, the nearby Jewish community of Cairo, Illinois, established Montefiore Congregation, also explicitly Reform, in 1894. The small congregation organized in 1863 had apparently collapsed sometime earlier, probably over issues of reform. The new group was also tiny—perhaps only fifty individuals—and had to make compromises to function effectively. Services were held on alternate Sunday evenings, a choice that may have been made to accommodate the "many travelling men" who attended services along with "all the Jewish citizens" of the town. Unlike in Paducah, where residents could afford to hire a rabbi, services in Cairo were led by Robert Bernard Sadler, a local clothing merchant. In 1897, Sadler was elected permanent rabbi though he was almost certainly not ordained. In 1899, he was even admitted to the Central Conference of American Rabbis on the recommendation of Rabbis Isaac Mayer Wise and Hyman Enelow of Paducah.[11]

Cairo's situation suggests some of the many problems facing small Jewish communities as they struggled to achieve stability and continuity and to maintain institutions that could continue to meet local Jewish residents' needs. The story of Portsmouth's Beneh Abraham from its 1858 founding through the early twentieth century attests that this was not an inconsequential achievement and provides a good indication of the sorts of communal concerns these small-town Jewish institutions were called upon to address.

Congregation Beneh Abraham was the most important, though not always the only, institution of Jewish communal life in Portsmouth, Ohio. Most local Jewish men maintained membership, though occasionally someone would drop—and usually later resume—his formal affiliation, often because of financial problems. A small group of men took seriously the business of running the congregation; they rotated the offices among themselves, raised money and kept track of funds, maintained the synagogue building, and dealt with communal crises as they arose. Congregational meetings were a forum for wrestling with the practical and philosophical issues of American Judaism in a small town.

It is clear, for instance, that despite liturgical reforms, kashrut remained an important observance for some Portsmouth Jews into the second half of the nineteenth century, and supervision of kashrut standards was the congregation's responsibility. In 1867, an outraged Matthias Schloss alleged that butcher A. H. Levi not only overcharged for kosher meat but also "that he dont keep his kosher meat in such a condition as our Jewish Religion will admitt, as I have seen myself a Piece of Hoge Mead and a Piece of Kosher Mead laing on the same Plate. I also believe that it is weight on the same scale and Cutt with the same Knife." A few years later, the board promulgated "Rules and Regulations between the Butcher and Shochet" to settle apparent disputes over the butcher's work schedules and fees.[12]

The religious school was also a source of concern. Nineteenth-century American Jews experimented with many formats for Jewish education, from day schools to private tutors. Supplemental schools (held after school, on Sunday mornings, or both) became the norm once most Jewish children attended public school, which was the case by midcentury. In small congregations, the Sunday school format, adapted from the Christian model, predominated; many of these once-a-week schools were taught by women. American Jews innovated in curricula, creating child-centered and age-appropriate texts that drew on the insights of American public school reform, rather than immediately immersing children in the original biblical and rabbinic texts, as was the practice in Europe. Not incidentally, the model of the American public school—where girls were educated equally—provided more opportunities for girls to obtain Jewish education than would have been the case if the European Jewish model had been followed. As with the public schools, synagogue school policymaking was vested in the community, especially the parents.[13]

Beneh Abraham's supplemental school, which met on both Saturday and Sunday afternoons, operated along these lines. It used special texts for teaching the Hebrew alphabet and grammar and *A Child's First Bible*, adapted by Rabbi Frederic de Sola Mendes, an important Reform rabbi in New York City. Initially the curriculum also included instruction in German, but this was dropped in 1877 as the parents themselves discarded the old language. (Congregational meeting minutes were recorded in German until 1872, and some sermons were given in German as late as 1878.) More troublesome were the logistics of a small school. When the congregation had the money to hire someone to lead services and preach, the person would double as schoolteacher. In 1877, with twelve children enrolled in the school, Isaac Stempel protested that it was too much for one person to handle. But the congregation's board reiterated very specific requirements: to "hold sabbath school up stairs from 2 to 4 P.M. both classes at one time, and to sit the children on the south side benches to prevent them from looking out the window. On Sunday he may divide them in 2 classes at different times. . . . Any other arrangements would be too expensable to keep up the school during the Winter."[14]

The congregational board had to resolve members' disputes, many of which are alluded to in meeting minutes. In January 1872, for instance, John Eisman and Abraham Nathan requested a special meeting to discuss "one of the most flagrant violations [that] has been perpetrated by one of the members," and a committee was appointed "to investigate the wholesale disturbance between the Congregation and Mr. E. Heidingsfield [Heidingsfeld]." The congregation also took responsibility for communal welfare. In November 1876, it paid Esther Silber's burial expenses and, nine months later, those of her husband. Several members volunteered to make arrangements for the six Silber orphans, the eldest of whom went to live with relatives and the youngest of whom went to Cleveland's Jewish Orphan Asylum. Isaac Mayer had never joined the congregation, but, perhaps at the urging of his wife, Emma, the board permitted the Mayer children to enroll in the religious school on a tuition basis. When Mayer died in 1875, his funeral was conducted by his fellow Masons, but at Emma's request, he was buried in the Jewish cemetery.[15]

Most of the board's meetings were occupied with calculations of income and expenses in an effort to keep the congregation solvent. Personnel was a large share of the budget and an administrative nightmare. Until the late nineteenth century, the need for rabbis in America far outstripped the supply; by and large, all but the largest congregations made do with unordained professionals, who had a job description of ḥazan, teacher and preacher, or minister, and who generally used the honorific title "reverend." Quality was as much a problem as quantity. In October 1879, a writer from San Francisco reported accusations against Jacob Vogelsdorff, the reverend at Wheeling's Leshem Shomayim, in an *American Israelite* column titled "The Pulpit Leper." He or she claimed to know that Vogelsdorff was a drunkard who had abandoned a wife and four children in San Francisco. Fumed the writer, "I have never dreamed of such a thing that he would even, with all his native cheek, present himself as a 'Rev.' in any pulpit, even in this country, where these titles are cheaper than mess-pork in Cincinnati." Though the notables of Wheeling responded immediately in Vogelsdorff's defense, the "pulpit leper" did not last more than a year with them.[16]

In the case of smaller—and therefore less wealthy—congregations, such as Beneh Abraham, finding any semiprofessional leadership was a source of perpetual difficulty, and quality varied widely. After Judah Wechsler, whose subsequent career was quite eminent, left Portsmouth in 1864, rabbis—or reverends, as the case might be—came and went with disruptive frequency, generally in a two-year cycle. A young man hired in 1870 died of tuberculosis during his second year in Portsmouth. He was followed by the very intriguing Simon Gerstmann. Born in 1833 in the Poznań city of Kalisz, Gerstmann came to the United States in 1852 or 1853, enlisted in the United States Army, and served as a private in the artillery for five years. Whatever the fantasies of European Jews about the wilds of America, Gerstmann lived them—he was even wounded in battle with Seminoles in Florida in 1856. After his discharge, Gerstmann embarked on the peripatetic career of a reverend. Having left Portsmouth after two years, Gerstmann continued to roam the United States, working in synagogues from the South to the Midwest to California, and back to the South and the Midwest. By the late 1880s, he settled in New York City, where he died in 1894.[17]

After Gerstmann's departure in 1873, Beneh Abraham elected Solomon Kaufmann of New York City to the position of minister, with the understanding that he should "conduct our services strictly Minhac [*sic*] America." Kaufmann must have pleased someone, because in August 1874, he married Betty Eichelstein, daughter of congregation president Mayer Eichelstein. Isaac Mayer Wise performed the ceremony, not neglecting to mention in his wedding prayer to "thank God that we have found in this free country a land where we can worship the God of Israel with the greatest freedom." Solomon and Betty Kaufmann's first child was born in Portsmouth in July 1875, but in 1876, they left Portsmouth. The "ladies of the congregation" presented their erstwhile leader with a gold-headed ebony cane as a token of their affection.[18]

Kaufmann's successor, Samuel Laski, came up the river to Portsmouth from Louisville, Kentucky, but stayed less than five months. Congregational records give no clue to the reason for this extremely brief tenure. The congregation then muddled along for some time, interviewing candidates and making offers, but not succeeding until mid-June 1877, when they hired Isaac Stempel of Williamsport, Pennsylvania. As suggested by Stempel's complaints about the school, it was a troubled relationship. When Stempel complained about work requirements, the congregation gave him notice, but six weeks later, they rescinded it. A year later, after A. H. Levi brought to the board charges against Stempel for "misconduct in the pulpit and slander of officers and members generally," they finally fired him. The board grudgingly agreed to provide a reference but made it clear they would "testify only as is due him, and nothing more."[19]

After this upheaval, once again facing the difficulties and uncertainties of hiring a new man, Beneh Abraham reverted to a solution seen in Cairo and often used by congregations at an earlier stage of development: they hired one of their own. It was none other than Mayer Eichelstein, Solomon Kaufmann's father-in-law, who had been president of the congregation for probably ten years. Eichelstein accepted the job in June 1879. A local hire was more reliable, and since he had another line of work (in this case, a liquor business), he was also cheaper. Initially offered $500 per year, Eichelstein ended up taking $450, much less than the $700 Stempel received in 1878 or the $900 Gerstmann received in 1872. And he continued to pay membership dues. There is no record of Eichelstein's Jewish educational background that might have qualified him for the post, though he probably received a traditional education as a youth in Germany. But he provided the sought-after stability for the Portsmouth congregation: he served as rabbi for seven years, until his death in 1886.[20]

The financial crisis that prompted the decision to hire Eichelstein was no doubt caused in large part by the economic depression of 1873–80. But an important additional factor (almost certainly related to the first) was that, through the 1870s and 1880s, the Jewish community of Portsmouth had stopped growing. In 1884, there were reportedly only about twenty member families.[21] This reflected a slowing in the town's phenomenal growth rate of the early nineteenth century. Between 1850 and 1860, the decade in which most Jews came to Portsmouth, overall population grew by two-thirds, and between 1860 and 1870, by three-fourths. In the 1870s, it crept up by barely 6 percent. The board of Beneh Abraham began to actively solicit memberships from young men.

There was a small trickle of new members in these years, Jews settling in Portsmouth for business reasons. Z. J. Kaufman took over the former Lehman, Richman location for his own clothing store in 1873; when he died seven years later, his wife and son continued the business. Felix and Sigmund Haas, nephew and uncle, came from Cincinnati to open the Haas Clothing Company. Several Haas women operated a millinery shop together. Most of the new residents had been in the United States for some time, up to twenty years. But in-migration was balanced by out-migration. By 1890, many members of the early Jewish families had scattered throughout the country: to Cincinnati, Chillicothe, Cleveland, and Springfield, Ohio, and to Louisville, New Orleans, Philadelphia, and New York.[22]

With a few exceptions, congregational officers continued to be drawn from the same pool of individuals and families, and board meetings became less frequent. Requests from the Union of American Hebrew Congregations for support of various national projects always received the response that the congregation was too small to undertake them. But the synagogue's needs were always met. In the summer of 1884, the congregation was forced to make repairs to its premises following February floods. Funds were collected not only from individuals and firms (Jewish and Christian) in Portsmouth but from a large network of Jews outside the city, including former residents such as the Dryfuss family, now in Zanesville in central Ohio, and the Ronsheims in Cincinnati. Leopold Eisman used his business contacts to solicit numerous small donations from firms in the garment trade, many in Cincinnati, though that city had also experienced the flood. The funds thus collected easily covered expenses.[23]

Eichelstein's death in 1886 precipitated another series of crises of professional leadership. Applications for the position included H. Pollock of Milwaukee and A. M. Bloch of Jackson, Mississippi. Both came for trial sermons, and in January 1887, Pollock was hired. But by December, he was fired on a petition from members complaining about "gross insults"; he was replaced by Bloch in January 1888. It was another disaster: in August, Bloch simply left town, apparently for another job.[24]

Fortunately for the congregation, the next hire was far more satisfactory. Abraham Schapiro assumed his duties as ḥazan and preacher at the High Holidays in 1888. A native of Poland who studied rabbinics in Breslau, Schapiro came to the United States in 1887 and spent a year in Philadelphia before coming to Portsmouth. There is some question whether he had been formally ordained, though he was clearly knowledgeable enough for the congregation.[25]

Ten years earlier, Mayer Eichelstein had provided stability to the congregation because his personal interests and professional abilities conveniently converged. Schapiro soon discovered the same convergence. The converse of Eichelstein, a local who became the rabbi, Schapiro was the rabbi who became a local. In 1892, he married Cecelia Schloss, whose family had been in Portsmouth since the 1860s. While still under contract as rabbi, Schapiro opened a bookstore with his wife, whose family was in the trade, and apparently business soon attracted him more than the pulpit, for in 1899, he attempted to resign from Beneh Abraham. Recognizing the dimensions of the dilemma, the board offered Schapiro a salary of $700 (up from $650) "if he would keep his store closed on Saturdays [and holidays]. He asked for a week to consider." With no evident options for the congregation, Schapiro—willingly or not, agreeing to the condition or not—continued in the post until the fall of 1901.

After that, he still occasionally led services, performed marriages, and *schechted* chickens (slaughtered them according to the laws of kashrut).[26]

One thing that kept Beneh Abraham and other small congregations from failing, either from lack of resources or from sheer exhaustion, was a comprehensive change in Hebrew Union College's approach to rabbinic training. The change was influenced by the emphasis developing in American higher education on the standardization of professional knowledge. HUC began to emphasize practical instruction along with the study of sacred texts and, in the 1890s, began with increasing frequency to let upper-level students have weekend pulpits as a sort of practicum. From the Reform movement's standpoint, these arrangements helped strengthen the movement by creating stronger links with more congregations.[27]

From the small congregations' standpoint, the system was vital to their survival. Starting in 1901, Beneh Abraham regularly employed an HUC senior, as did the congregation in Henderson. Being close to Cincinnati, Ohio Valley congregations had no difficulty finding an available student, and, as HUC expanded and then mandated the student pulpit program, the inconsistency of annual changes was offset by the reliability of the placement system in providing someone. Although the Reform identity of such congregations was probably never in doubt, constant interaction with the movement made it possible for them to feel truly a part of a larger Jewish community.[28]

Beneh Abraham's story shows how important the survival of their unique Jewish communal life was to small-town Jews, despite the obstacles they encountered. Using their own creative strategies and the resources of the institutional American Jewish community, they worked hard to ensure this survival.

In the late nineteenth century, as West Virginia began to seriously exploit its mineral and petroleum resources, Jewish institutions emerged in two of the state's Ohio River cities, Huntington and Parkersburg. In both cases, the increased organization and professionalism of Reform Judaism was central to their success. Times had changed. The small communities of the mid-nineteenth century had seen themselves as independent and self-sufficient entities; by the early twentieth century, small communities were virtually missionary outposts.

Hoping to expand its reach and affiliation level, the UAHC had begun in the 1880s to emulate successful Protestant strategies and experiment with circuit preaching, that is, sending rabbis to conduct services and assist with Jewish education in locales without professional Jewish leadership. In 1894, the Committee on Circuit Work was expanded and bureaucratized, and by the turn of the century, it reached some fifty towns, mainly in the South and Midwest. In 1904, Rabbi George Zepin took the helm of the expanded Board of Synagogue Extension, which, in addition to recruiting new UAHC affiliates, provided to small congregations resources such as educational materials and prepackaged sermons. By using rabbis of larger regional congregations as district supervisors, Zepin was also able to link the small communities with the larger American Jewish world. In addition to rural Jewish communities, the board targeted "scattered Jewish groups inside cities of all sizes." Both Huntington and Parkersburg were in this category.[29]

Huntington did not even exist until 1871, when railroad magnate Collis P. Huntington developed it as a river terminus for the Chesapeake and Ohio Railway, close to the mining region. A year later, Samuel and Dora Gideon, recent immigrants from Germany, moved to Huntington from the tiny Ohio River town of Manchester, in Adams County, about forty miles west of Portsmouth. The following year, a letter to the *Israelite* reported that there were two Jewish families and four single young Jewish men among Huntington's population of 2,800; all were in the clothing business but one, who "buys and sells everything." The Jewish population continued to grow. In 1888, the Gideons' daughter Ida married Moses ("Mike") Broh, a Cincinnati native who had recently moved to Huntington. Eventually several of Mike's nine siblings and his parents joined them. Huntington was immediately part of the large Ohio River Valley Jewish network: the Brohs were from Cincinnati and had business and marriage connections not only there but also in Parkersburg and Ashland, Kentucky.[30]

In 1886, Huntington Jews followed the pattern of earlier German Jewish communities, founding a Reform congregation that they called Ohab Sholem; a cemetery association was founded the same year. There was also a Jewish social club, the Ladies' Hebrew Benevolent Society, and later a branch of the Jewish Chautauqua Society. Though in 1892, the congregation was able to buy its own building, it did not employ a rabbi. Rather, religious services were lay led, often by Sam Gideon, a founder and for many years the president. In 1903, the congregation expressed an interest in the UAHC's synagogue extension work and hosted director Zepin for a visit in November. Zepin offered the services of Leon Volmer, rabbi in the state capital of Charleston, and discussed with the group the possibility of setting up a circuit among Huntington; Ironton, Ohio; and Ashland and Catlettsburg, Kentucky. Whatever the results of these initial conversations, by 1916, the HUC rabbinical student posted to Huntington was also doing extension work in Ironton and Ashland.[31]

The Jews of Parkersburg presented more of a challenge. By the late nineteenth century, the community was well established, many residents having arrived thirty or forty years earlier. They had still not formed any religious association, however, and held only ad hoc High Holidays services. Despite the trend for nineteenth-century American Jews increasingly to identify Judaism solely as a religion, renouncing notions of nationhood and peoplehood and downplaying ethnicity, the Jews of Parkersburg were resolutely an ethnic entity. They organized a panoply of secular organizations. One was the Progress Club, a social club started in 1888 by second-generation members of the Newberger, Prager, Epstein, Nathan, and Rauch families; in 1900, its membership represented a majority of the Jewish population of Parkersburg. There were a Ladies' Sewing Society and a Hebrew Ladies' Aid Society as well.[32]

In 1875, Isaac Mayer Wise had failed to inspire Parkersburg's Jews to religious observance, and twenty-one years later, Charles Levi, assistant rabbi to the aged Wise at Bene Yeshurun in Cincinnati, made another attempt—probably under the auspices of the Committee on Circuit Work. "He was successful," the B'nai B'rith monthly, *Menorah*, reported, "in so far that services were held during the holidays and a committee appointed to raise subscriptions with a view of having their own temple."[33]

Apparently, Levi was successful only in so far as he extracted this promise, because in 1903, the UAHC again turned its institutional eye on Parkersburg. Because of this new circuit-riding program, the *American Israelite* predicted, "the time seems to have come for many communities that hitherto have borne reputations for heedlessness in matters religious to live down that reputation. . . . In many cities the apparent religious indifference is merely the result of the lack of leaders. This appears to have been the case in Parkersburg. The people are, almost to a man, desirous of having religious services, and especially a Sabbath school. But there is wanting the leadership of a minister."[34]

No longer was congregation formation expected to be the responsibility of each community's Jewish elite; the UAHC had now taken in hand having it done professionally. With this in mind, Zepin called a meeting on November 17, 1903, in Parkersburg, at which he offered that Rabbi Harry Levi of Wheeling could come twice a month to conduct services. The idea was discussed, in the words of the *American Israelite,* "from various points of view" (perhaps indicating some controversy), and an organizational structure was set up. Twenty-eight men signed on as charter members.[35]

This approach seems to have had limited success. A community history credits the Progress Club during this period with hosting religious services, led by a member, at its club rooms on downtown's Juliana Street; apparently the rabbi came from Wheeling for weddings and funerals. But in this case Zepin may have underestimated the critical role of lay leadership in sustaining the local congregation. With or without the visits of a circuit-riding rabbi, it was another six years before the basis of a permanent congregation was laid in Parkersburg. On October 25, 1909, twenty women and men gathered at William A. Hersch's United Woolen Mills building and gave themselves the temporary name of the Parkersburg Hebrew Congregation. The group described itself as "semi-reformed"—an odd designation that, along with some issues that quickly arose within the group, suggests yet another reason for the community's avoidance of organized religion: a conflict between loyalties to Orthodoxy and Reform.[36]

At subsequent meetings in the next few weeks, a constitution and set of bylaws were adopted, as was the name B'nai Israel; a resolution that the congregation use the *Union Prayer Book*, now the standard of the UAHC and classical Reform, did not pass. A rabbi was hired in the fall of 1909, a recent immigrant from France who was apparently known to national Reform leader Rabbi Stephen S. Wise. He left the post in the fall of 1910, and his role in the intramural conflict is unknown. But in the spring of 1910, there was agitation in favor of holding Orthodox services for Passover. Within two years, the group had apparently fractured, for congregational minutes report that a motion was passed "to allow the Orthodox Cong[regation] the use of the New Place of Worship of the Reform Cong. to hold Minion [minyan] in anytime so it does not conflict with our Services."[37]

Not that a building for the Reform contingent was in sight. In 1910, a proposal to set up a building fund was voted down. For a while the group met in Hersch's building. Later various meeting rooms were rented, including those of the new B'nai B'rith lodge established in 1915. (These rooms were in the Wood County Bank building.) In 1930, the congregation received a bequest of $2,000 toward a building fund, and in 1935, members agreed in principle to a building fund assessment of $250 each.[38] But it was not until 1949 that a building was actually completed, on the basis of generous pledges from eight individuals. Only two of these individuals were from families that had been in the congregation since its inception. Several others had joined in the late 1920s. It seems that with a change of personnel, the Parkersburg Jewish community had finally left behind whatever ambivalences or hostilities had existed before and pulled together under the banner of Reform. The community preferred to ignore much of its turbulent past and delayed development, characterized brightly by a temple history as "slow but steady progress." In 1956, B'nai Israel celebrated a centennial with a Friday evening service, official temple history, and exhibit. Perhaps the congregation, now having an institutional identity and a new institutional building, also felt the need for an institutional past, but it is unclear what event 1956 was the centennial of.[39]

Thus small Jewish communities persisted in the towns of the Ohio River Valley. Even though their geographic location was no longer advantageous, they had secured a certain psychic location. On the one hand, they could see themselves as part of regional and even—through the UAHC—national Jewish networks. On the other hand, they occupied, by and large, a defined and increasingly comfortable niche in their towns of residence.

Small-town Jewish life is often caricatured as one of two extremes, excessively vulnerable either to the quicksand of assimilation or to the menace of backwoods antisemitism. Neither extreme is accurate. There certainly were intermarriage and assimilation. In Gallipolis, Ohio, for example, only three of Abraham and Amelia Moch's six children, born between 1878 and 1890, married, and all married non-Jews. Two spent their lives in Gallipolis, and nothing in their obituaries suggests that they retained any Jewish connection at all. To the contrary: their funerals (and that of a sister who died in northern Ohio) were conducted by Protestant clergy. One obituary simply alluded to the fact that the deceased's "grandfather lived in France, and his grandmother resided in Germany"—evidently the way family members remembered their past when questioned by the local newspaper.[40] In Paducah, Kentucky, however, virtually all members of the Dreyfuss extended family who were born in that same generation, and still living in the Ohio River Valley, married other Jews. Only in succeeding generations, and as descendants dispersed throughout the country, did intermarriage become significant in the family.[41]

Small-town Jews did have options, and they exercised those options within a context both constricted by antisemitism and opened up by common citizenship. Their lives, whether they were in-married or intermarried, and their congregations, if they had them, were part of the fabric of small-town life in the Ohio River Valley. Jews continued to move out of and into smaller cities and towns. By the end of the nineteenth century, currents of Jewish history would begin to transform even small communities in important ways.

The transformation was particularly dramatic in Marietta, Ohio. There, Jews bonded socially as an ethnic group before they took any steps toward religious organization. In March 1898 this group came together to celebrate the wedding of a young Romanian immigrant couple who had recently arrived in Marietta. The wedding was the subject of breathless curiosity in the local papers. "In all the hundred and ten years of Marietta's history there has never been performed here a wedding ceremony according to the Hebrew rites," the *Marietta Register* pronounced—probably accurately. "But at half-past five o'clock, to-night, there will be such a ceremony." The groom was Israel Evin (he used the English name Edward), a shoemaker; the bride was Yetta Feicke.

Yetta's sister and brother-in-law, Jenny and Nathan Newman, lived in Marietta, and the ceremony took place at their home, which was also the location of Nathan's tailoring business.[42]

The local German-language newspaper, *Die Zeitung*, had a two-paragraph article on the event, but both of Marietta's English-language papers described at some length Jewish wedding customs—or, in any event, their understanding of them. The *Marietta Times* reporter seemed most intrigued by the sight of "the Rabbi, groom and other gentlemen with their hats on." At the dinner following the ceremony, toasts were given by both Jewish and non-Jewish guests. The *Times* reporter was also invited to make a toast, and quite joined in the jollity of the occasion. He seems to have been a special friend of one of the guests, the liquor merchant Peretz Fragner, and got in several digs at his expense, for instance, that "Mr. P. Fragner made at least sixteen speeches and was always applauded—when he sat down." (As a play on his Hebrew name—and perhaps as a nod to the stereotyping of his business—Fragner anglicized his name to Patrick and used the nickname Patsey.) "One of the very pleasant features of the evening," the reporter continued, "was the singing in Hebrew, German and English which was led by Mr. [Morris] Miller. . . . The festivities were closed with dancing. There was no Miriam with a timbrel but some sons of Ham [!], with more modern instruments, made the music. We are notified that there will soon be another Hebrew wedding and are sure it will mean another 'hot time in the old town.'"[43]

While clearly conveying the happy mood of the wedding, the reports were confused about some details, even the correct name of the officiating rabbi: the *Marietta Times* gives it as Terscheid, the *Marietta Register* as Kirschwell, and *Die Zeitung* as Abraham Hirschwell. (The marriage license says Tieschwell.) The *Times* said he was from New York, but the *Register* claimed that he was "the Rabbi of the Marieta [*sic*] congregation, called the Congregation of Peace." The *American Israelite* was confused by this information when it picked up the story from the *Register*. "We believe this is the first time this congregation has been heard from," they noted. "We do not remember ever before hearing that there were any Jews in Marietta much less that they had a congregation, and a rabbi, and we never saw Marietta on a charity subscription list. Let us hope for better things in the Future." Only three months later, the *American Israelite* had the opportunity to mention Marietta again, this time reporting on the dedication of a Jewish cemetery there, an event that was celebrated "by a banquet and jollification." As *Die Zeitung* reported, the fundraising was done by "our Israelite neighbors" through social events such as a ball "with the best of their society."[44]

When, two years later, a congregation was organized in Marietta, the impetus came from a new source: the appearance of a large group of new residents who had arrived from new places. Already by 1898, the community was becoming more diverse, on the evidence of the group that gathered for the wedding at the Newman house. Some, such as Joseph and Lena Josephy, were native-born Americans from Cincinnati, descendants of the German Jewish immigration. "Patsey" Fragner and a number of others were born in the Austro-Hungarian Empire and immigrated mostly in the 1880s, though Fragner had come in 1866. (The "Austrians" were almost certainly not from present-day Austria but rather from Galicia, a province of medieval Poland annexed by Austria in 1772.) Morris Miller was Russian born, as were his wife and their children. The geographic origin of Jews immigrating to America was shifting eastward, and its cultural profile was shifting as well.[45]

In the 1890s, the influx of east European Jews into Marietta accelerated. By 1910, about two dozen families, most of them part of a large extended family group, had settled in the city. When, in 1900, an organized congregation appeared in Marietta, it was Orthodox—east European style. The coincidence of east European immigration with new economic opportunities in Marietta and other Ohio River towns would be a challenge—and sometimes a boon—to these towns and their Jewish communities.

CHAPTER 8

The East European Immigration and the Reconfiguration of Community

Between 1880 and 1924, some 2.25 million Jewish immigrants arrived in the United States, overwhelming the existing American Jewish population of 250,000. The wave started slowly. Between 1871 and 1880, there were about 1,500 Jewish immigrants per year, making up only about one-half of 1 percent of all immigrants to the United States. In the following four years, 1881 through 1884, Jewish immigration was almost 75,000 persons, an average of more than 18,000 per year, constituting 3 percent of all immigration. The wave continued to surge, cresting at 154,000—14 percent of all immigration—in 1906.[1]

The flood was precipitated by deteriorating conditions in those areas of eastern Europe—Ukraine, Belarus, Lithuania, Poland, Romania, and Galicia—that were then home to fully 75 percent of the world's Jews. In the Russian Empire, where most lived, there was a sudden and violent increase in antisemitism in the late nineteenth century, reflecting wrenching economic dislocations and the conflicts accompanying the rise of revolutionary politics. With an autocratic government and a society only a step away from feudalism, Russia was not modernizing gracefully, and Jews often bore the brunt of conflicting policies. Throughout the nineteenth century, they suffered under repressive measures designed to undermine traditional communal authority, damage Jewish economic life, and coerce assimilation and conversion to Orthodox Christianity.

Although Jews in central Europe had experienced discrimination and repression, it was almost mild compared to the harshness and violence of the Russian situation. The so-called May Laws of 1882, instituted in the wake of the assassination of the liberal Czar Alexander II in 1881, revoked most of the few gains Jews had achieved in the mid-nineteenth century, severely restricting rights of residence and access to schools and professions. The czarist government now sanctioned—perhaps even encouraged—physical violence against Jewish persons and property; pogroms (the Russian word means "devastation") were widespread, frequent, and vicious. Some Russian Jews responded by committing themselves to revolutionary politics. Others, inspired by Zionism, moved to Palestine to begin to rebuild the Jewish national homeland. Many chose a route of greater economic promise: immigration to America.

The memory of the east European experience tends to dominate contemporary American Jewish life—not surprisingly, since the present-day Jewish community is dominated by their descendants, and the vibrant and diverse American Jewish culture of today is unimaginable without this immigration. This is true even for the Ohio River Valley, where German American Jewish life had developed in its classic form, for the cultural and demographic reinforcements provided by the east Europeans secured the survival of many small Jewish communities well into the twentieth century. But in each of these towns, the experience of the east European influx was influenced by specific local conditions.

A critical factor in the east European experience—and an important difference from the central European experience in the earlier nineteenth century—was the destination, as much as the size, of the migration. By the late nineteenth century, America's industrial cities were the sites for economic mobility; country peddling and small-town merchandising no longer offered as much promise. Although many Jews in the Russian Empire were, like the Germans, petty merchants, many were artisans or even, already, industrial workers. America's cities attracted the bulk of east European Jewish immigrants because there new arrivals, even the unskilled, both men and women, could best hope to earn a living, especially in the burgeoning garment manufacturing business, and because there, where Jews were but one of a wide diversity of immigrant ethnic groups, they could adapt to American life within a familiar religious and ethnic context. As industries developed in the Ohio River Valley, aided by the option of river transport for coal, steel, and other products, Ohio River Valley cities also benefited from the mass migration. Jewish populations boomed in Pittsburgh, Cincinnati, and Louisville; expansion was also notable in the regional cities of Wheeling, West Virginia, and Evansville, Indiana.

Smaller cities and towns in some parts of the Ohio River Valley, especially the upper valley close to Pittsburgh, also experienced Jewish population growth in the late nineteenth and early twentieth centuries. As Pittsburgh's hinterland developed, some immigrants moved to the small river towns near the city that were an extension of urban concentration and development. Few of the Ohio River towns south of Wheeling received substantial immigration.

But even in these places, some opportunities existed, and some east Europeans Jews took advantage of them. Like the Germans before them, they provided commercial services rather than an industrial labor force. Their migration replenished Jewish populations, even if it was only at (or, in many places, below) replacement level or only for a short time. In any event, population movement enabled small Jewish communities to survive well into the twentieth century.[2]

The integration of the new immigrants was a challenge for all existing American Jewish communities. In many respects, the new, large wave of Jewish immigrants from eastern Europe had much in common with the earlier, smaller wave of Jewish immigrants from the German-speaking countries. When they left Europe, both groups were largely traditional religiously, socially, and economically; both had suffered oppression and discrimination; and both wished to—and worked to—maintain their Jewish identity while becoming American. But by the time the east Europeans arrived in America, it was the differences between the groups that loomed large. The America into which the east Europeans poured was vastly different from the America that had greeted the Germans, and the Germans' decades-long experience adapting to a changing American scene put them at a distance from their east European cousins.

In many cities, economic and social class disparities within the Jewish community were reflected in residential patterns. In Louisville, the east Europeans concentrated in the downtown Preston Street neighborhood, often referred to as a shtetl (an eastern European Jewish village), whereas German Jews lived several miles away, in residential neighborhoods south of Broadway. When the east European influx began, Cincinnati's German Jews had already begun to move to suburban Avondale from downtown, where immigrants soon clustered. Pittsburgh's older Jewish neighborhood, the Hill District, became at the turn of the century increasingly poor; wealthier Jews, such as the Kaufmanns of department store fame, were now in Squirrel Hill.[3]

Affluent urban German Jews took on the responsibility to provide social services for the immigrants, both despite the disparities and because of them. The Germans recognized their deep Jewish connection to the newcomers but also found them sorely in need of civilizing influences. In Pittsburgh, for example, the Hebrew Benevolent Society in 1883 opened a homeless shelter for Jews, supported solely by members of the Reform congregations Rodef Shalom and Tree of Life. In Cincinnati, German Jews founded the Cincinnati Charity School, the Society for the Relief of the Sick Poor, and the Jewish Foster Home, among other institutions, in the 1880s and 1890s. Louisville's established community opened a Young Men's Hebrew Association, settlement house, and Jewish hospital for the new arrivals. Even when the east Europeans established their own self-help institutions, the stigma of being "projects" of the wealthier Germans was a source of resentment for many decades to come.[4]

Beyond their economic integration and social acculturation, the Germans practiced an American Judaism that was barely recognizable to the east European immigrants. In the Russian Empire, economic, social, demographic, and political circumstances all conspired to thwart the development of religious reform. Although by the end of the nineteenth century, significant numbers of Russian Jews, both in the cities and the villages, were not religiously observant, the religion they were not practicing was traditional rabbinic Judaism. And while many opted for nonreligious ideological alternatives such as Zionism, Bundism (Jewish socialism), and secular Yiddishist culture, the largest proportion remained traditionally observant. The American Jews in the Reform movement, on the other hand, were becoming ever more radical and removed from traditional belief and practice. This ideology, known as classical Reform, which dominated the movement until the 1930s, emerged through two events that took place in the Ohio River Valley.

In 1883, in Cincinnati, Hebrew Union College celebrated the graduation of its first class of rabbis and the tenth anniversary of the founding of the Union of American Hebrew Congregations with the notorious "*treyfe* banquet." A lay organizing committee had approved and ordered—from a Jewish caterer—a menu that started with "Little Neck Clams" and proceeded to further violations of traditional Jewish dietary laws. (Interestingly enough, while they served shellfish and meat-and-dairy mixtures, there was no pork.) With Wise and other movement leaders dismissive—even contemptuous—of the shock and hurt feelings of the observant participants, it was clear that such inattention to Jewish law was becoming not only the norm in America but even the desideratum.[5]

At a meeting in Pittsburgh two years later, a rabbinical conference produced the ideological manifesto of this new orientation. The ideals of classical Reform were articulated in the Pittsburgh Platform of 1885, a statement prepared by a group of younger rabbis dominated by Kaufmann Kohler, son-in-law and spiritual heir of David Einhorn. The platform's eight planks codified a universalist, rationalist, and spiritualized position; they rejected kashrut and other traditional practices and declared that Jews are "no longer a nation, but [only] a religious community." Taking a broad and generous view of other religions and of the human capacity for reason and progress, the rabbis reinterpreted the ancient concept of the Messiah as an ideal of social justice for all humankind. At the same time, the rabbis rejected more radically universalist positions, such as that of Felix Adler's Ethical Culture, by emphasizing the special heritage and mission of the Jewish people.[6]

These two events represented the high-water mark of the Ohio River Valley's importance in American Jewish religious life. The new platform's promulgation from Pittsburgh was of course somewhat accidental (the rabbis could have chosen another city in which to meet), but its role as the ideological explanation of trends evidenced by the Cincinnati banquet highlights the Ohio city's leadership role. Yet this preeminence was already beginning to slip. The success of classical Reform was not the success that Isaac Mayer Wise had envisioned—that is, of a united liberal American Judaism—for it led to the disillusion and defection of moderate reformers.[7] And the demographic change created by immigration strengthened and augmented the existing American institutions of traditional Judaism. "Henceforth," notes historian Michael Meyer, "it would be as only one of the 'branches' of American Judaism that Reform would shape its narrower destiny."[8]

Though classical Reform was very different from the Reform that Isaac Mayer Wise had promulgated to small towns in the mid-nineteenth century, it found a sympathetic reception there. Through participation in the UAHC, the small communities of the Ohio River Valley assimilated the new outlook. In Portsmouth, Ohio, for instance, Beneh Abraham maintained a firm Reform orientation and UAHC loyalty. In 1895, the board voted unanimously to recommend the adoption of the newly published classical Reform *Union Prayer Book*, a largely English-language liturgy, which emphasized ethical principles and abbreviated important sections of the traditional liturgy (including the Torah and prophetic readings) while omitting others entirely. The members of Beneh Abraham's board were businessmen, not philosophers, but the optimistic and progressive tone of the new Reform no doubt appealed to them. Reform was now an integral part of their identity as Jews, so they responded positively to Rabbi Abraham Schapiro's assertion that it "is almost a necessity to adopt the new Union prayer books as nearly all reformed congregations are using them."[9]

By the turn of the twentieth century, then, American Jewry's religious landscape had been drastically altered, by the UAHC's move away from tradition, on the one hand, and on the other hand, by the appearance of a multitude of traditional (usually designated Orthodox) congregations reflecting the regional diversity of the immigrants. In Pittsburgh, for example, there were new Orthodox congregations for Jews from Lithuania, Russia, Poland, Hungary, Galicia, and Romania. In Cincinnati, which already had two Orthodox synagogues, founded in the mid-nineteenth century (one German, one Polish),

Orthodox congregations multiplied. Four new Orthodox congregations were established in Louisville in the 1880s and 1890s. The UAHC, which had once aspired to unite all American Jews, by 1907 represented less than 10 percent of the estimated 1,700 congregations in the United States.[10]

Social, cultural (especially linguistic), and religious differences separated east European Jews from the communities of the central European immigrants in small towns as well as in cities. In most small towns, east Europeans formed their own—Orthodox—congregations. In a few places, established German Jews gradually brought the new east European arrivals into the Reform fold. In some towns, Jewish institutions appeared for the first time in the mass migration era. What happened in Ohio River Valley towns varied greatly depending on the extent of east European immigration and the existing situation of the local Jewish population. But in any event, with such small numbers, neither group could afford to ignore the other completely.

In the regional cities of Wheeling and Evansville, where the Jewish population would reach over one thousand in the early twentieth century, Jewish communal life developed much the same way it did in the largest cities, Pittsburgh, Cincinnati, and Louisville. As a result of earlier conflicts, Evansville had by 1870 two congregations: one Reform, B'nai Israel, and one Orthodox, B'nai Moshe. B'nai Israel was prosperous and proper. B'nai Moshe was small but committed; in 1880, there were only twenty-five member families, but they had a small synagogue and a Hebrew day school for twenty pupils, taught by their full-time rabbi. As more east Europeans moved to Evansville, this congregation grew to about fifty families by 1900.[11]

With the arrival of the east Europeans, the economic and social gap between Reform and Orthodox began to widen. B'nai Israel members made their livings from banking, law, and manufacturing. B'nai Moshe members were small-scale merchants, such as pawnbrokers and dealers in secondhand goods. A county history from 1897 noted that B'nai Israel "numbers among its members some of the wealthiest and most prominent business men in the city." In fact, all of the prominent Jewish citizens listed in the history were German Jews—and all were members of B'nai Israel. At the turn of the century, the two synagogues were only about a block apart in a neighborhood just northwest of the commercial center. But the Orthodox Jews tended to live close to downtown, whereas the Reform Jews lived farther away, in exclusively residential neighborhoods. In 1902, B'nai Israel erected a new building, closer to the members' neighborhood.[12]

Evansville's veteran German Jews were quickly outnumbered. In 1907, community leaders estimated that the city's Jewish population of 850 was 75 percent German and 25 percent Russian; by 1912, the breakdown of the 1,000

Jews was "German and Russian in equal parts." The two groups of Jews usually moved in separate circles. Reminiscing in the 1980s about his childhood in the 1910s, one Evansville native from a German family commented that the east Europeans "certainly didn't have association with the part of the Jewish community that we associated with. . . . There was very little traffic between the two [groups]. It was snobbery of an extraordinary kind. . . . When we grew up my sister picked up a Yiddish phrase or two and my father forbad her ever to use them. It was strict by order that no one in the family ever use Yiddish expressions. It was below us. It was demeaning to do that."[13] There were also difficulties between the older German members and the newer east Europeans in the Orthodox community of B'nai Moshe, and sometime around the turn of the century, the latter founded their own congregation, Adath Israel.

Germans and east Europeans also remained separate in Wheeling. The German Jewish community was solidly middle and upper middle class by the 1890s, still concentrated in the traditionally Jewish clothing and dry goods businesses, and closely knit through business and marriage relationships. Their congregation, Leshem Shomayim, with about one hundred members, continued to be in the forefront of radical Reform, adopting a markedly Protestantized liturgical style. After using the Einhorn prayer book for years, Leshem Shomayim adopted the *Union Prayer Book* with alacrity. And in April 1892, the congregation completed and dedicated an expensive Moorish-style synagogue on Eoff Street.[14]

Before the 1890s, there had been a few non-German Jews in the community, though they were not very visible. Soon Wheeling was the preeminent industrial town in West Virginia, part of the major industrial region surrounding Pittsburgh; industrialization and its concomitant immigration greatly increased the city's ethnic diversity generally. By 1906, approximately 20 percent of the five hundred Jews in Wheeling were east European immigrants, and both the number and the proportion were growing steadily. Leshem Shomayim responded as did other German communities, organizing social services for, as the congregation's rabbi Harry Levi put it, "the poor, forlorn, homeless creatures . . . these unfortunate co-religionists." Responsibilities for social welfare were divided between the existing Ladies' Hebrew Benevolent Society, which attended to impoverished Jewish residents, and the new Relief Society, which provided for transients.[15]

The east Europeans in Wheeling quickly developed their own spheres of activity. Some opened small stores, and others peddled junk; many were cigar makers who had learned the trade in Pittsburgh. The large number of single men employed as stogie makers supported the existence downtown of several small kosher restaurants, such as Levy's on Eleventh Street. Orthodox Congregation Ohev Sholem was organized around 1914; it met in various rented locations in downtown Wheeling, where most of the fifty or so members lived. By 1920, the Jewish population of Wheeling had grown to around one thousand, largely as a result of the immigrant influx.[16]

In two other West Virginia industrial towns with smaller, more recently organized communities, the new immigration also created divisions. In Parkersburg, where a congregation was finally organized in 1909, after fifty years of Jewish settlement, the addition of east Europeans almost immediately accelerated its breakup into Reform and Orthodox factions. In Huntington, because of the newness of the city, German Jewish hegemony did not last very long at all. Congregation Ohab Sholem attempted to absorb all local Jews, though tensions over the direction of the congregation appeared as early as the 1880s: the congregation used the *Union Prayer Book* after its publication in 1896 but made Orthodox services available for the High Holidays. Though not a member of the UAHC, the single congregation could stretch only so far. Around 1910, with at least one hundred Jewish residents in the city and a much greater diversity of backgrounds, the traditionalists, including many recent immigrants from eastern Europe, founded Orthodox congregation B'nai Israel, which soon erected its own synagogue, employed its own full-time rabbi and a shoḥet, and established its own cemetery.[17]

It is not apparent that intracommunal differences were extremely contentious in Parkersburg or Huntington. Perhaps because these two towns did not have long histories of institutional unity, separation by religious preference was easier. Reform and Orthodox Jews continued to mingle at B'nai B'rith and other communitywide meetings. In Parkersburg, the two groups shared meeting space, and in Huntington, some children from the Reform congregation attended the afternoon Hebrew school run by the Orthodox.[18]

In some small towns, the Jewish community managed not to fragment. Newcomers were folded into the existing communal and social structure, though not always with the greatest of ease. In late-nineteenth-century Paducah, Kentucky, the Jewish population barely increased despite steady increases in the town's total population. Some east Europeans in Paducah who desired communal affiliation joined the German-dominated Reform congregation, but there was always a certain social distance. In Paducah, as elsewhere, German Jews were the benefactors, and many east Europeans the recipients of charity; the local Federation of Jewish Charities originated in 1917 as a German project to assist the east European immigrants.[19]

Newcomers were also a challenge for well-established small Jewish communities such as Portsmouth. Though it was never large, the Portsmouth community was by the turn of the century a stable and prosperous group. In 1906,

Congregation Beneh Abraham purchased the building in which it had rented space for many years; it later resold the building, bought a lot at Eighth and Gay streets, and, in 1923, dedicated the cornerstone of a new temple. The new temple, a solid, Romanesque brick structure, was possible because of the community's affluence. The lead gift came from congregation president Simon Labold, the son of Bavarian immigrants, who came to Portsmouth from Cincinnati as a young man in the 1880s; by the 1910s, Labold, president of First National Bank, was able to pledge the phenomenal sum of $10,000 to the congregation's building fund.[20]

The move was also made possible—and necessary—by a surge in membership. As late as 1896, the congregation had only thirty-seven individual members, representing even fewer families; in 1926, there were eighty-one, with two dozen children in the Sunday school.[21] Much of this growth was fueled by the settlement in Portsmouth of Jews of eastern European background.

The integration of newcomers was gradual. When, in 1894, Joseph Lopinsky, a Polish Jew, applied for congregational membership, several men objected that he had not been in town long enough—almost certainly a cover for hesitation about this particular individual, since length of residence had never before been a problem. Hedging their bets, the congregational board accepted Lopinsky provisionally while amending the bylaws to provide for a committee to investigate "the character and qualification of the applicant." The board accepted Lopinsky into full membership the next month.[22]

Timing of immigration and place of origin could also be factors in ease of integration. Henry Atlas and Samuel Horchow provide two examples. Born in rural Hungary, Atlas emigrated as a teenager in 1880 and opened his first store in Portsmouth in 1895. He quickly prospered. In addition to the synagogue and B'nai B'rith, Atlas joined the Masons and the Elks. He adopted the values and goals of his new community, and the community in turn opened up to him; one of the Atlas daughters married a member of the Levi family, which had been in Portsmouth since the 1850s. Featured in a 1924 *Portsmouth Daily Times* series, "Men Who Helped Make Portsmouth," Atlas observed that when he came to Portsmouth, it was a "conservative little town, and the stranger was regarded with suspicion. Now that attitude has changed."[23] Atlas was part of the change, joining his formerly suspicious neighbors in the local booster culture of the 1920s.

Horchow was born in the town of Brody in Polish Galicia and came to the United States in 1891. Two years later he opened a furniture store in Portsmouth. Like Atlas, he was a club man, belonging to the Masons, Elks, Knights of Pythias, and Modern Woodmen, in addition to B'nai B'rith and, of course, Congregation Beneh Abraham. He was a booster: member of the chamber of commerce and president of the Bureau of Community Service.[24]

Atlas and Horchow were both from regions that, in the nineteenth century, lay within the Austro-Hungarian Empire, straddling central and eastern Europe. These regions were influenced by German culture, which probably made it easier for them than, say, for a Russian Jew to adapt to an American Jewish community still infused with a sense of Germanness. Their success was accelerated by their ability to attach themselves to a Jewish community that had already achieved social acceptance.

Initially, the economic differences between Germans and east Europeans in Portsmouth were considerable. The Germans were almost exclusively merchants; more east Europeans were employees, for instance, the foreman of Portsmouth Shoe Company. Those east Europeans who were merchants had smaller, less prestigious establishments, like pawnshops and junkyards.[25] But these families too reached the middle class in Portsmouth by the 1920s. With a few very wealthy—but even fewer poor—constituents, the Portsmouth Jewish community's homogeneity reinforced its stability.

The process of integrating non-German Jews into an established German community was influenced by the close-knit nature of the Portsmouth community. Small-town societies may often be cool to outsiders, but once one becomes an insider, these societies are usually reliably loyal. And in a small community, the disadvantages of exclusivity far outweigh the challenges of inclusivity—especially when exclusivity is a bad decision in terms of the financial viability of the group's institutions. From the 1890s on, as the percentage of east Europeans in the American Jewish population increased exponentially, so too did the percentage of Beneh Abraham's membership. The old German families maintained a strong hand in communal affairs, but east Europeans eventually rose to leadership; though unused to Reform, most were eager to benefit from the social stability and prestige the congregation carried in Portsmouth.

As older communities received reinforcements, new Jewish communities and congregations sprang to life in the mid–Ohio Valley in the late nineteenth and early twentieth centuries. Across the river from Cincinnati, the villages of Covington and Newport, Kentucky, developed their own Jewish identities. A few Jewish families had lived in this Cincinnati hinterland in the mid-nineteenth century, but in the late nineteenth century, as the expansion of Cincinnati's regional economy brought northern Kentucky into its metropolitan orbit, east European Jewish immigrants moved into Covington and Newport's poorer neighborhoods, sometimes after a sojourn in Cincinnati. (In fact, though Covington and Newport were in 1900 Kentucky's second- and third-largest cities, after Louisville, they were still considered satellites of Cincinnati.) In 1897, United Hebrew Congregation, an Orthodox synagogue, was incorporated in Newport; in 1905, the congregation dedicated a refurbished former Christian church as its synagogue. Covington Jews also began around 1906 to organize an Orthodox congregation; in 1915, they bought a building lot, and they dedicated their synagogue the next year.[26]

In two other towns near industrial areas on the south bank of the Ohio, Orthodox congregations sprang up around the turn of the century. In Ashland, Kentucky, near Huntington, West Virginia, new east European immigrants formed their congregation in 1896; the few German Jews who lived in Ashland in earlier decades had not formed their own organizations, preferring instead to join Beneh Abraham in Portsmouth. The small Jewish population of Moundsville, West Virginia, about a dozen miles downriver from Wheeling, started a congregation in 1909.[27]

One important facet of industrialization in the upper Ohio Valley was the development in the late nineteenth and early twentieth centuries of oil and gas production. This industry was the economic base for the expansion of the Jewish community in Marietta, Ohio. Once home to just a few German Jews, Marietta was rapidly settled by Jews from the Russian Empire, including many from an extended clan that included the Rabinovitz, Brachman, and Beren families. Many of these family members hailed directly from the small Latvian town of Plavinas, southeast of Riga, near Lithuania. At the end of the nineteenth century, Plavinas was close to half Jewish and was part of the strongly traditionalist religious culture of Lithuanian Jewry. The pioneer of this chain migration seems to have been Dave Rabinovitz, who immigrated to the United States in 1891 and was settled in Pittsburgh by the United Hebrew Charities of New York. Once the chain migration had begun, most of the new immigrants came directly to Marietta, where they found an economic niche on the periphery of the local oil industry. The enterprising arrivals would scour the oil fields for scrap metal, rope, and other abandoned materials, which they would collect and resell. The pace of oil production meant that this work was, if difficult, reasonably profitable, and the "recyclers" became a staple of the industrial scene. When Morris Miller, a Russian immigrant, died in 1907 after being struck by a train while driving his junk cart out to an oil field, a local newspaper commented that "the aged Jew" was "a familiar sight on the streets of this city as he drove his one horse wagon from place to place on his daily rounds."[28]

Some immigrants got into oil production. Whereas at least a dozen Marietta Jews listed their business in the 1900 census as "junk," Herman Appleman, an early arrival and Rabinovitz relative, was already an "oil well supervisor." Most of these east Europeans at first lived in the neighborhood around Hart and South Fourth streets, near the Ohio River, often next door to or on the same lot as their businesses. In 1908, a visitor from New York observed that all of Marietta's Jews seemed "more or less prosperous." In fact, as early as 1902, about half of all Jews in Marietta, including even the newest residents, owned real property.[29]

Though they had no doubt been meeting informally for communal worship for some years, by 1900, the community had reached sufficient numbers (perhaps as many as one hundred individuals, including children) to organize a formal congregation—an Orthodox congregation, which they named Binae Israel. Most of the founders were from the core families, including president Herman Appleman, but other east Europeans also participated, including Nathan Newman and his new brother-in-law, Edward Evin. In the early years, membership numbered about two dozen men. They hired E. M. Mosinter as an all-purpose communal functionary—to lead services, teach, circumcise baby boys, and provide kosher slaughter; he and his wife also ran a small grocery. Mosinter was succeeded by a number of men who kept the job for only two or three years, but some stability was achieved when Aaron Axelrod held the position from 1918 until the early 1930s. The community had its own cemetery, a tract of land on Cisler Ridge purchased in 1902, and a synagogue, in a converted house on Hart Street purchased in 1903. Herman Appleman was the largest single contributor to the synagogue and cemetery purchases and also made several loans that he later forgave.[30]

Marietta's Orthodox community was extremely close-knit, and there were a number of marriages among the family groups. The community was very strict in its observance of Jewish law and well connected in the American circles of traditionalist Lithuanian Orthodoxy. In 1909, Sarah Rabinowitz, Isaac Hertz Rabinowitz's eighteen-year-old daughter, married Bernard Revel, a rabbi and scholar who later founded and served as first president of Yeshiva University. Writes Revel's biographer, accurately, "The worldly Jewish residents of the thriving Marietta community were enchanted by him." The local press made the most of the event. The *Marietta Register-Leader* pronounced it "one of the prettiest Jewish weddings to occur in Marietta in some time," though the paper got many of the details wrong, including, in one reference, the groom's name. The *Marietta Times* account was even more grandiose: it was "an important event in Hebrew circles all over the country." After all, the bride was "very popular and highly educated," and the groom was "one of the most brilliant Hebrews of the country."[31]

Evidence of these Mariettans' religious position and connections can be found in the fact that the officiants at the Rabinowitz-Revel wedding were two of Revel's mentors, Bernard Levinthal of Philadelphia and Moses Simon Sivitz of Pittsburgh. These two rabbis were leaders of Agudat Harabbanim, a leading rabbinical group that firmly opposed any Americanization of Judaism. Sivitz, who had introduced the couple, was considered by Marietta Jews their *mara d'atra* (local rabbinic authority), to whom they turned with questions of Jewish law. In Marietta, then, traditionalist east Europeans dominated the Jewish landscape, maintaining strong institutions and social cohesiveness. Coming into town almost en masse, they had no need to assimilate to or in any other way deal with a preexisting local Jewish elite. Other east European Jews were part of the community whose nucleus was the Latvian families, but the non-Orthodox Jews already in town—especially since they had not organized communally—were barely relevant.

Particularly remarkable in this period was the growth of Jewish communities in the small towns and cities on the Ohio River in the industrial region anchored by Pittsburgh. The iron, steel, and coal industries were already active here in the early nineteenth century, but before the advent of railroads in the 1850s, the hinterland was relatively isolated from Pittsburgh. After the Civil War, the countryside quickly became integrated into the city's industrial expansion, an expansion that would not have been possible without easy transport and access to western markets via the Ohio River. The river winds downstream for approximately thirty miles from its origin in the heart of Pittsburgh to the Ohio border, past the Pennsylvania towns of McKees Rocks, Coraopolis, Aliquippa, Monaca, Rochester, Beaver, and Midland; it then makes a sharp southward bend, thus encompassing within the Pittsburgh hinterland the larger towns of East Liverpool and Steubenville, Ohio, and Weirton, West Virginia, with Wheeling at its outer edge.

As the industrial upper Ohio Valley developed, so did its Jewish communities. In less than forty years, Pittsburgh's Jewish population grew more than tenfold, surging from 5,000 in 1890 to 53,000 in 1927. Soon both seasoned German Jews and recently arrived east Europeans began flowing into the smaller cities and towns of this extended hinterland.

Because of the types of economic resources and the industrial emphasis, these places developed as industrial towns, in sharp contrast to the small towns that functioned primarily as service centers for agricultural regions. Steubenville and East Liverpool became centers of regional industry: steel in Steubenville and ceramics in East Liverpool. Most of these towns had always had one or two Jewish families but no Jewish communal organization. Now, at the turn of the twentieth century, new Jewish residents, following the traditional Jewish commercial path, re-created the economic pattern of the mid-nineteenth-century German Jewish immigrants in a more thoroughly industrialized and ethnically diverse context.[32]

As Ewa Morawska has thoroughly detailed in her study of Johnstown, Pennsylvania, social organization in small American industrial cities and towns was influenced by patterns of relationships carried over from the old country. Particularly noticeable was a continued ethnic division of labor, with a concentration of Jews in small business.[33] Even in large American cities with a substantial Jewish working class, very few Jews worked in heavy industry; the majority of the Jewish labor force in New York City was in the garment business. Around 1900, perhaps only thirty or forty Jewish men labored in the large Pittsburgh steel mills, and no more than a few hundred total in other plants such as Westinghouse. Rather, the largest manufacturing segment for Jewish employment in the city—for men, women, and children—was cigar making.[34] Even in large cities, most Jews made their livings through commerce.

The pattern that Morawska identified in small industrial towns is certainly well demonstrated by East Liverpool. A few Jews were employed as wage workers in East Liverpool's numerous potteries. Almost all Jewish families earned their livings through retail, and the type of business was often related to their ethnic origins. Many of the Germans were in dry goods or ready-to-wear: the Erlangers' store sold menswear; Gus Bendheim sold shoes. The east Europeans were in a wider range of pursuits, but many of these still historically associated with Jews. Some dealt in scrap metal and junk, a few had small groceries, and another few had small businesses in more upscale lines, such as jewelry, furniture, or tailoring. Morris Sarbin ran a tavern.[35]

The overall ethnic diversity that was a feature of these upper Ohio Valley towns contrasted strongly with the populations of most of the towns downriver. The diversity encompassed varied southern and eastern European populations—Italian and Greek as well as Slavic—that made up the mass migration to America's industrial centers in that era. As a result, the social demography in the small upper valley towns was more like that of the large industrial cities like Pittsburgh than of remote county seats like Portsmouth.

Jews were an integral part of this ethnic variety. For example, Steubenville's population zoomed 60 percent (from 14,000 to 22,000) in the first decade of the century, much of the growth attributable to a large number of new southern and eastern European immigrants, predominantly Italians but also Hungarians, Poles, and Russians (including many Jews). The 1900 U.S. census listed 46 Russian-born residents in all of Jefferson County. By 1910, there were 830 in Steubenville alone, a sizable percentage of whom were Jews. Most of Steubenville's ethnic groups, especially those of recent settlement, lived in a few distinct residential areas. For instance, many Russians, both Jews and non-Jews, lived in a few blocks of Eighth and Ninth streets. Likewise, in nearby East Liverpool, the east European Jewish immigrants lived in the east end of town, a modest neighborhood with its own business district, which was also home to a large and varied ethnic population, mostly Catholic.[36]

Unlike the smaller downriver communities, these upper valley communities were dominated by east Europeans. According to the 1910 census, Steubenville's Jewish population of approximately three hundred individuals was three-quarters Russian or Polish, with many Hungarians but only a small percentage of Germans. This situation also prevailed in the western Pennsylvania and West Virginia towns north of Wheeling. Because of overall ethnic social stratification and residential segregation in the upper valley towns, differences of background within the Jewish population were particularly salient. The identification as a specific type of Jew—German or east European—was reinforced by the social structure and remained an important part of locals' Jewish identity until the mid-twentieth century.

Not surprisingly, the new congregations established in the upper valley towns were almost uniformly Orthodox. One began meeting in Steubenville in the late 1880s and was formally incorporated in 1892 as B'nai Israel. In 1903, with membership numbering sixty men, B'nai Israel purchased for a synagogue a small but elegant building on South Fifth Street, a former church built in 1835. A mikvah was installed in the building that same year, and two years later, the congregation purchased land for a cemetery on Sunset Boulevard. The congregation engaged immigrant "reverends" for the roles of ḥazan and shoḥet, M. S. Peiros from 1897 to 1906 and Isaac Caplan from 1906 to 1923.[37]

Steubenville's Orthodox Jews maintained connections with the rapidly growing Orthodox community in Pittsburgh. The 1903 dedication of B'nai Israel was attended by Rabbi Aaron Ashinsky, Pittsburgh's leading moderate Orthodox rabbi, as well as—interestingly enough—by Wheeling's ultra-Reform rabbi, Harry Levi. Ashinsky cultivated connections throughout the upper Ohio Valley, soliciting support for major communal projects in Pittsburgh, such as the Hebrew Institute. Teachers trained at the institute were hired in Steubenville. Isaac Adler may have been one of these; around 1910, he ran the already-established Talmud Torah for boys and also organized a Sunday school for girls (an uncommon innovation for an Orthodox synagogue in this era) with the assistance of Rabbi Ashinsky.[38]

Orthodox congregations also sprang up in western Pennsylvania towns. McKees Rocks, Pennsylvania, only a few miles from downtown Pittsburgh, was the site of several large iron and steel companies set up in the 1880s; Jews there started their own synagogue in 1903. Thirty miles downriver from the city was Midland, whose population more than quadrupled in the 1910s as its steel mill expanded; in 1918, the nearly 100 Jews in Midland chartered their own Orthodox congregation. Jews in Coraopolis, which is also quite close to the city, founded a synagogue in 1923, when the Jewish population was over 200, though a Ladies' Aid Society was already active. In 1927, Tree of Life congregation was started in Rochester by some of its 100 Jews as well as residents of the neighboring, even smaller, river towns of Monaca, Beaver, Freedom, and Conway. The steel industry expansion in the 1910s caused the population of Aliquippa to spurt from 3,300 in 1910 to more than 15,000 in 1920, with a concomitant growth in the Jewish population. One group of Hungarian Jews clustered in the older part of town, near the Ohio River, in West Aliquippa, where they attended Orthodox congregation Beth Jacob, organized around 1912. Another, larger group lived in the Woodlawn section, where Agudath Achim, also Orthodox, was chartered in 1919. That year, there were perhaps 300 Jews in a total local population of 2,000—about 15 percent of the total, a high percentage.[39]

The upper valley featured some "instant" industrial towns, such as Ambridge, Pennsylvania, and Weirton, West Virginia, populated largely by iron and steel workers. Virtually all their Jewish residents were east Europeans and merchants. Ambridge was a company town of the purest variety, built in 1903 for the American Bridge plant of U.S. Steel. The population more than doubled between 1910 and 1920, bringing Jewish merchants, who chartered Beth Samuel Synagogue in 1914. By 1920, there were about two hundred Jewish residents in a very ethnically diverse population that was more than one-third immigrant.[40]

The city of Weirton grew up along with a steel mill built in 1909 by Ernest Weir. Jews were among the first residents that same year: Sam Geffner, a Romanian immigrant whose first occupation was peddling, came from Pittsburgh to set up a small store in the new town. By 1916, there were approximately fifteen Jewish families in Weirton, totaling about seventy individuals. That year, the families banded together to form a small Orthodox congregation named Beth Israel. At first they met in a rented hall and used a Sefer Torah borrowed from a congregation in nearby Steubenville; in 1924, they bought a building lot at the corner of West Street and Virginia Avenue, and three years later, they dedicated a small structure for a synagogue.[41]

Because East Liverpool's growing Jewish community included a number of German Jews who had been in the United States for many years before moving to town, two congregations—one Reform and one Orthodox—arose within a few years of each other. Beginning in the 1880s, a small group, largely German families, held Reform High Holidays services in private homes. In 1894, the group designated itself Congregation B'nai Israel, and in 1909, it affiliated with the UAHC. At first the congregation was tiny; only twenty men were charter members. In its early years, the congregation rented space from various fraternal organizations, including the Elks, Moose, and Odd Fellows, until starting construction on a building in 1921. Rabbis from Reform congregations in Wheeling, Cleveland, or Youngstown would visit occasionally to lead services, especially the religious school's confirmation services. In the early twentieth century, the Orthodox east Europeans also organized, first as a minyan, gathering informally for prayer, and then as a formal congregation, B'nai Jacob, in 1904. This group also met in private homes and then in a rented hall until a building was constructed on East Third Street in 1915.[42]

In Bellaire, Ohio, across the Ohio River from Wheeling, the dynamics of industrialization and the mass migration turned a small country town with a few German Jewish merchants into a small manufacturing city whose Jewish community was dominated by east Europeans. In the mid-nineteenth century, some 50 or 60 Jews lived in Bellaire—including, at one point, Rabbi Judah Wechsler—and they had some sort of organized Jewish society, though whether it was a formal congregation or a benevolent society is unclear. By the turn of the century, as east European immigrants settled in larger numbers, the town had two congregations for a Jewish population of probably no more than 125. The Reform congregation, called Sons of Israel, was composed largely of German and Alsatian Jews, many of them clothing merchants; Agudas Achim was Orthodox and largely east European.[43]

Soon a significant expansion in Bellaire's Jewish population came from a new influx of east Europeans. By 1907, the Jewish community totaled 250 or 300 persons, and Russian- and Romanian-born Jews outnumbered Germans 70 percent to 30 percent.[44] A substantial number of the new immigrants, close to half of the Orthodox population, had come to town under the auspices of a national Jewish organization, the Industrial Removal Office (IRO). The story of the IRO in the Ohio River Valley illustrates the challenges that faced the American Jewish community as it grappled with integrating a huge new population in the new conditions of the industrial age.

The IRO was founded in 1901 to promote immigrant Jewish settlement in cities and towns in the interior of the United States. The mass migration—some twenty million persons arrived in the United States between 1880 and 1920—put tremendous pressures on American cities. With housing at a premium and large numbers of newcomers seeking shelter and community, ethnic immigrant ghettoes—overcrowded, unsafe, and unclean—coalesced in all the major cities, arousing concern, anxiety, and fear in many Americans. Could "this queer conglomerate mass of heterogeneous elements"—as the generally sympathetic journalist and reformer Jacob Riis described them—ever truly assimilate American values and behaviors? Though all immigrants were suspect, there was particular concern about what one decidedly unsympathetic journalist called "the great Jewish invasion."[45]

The founders of the IRO, mainly wealthy German American Jews, were alarmed at the increase in antisemitism that accompanied increased immigration. They worried, not unreasonably, that this would fuel sentiment in favor of restricting immigration, at a time when so many Jews, especially in Russia, needed a place to go. A classic example of the Progressive era's faith in social engineering, the IRO's strategy was to stem antisemitism, and thereby save open immigration, by "normalizing" Jewish occupations and broadening Jews' geographic distribution. "Traveling agents" were sent throughout the country to scout for job opportunities and to cultivate support among local Jews; job placements were then made from the New York office. Before disbanding in 1922, the IRO relocated 79,000 immigrants to 1,670 cities and towns across the United States.[46]

In view of the planning, money, and hard work invested, the IRO has usually been judged a mixed success at best. Many of the small cities and towns in the Ohio River Valley seemed ideal by IRO criteria, which identified "open space" with healthy living and immigrant conformity with Americanism. These towns were local economic centers, seemed to exemplify American civic virtue, and had established Jewish communities. Yet few immigrants were ever placed in the Ohio River towns by the IRO, and those who were seldom stayed long. Indeed, success and longevity could not necessarily be predicted based on the size of the city in which the immigrant settled, the size of the Jewish community already there, or its distance from a major city. Success stories came out of some small towns, whereas turnover rates in some cities, such as Columbus and Detroit, were very high.

The IRO came to the small communities of the Ohio River Valley in the wake of the depression of 1907, hoping that expansion into new areas would offset job losses in areas where immigrants had already been placed. This strategy was only partly successful. Immigrants were indeed sent farther from New York than before, many to the central states. In fact, Ohio was first in the number of "removals" (as the IRO's immigrant clients were called), with some ten thousand resettled.[47] But economically depressed small towns were no better than economically depressed cities. In 1908, traveling agent Henry Goldstein visited Ironton, Ohio, and wrote back to IRO general manager David Bressler in New York, "Coming in to Ironton my first impulse was to get out as soon as I got in but as no train goes out until to-morrow morning I made my investigation which only confirmed my first impressions." Goldstein did not even attempt to form a committee to support the IRO from among the ten local Jewish families. In Goldstein's opinion, "The town is dead and I feel no one we might send could be satisfactorily placed or would stay."[48]

But economics was only part of the story. Equally critical was that individual and group personalities could thwart or aid the IRO's scheme. These factors—immigrants' social and cultural attitudes and needs, and the ability of established Jewish communities to meet those needs—were, of course, closely related. From the outset, the IRO knew it had to deal with German Jews' ambivalence and to open immigrants' minds to the possibilities of living in the American interior, away from the ethnic supports of New York. Traveling agents attempted to bridge the gaps between immigrant and settled Jews and among the settled communities.

Lack of cooperation between segments of the community, as occurred in Evansville and Steubenville, limited the chances for success. But even decent intracommunal relations, like decent economic conditions, did not guarantee it. Immigrants unfamiliar with the American interior, insecure in the English language, or unused to substantial interactions with Gentiles were often uncomfortable in small-town settings, and there were limits to what settled Jews, especially of a different immigrant background, could do about it. The Jewish community of Portsmouth was sympathetic to the IRO's project, but the town was of limited appeal to new immigrants. In the judgment of one IRO official who visited Portsmouth, "The people here are very nice but they have neither a permanent Rabbi nor a Bnai Brith lodge—hence a sort of a lukewarm Judaism." He warned, "It is best for people still here [in New York] to understand that they [immigrants] can not live with Jews not kosher." In this view, the social stability created, at great effort, by the Reform strategy was not worth the cultural cost to immigrants.[49]

Bellaire was one of the IRO's few certifiable success stories in the Ohio River Valley, and that story exposes a factor for success that trumped others. Not only did many immigrants come to Bellaire under the auspices of the IRO, but a majority remained. Many of those who left went to other small towns; the IRO was quite gratified that, as the agent reported, "none went back to N.Y." IRO agent Stanley Bero wrote to general manager Bressler in 1907, "I was never so pleased in all the days of my travels, as I was at Bellaire where at the orthodox synagogue I met about 15 of the heads of families sent here by the

IRO. The city is very poor industrially and the Jews are not as well fixed as in Wheeling. Our people all make a fair living[;] most peddle junk."[50]

The removals were also satisfied. At his Bellaire meeting, Bero told Bressler, "they drew up resolutions expressing their gratitude to the IRO which will be sent to you and copies will be sent to the Jewish press of New York. . . . I spoke in Yiddish, [and] the people assured me that they not alone understood but felt my words. It would have done your heart good to be here. I know it made me feel proud and I shall use this town as proof in the other towns." A year later, in 1908, another IRO agent, Henry Goldstein, also spoke enthusiastically about Bellaire as "a town of excellent opportunities for our people." Though some layoffs had recently occurred, Goldstein thought that these were temporary economic setbacks. (In fact, Goldstein noted, Ohio's progressive child labor regulations forced industries to hire young men rather than boys, providing opportunities for immigrant men.) The local Jews "reported that there was little or no Rishus [antisemitism] in this town." Goldstein looked up former removals and reported that though more had left town than Bero thought, a large percentage had settled permanently, making a living as small-scale merchants or artisans.[51]

What accounted for this success? The economic situation in Bellaire was not especially promising. There was no unusual degree of intra-Jewish cooperation. The IRO attempted to establish working relationships with both the German Reform and the east European Orthodox contingents, but it seems to have relied more heavily on the Germans, undoubtedly in the hope that their overall prosperity and social standing would be helpful. Despite their sense of noblesse oblige, the German Jews in Bellaire were not especially enthusiastic about the project. Bero observed that their reluctance "was due to the attitude of A. Luchs who foreshadowed the risks in having people come here of the character etc that the average immigrants represent. . . . Try to send a good fellow at first—so that they may not fear to receive a large quota."[52]

It was self-help that made for the IRO's success—the personal contacts of the less-established east European immigrants, especially former removals, even though these people were the least likely to have much by way of financial resources. East European Jews brought their relatives and landsleit to settle near them, often through the IRO. The Orthodox east Europeans spoke the same language and understood the special needs of their fellows. Sam Kapner hired some for his enamel works. At one Jew's urging, a local Gentile baker agreed to hire an immigrant who would be allowed to observe Shabbat—a not inconsiderable concession. By 1912, Bellaire's Jewish population had soared to more than four hundred. The population growth, and its particular pattern, created a Jewish community that was tightly and intricately interconnected through marriage and work. The IRO, by providing opportunities for a few individuals, helped create an entire new immigrant community in Bellaire by fostering the process of chain migration and self-help.[53]

The east European immigration gave an infusion of energy to Jewish life in the Ohio River Valley in the early twentieth century. Through the first half of the twentieth century, the small towns provided comfortable contexts for social and economic life and a modest level of Jewish activity. Pittsburgh, Cincinnati, and Louisville remained diverse and active Jewish communities. But as the profile of American Jewry continued to change, the small-town community was losing its appeal.

CHAPTER 9

Communities at Maturity

Though the occasional reinvigoration of the river economy might boost a town for a while, the importance of the Ohio River to Jewish settlement was strongest in the mid-nineteenth century and essentially ended at the end of the century. Over the course of the first half of the twentieth century, at various points, the Jewish populations in the small towns of the Ohio River Valley reached their peak. Some communities began to collapse; others shrank. Yet in the period before World War II, most towns continued to have viable Jewish institutions and active Jewish communal lives. Jews in the small towns of the Ohio River Valley shared many of the experiences and concerns of other American Jews while also dealing with challenges particular to their settings.

The first few decades of the new century were critical for the development of American Jewish culture. The east European mass migration had increased Jewish numbers such that by 1940, Jews were almost 4 percent of the United States' population—the highest percentage in American history. A distinctive ethnic style developed, blending the Yiddish folk heritage and selected traditional religious practices with American domesticity and consumer culture. This new ethnicity was created largely in the cities, and most particularly in the Jewish neighborhoods of New York: by 1927, almost half of all the Jews in the United States lived in that city, forever cementing an identification of people and place that continues to influence American popular culture.[1]

East European Jews who settled in small towns shared many of the inherited cultural traits. But unlike their urban cousins, small-town Jews did not spend their days in an intense Jewish subculture, and in this respect, their experience was far more like that of their predecessors from the mid-nineteenth-century central European immigration. The inner life of the local Jewish community, expressed in various institutions, was lived in tandem with the outer life of small-town American boosterism. On the one hand, synagogues, sisterhoods, B'nai B'rith, and other auxiliary and independent organizations were going strong. On the other hand, Jews were an important component of the local business community and active in civic affairs; their children attended local public schools with largely Christian classmates.

A variety of organizations continued to play a role in Jewish life in the small river towns. A legacy of the German era, B'nai B'rith experienced something of a renewal of importance in small Jewish communities in the early twentieth century, as its national profile became increasingly midwestern and middle class.[2] New lodges were founded in McKeesport, Pennsylvania, in 1904; in East Liverpool, Ohio, in 1915; and in Huntington, West Virginia, and Steubenville, Ohio, in 1916.

Some communities spawned elaborate organizational structures usually more typical of larger Jewish communities. In Steubenville, for instance, in addition to B'nai B'rith and the Ladies' Aid Society (founded in 1902), there was a Young Women's Hebrew Association (1917), a young men's social club (1919), a synagogue-sponsored Boy Scout troop, and a Young Men's Hebrew Association Juniors Club that used the slogan "Keep Jewish Boys Jewish" (indicating a common fear in America). The proliferation of organizations was noticeable even at the time, and the community seems to have overextended itself. "In the last ten years," a communal publication noted in 1925, "many organizations were formed, almost all of which failed on account of the lack of interest on the part of the members."[3] This was perhaps an unfair judgment on a community that numbered only about four hundred souls, especially since the organizations mentioned above were still active.

The synagogue remained the central, dominant institution of small-town Jewish life. Reform congregations seemed to prosper: in 1922, Congregation B'nai Israel in East Liverpool moved into a new building; Beneh Abraham in Portsmouth built a new one, architecturally quite similar, in 1925. With east European immigrants becoming more at home in America, Orthodox congregations also flourished. The Orthodox congregation in Bellaire was able to obtain its own building, a renovated private home, in 1923; the one in Steubenville was able to hire a full-time rabbi for the first time that same year. In 1921, the Marietta congregation moved uptown, away from the flood plain that was the area of first settlement. The new property included a second-floor apartment to accommodate a visiting rabbi. In Wheeling, increasingly affluent east European Jewish families moved out of downtown—"out-the-pike" in local parlance—toward Oglebay Park and nicer residential neighborhoods. In

1924, they organized a suburban Orthodox congregation, Synagogue of Israel, with its own building and a rabbi. New Orthodox congregations in the Pennsylvania towns of Coraopolis and Rochester started in 1923 and 1927.[4]

The small Jewish communities on the Ohio River—both Reform and Orthodox—continued in the twentieth century the voluntaristic practices that had enabled them to survive in the nineteenth. In the tradition of mutual assistance, the Orthodox congregations in Wheeling, West Virginia, and neighboring Bellaire, Ohio, cooperated on a ḥevra kadisha and sometimes shared rabbinical services. The laity continued to fill vital roles. At Bellaire's Reform congregation, Sylvan Blum handled most liturgical duties as "lay reader" for more than twenty years, even participating in such ecumenical activities as the popular pulpit exchanges with Christian ministers.[5]

The necessary reliance of small communities on nonrabbinic leadership provided some interesting options for innovation. The Ohio River Valley was the first forum for the career of Avis Clamitz Shulman, a pioneer in women's rabbinic education. Raised in a radical Reform congregation in Chicago, Clamitz studied at Hebrew Union College, the only woman there at the time. In 1929, she earned a bachelor of Hebrew letters degree, the prerabbinic degree, but demurred when some faculty members wished her to push forward as a test case for women's ordination. That year, she married Rabbi Charles Shulman, who had served at Wheeling's Eoff Street Temple since 1927. Clamitz Shulman used her prerabbinic education as a popular lecturer on Jewish topics and, her biographer points out, occasionally "as a sort of unofficial rabbi in cities such as Parkersburg, Wheeling, and Fairmount, West Virginia." In addition, she conducted services and lectured at least once at B'nai Israel in East Liverpool.[6] (The Shulmans left Wheeling in 1931.)

The dominance of synagogues in the institutional life of the small Jewish community was in marked contrast to the situation in the big cities, where secular organizations led in membership and communal power. In most cities, a proliferation of organizations reflected a social and ideological fragmentation of the Jewish community along political and religious lines. Such differences—while real—were far less salient in small towns. Urban Jewish communities often experienced tensions between religious and secular, "cultural" Jews, but small towners found it no particular contradiction to belong both to the socialist, antireligious Workmen's Circle (for example) and to the local Orthodox synagogue.[7] Small-town organizations that were synagogue sponsored or synagogue connected played a vital communal role by casting a wider net into the local Jewish community. For instance, of the ninety members of Steubenville's Ladies' Aid Society in 1925, probably one-fourth were women who were not wives of synagogue members, thus keeping these families connected to the Jewish community in another way.

As this suggests, women's organizations continued to be, as in the nineteenth century, central to the structure and operation of the Jewish community. In the small town, these organizations were the synagogue sisterhoods, which were both connected to and yet, to some degree, independent from the institutional synagogue itself. In East Liverpool, for example, the Sisterhood of Temple B'nai Israel was an important power center that interacted with other segments of the community. In 1920, the sisterhood, founded in 1919, had absorbed the Jewish Ladies' Aid Society of East Liverpool and Wellsville, creating a single women's organization responsible both for support of the congregation and for charitable work in the community generally.[8]

Throughout the 1920s and 1930s, the sisterhood was a powerful fund-raiser for the congregation, in some years forwarding as much as $1,000 to the temple board. This was in addition to the funds raised for other projects both within and beyond the congregation; in fact, the women were probably more productive than the men of the congregation in terms of the proportion of members involved in ongoing fund-raising activities. The women engaged in numerous small-scale fund-raisers: card parties, sewing parties, catering, bazaars, calendar sales, rummage sales, food sales, flower sales, apron sales. (In contravention of Jewish law, but reflecting their own practice and that of their non-Jewish neighbors, such sales were usually held on Saturdays.) There were a few big events: concerts, dinner-dances, and communitywide turkey dinners. The sisterhood paid for Hanukkah gifts and Purim treats for the Sunday school, children's activities, confirmation gifts, library books, and even teachers' salaries; they also contributed to HUC scholarship funds. The women provided flowers for the sick, supported Cleveland's Jewish Orphan Asylum and other hospitals and agencies, and volunteered in the city hospital.

The sisterhood provided real leadership opportunities for women, which they took very seriously. In East Liverpool, women whose husbands were congregational officers dominated the sisterhood, but their hegemony was not uncontested. In the first thirteen years of the organization, there was only one president, Belle Rickersberg—and several attempts (the last successful) to instate term limits.

The question of sisterhood leadership also encompassed an ongoing debate about the role of the congregation as a focus for activities that went beyond its own members. The males-only board of B'nai Israel was apparently anxious to keep some control of the independent sisterhood. In 1923, Gus Bendheim, whose wife, Flora, was sisterhood treasurer during Belle Rickersberg's tenure, persuaded the sisterhood that it should not be open to all Jewish women, but henceforth only to those whose husband, father, or brother was a temple member. (This proposal was formally moved by Flora Bendheim.) Furthermore, he persuaded them to consolidate their funds with those of the temple. Gus Bendheim patronizingly stressed that "the religious spirit [is] of primary importance coming before social importance in the Sisterhood."[9] This statement undoubtedly missed the point in the minds of many women (why are religious and social life mutually exclusive?), but equally undoubtedly, this change reflected the victory of the male-dominated institution in the competition for allegiance and financial support in a community with limited resources. Yet among the forty-three members of the sisterhood at the time were eight women whose families belonged not to the Reform but to the Orthodox congregation, B'nai Jacob, so there seems to be evidence that the boundaries Gus Bendheim wished to secure remained rather more permeable.

This debate about the boundaries of the sisterhood in East Liverpool reflected the persistent question of relations between veteran Jewish residents from families of German background and east European newcomers. Though in many cities, cultural differences between German and east European Jews remained until the post–World War II era, the barriers began to break down in the 1920s with the virtual cessation of immigration and the increased acculturation of immigrants. In small towns, in fact, this breakdown proceeded more quickly than in cities, where large populations could easily support various Jewish subcommunities.

One meeting ground was philanthropy. In large cities, Jews of different backgrounds met uncomfortably as both dispensers of charity (the wealthier, more acculturated Germans) and recipients (the more recently arrived east Europeans). Though small towners also played these roles, the size and informality of the community enabled quick and flexible responses to needs, responses that also enhanced informal contacts. In East Liverpool, in the middle of a B'nai Israel sisterhood dinner-dance at the Moose Hall one spring evening in 1920, the women held an emergency meeting to assist a sick Jewish man with travel expenses to New York for medical care. This man, who was given $30, was an east European member of the Orthodox congregation, B'nai Jacob. On another occasion, the sisterhood responded to a poor Jewish woman from the nearby hamlet of Salineville, who had just given birth in the East Liverpool hospital. The women arranged to pay for infant care, care for the family's older children, and a housekeeper. Like professional social workers and lay "friendly visitors" in urban ghettos, Belle Rickersberg and Fannie Stein were delegated "to investigate the home conditions in Salineville."[10] But this was not an urban ghetto with thousands of needy people and large, mutually distrustful German and east European communities. Mutual reliance and obligation crossed shorter bridges in the small towns as Jews of all backgrounds were forced to share resources.

The dynamic of the east Europeans' acculturation also began to build bridges in religious life. Throughout the first few decades of the twentieth century, some east European Jews began to move into the institutions of Americanized Reform. Sometimes this shift was driven by educational needs. In traditional mode, most Orthodox synagogues did not provide Jewish education for girls, yet many modern parents did not want to ignore the value of Jewish education for their daughters. Many would, as in East Liverpool, Ohio, or Ashland, Kentucky, send their sons to the traditional Orthodox ḥeder (an intensive afternoon school) to study Hebrew and rabbinics and send their daughters to the Reform temple's less rigorous Sunday school, where they studied Bible and ethics rather than Hebrew or rabbinics. In Covington, Kentucky, the Orthodox congregation opened a Sunday school for girls (who could not attend ḥeder with the boys) and hired as teachers students from the Reform seminary across the river in Cincinnati.[11]

In the 1920s and 1930s, more and more east Europeans, especially those of the second generation, began to actively prefer Reform to Orthodoxy. One example of this phenomenon was Congregation Agudath Achim in Ashland, Kentucky, founded by east Europeans in 1896 as an Orthodox congregation. As early as 1915, biweekly Reform services were conducted by a student rabbi from Hebrew Union College, and in 1921 the congregation joined the Reform movement. Not surprisingly, this change was not uncontested: the move to Reform led to the secession of some members, who constituted themselves as a new Orthodox congregation, House of Israel.[12]

The following year, a group of Steubenville Jews formed that town's Reform congregation, Temple Beth El. The early membership included several German Jewish families who had been in Steubenville for some time (some were second generation and several were related by marriage) without their own religious organization. But the main instigators of the new congregation were east Europeans, as were the majority of the members, some of whom had been—and some of whom remained—members of the Orthodox Congregation B'nai Israel. Echoing the rhetoric of their nineteenth-century predecessors, the founders of Steubenville's Beth El desired, in their words, "a more modern approach to Judaism." The new congregation dedicated its own temple building in 1924.[13]

The appeal of a "more modern approach" can also be seen in the response of the Orthodox congregation. In 1923, the same year Beth El was formed, B'nai Israel hired its first permanent rabbi, Henry R. Goldberger, who made two significant changes in the direction of modernization. One was to institute a late Friday evening service, a practice that had become the norm in Reform congregations by the 1880s. The rationale was that a service at a fixed time would better accommodate the typical American work schedule and that featuring a lecture or long sermon would cultivate interest—and thus increase attendance—in a way that praying didn't. To be sure, B'nai Israel proudly promoted its late Friday evening service as "an inspiration and a great source of Jewish education for young and old."[14] (It is important to note, however, that at B'nai Israel, this service was in addition to one at the traditional time of sunset.)

Under Goldberger's guidance, the congregation also revised its educational program, reducing the number of hours of Hebrew instruction in favor of emphasizing Sunday school, as had been the trend in Reform. (In fact, by the early twentieth century, Reform had abandoned the teaching of the Hebrew language altogether.)[15] During the 1920s, Jewish education in the United States was in serious crisis: in New York City, only about one-fourth of Jewish children were receiving any formal Jewish education. The proportion was undoubtedly higher in a smaller community such as Steubenville, where—unlike New York—Jewishness was not just "in the air." But Goldberger's changes may have reflected a similar concern for the number of families willing to commit to Jewish education. Even so, there were limits to the congregation's desire to change: when the rabbi and cantor suggested that a girls' choir provide music for the late Friday evening service (mixed choirs being very popular in Reform), the idea was promptly quashed. Steubenville's Orthodox were not quite ready to transgress the traditional prohibition on men's hearing women's voices in the synagogue.[16]

As community social and institutional structures were changing in the 1920s, so too, it seemed, were relations between Jews and their non-Jewish neighbors. Initially, it was the demands of World War I that brought this change to light. "The impressive joint efforts of Protestants, Catholics, and Jews during the war years," writes historian of American religion William Hutchison, "displayed what had been happening, over a number of decades, to intergroup relations and the traditional Protestant hegemony. . . . It became evident to anyone who was paying attention . . . that the traditional religious mainstream was widening into a triple mainstream."[17]

One such piece of evidence was a 1916 fund-raising campaign organized by Jews in East Liverpool, Ohio, for European Jewish relief. The campaign was very successful in garnering support from the general community for the work of the American Jewish Joint Distribution Committee (often referred to as the Joint). East Liverpool's mayor served as honorary chairman of the campaign, and non-Jews, including Catholic and Protestant clergy, participated actively. The pastor of First Baptist Church made it the centerpiece of his sermon that week. The *East Liverpool Evening Review* encouraged these efforts in a major editorial of January 24, 1916. "No race of people are greater sufferers from the European war than the Jews," the editorial asserted. "Usually proudly able and willing to care for their own financial obligations of charity, in this case the need is so appalling that appeal is necessary from them outside of their own nationality. . . . There is a little handful of Jews in the city who can personally take charge of the work. . . . Notify Gus Bendheim, Leon Rubin or William Erlanger [to contribute]."[18]

Over $1,500 was raised in just three days in East Liverpool and Wellsville, Ohio, and Chester and Newell, West Virginia. Though this sum was but a drop in the bucket of the Joint's eventual astounding total of $20 million, the effort was an important expression of East Liverpool Jewry's sense of Jewish unity on the national level and sense of belonging on the local level. The *Evening Review* praised "our fellow citizens of Jewish nationality" and suggested that "gradually, but most certainly, hyphenation in our American life will be considerably diminished by the experiences drawing us together, forced on us through the European war and by the problems we must face for the sake of our common safety."[19]

The nature of "hyphenation" was a prominent theme in American civic discourse and social theory, for both Jews and non-Jews, in the early twentieth century. On the one hand was the model of the melting pot, a metaphor that was elaborately developed in a 1908 play of that title by Israel Zangwill, a British Jewish writer. Zangwill glamorized a scenario in which all cultural differences among Americans would be melted down to create an amalgam, a new entity, the American. Others not only challenged the notion that a melting pot effect was at work but also negated its desirability, which, they charged, often really meant conformity to Anglo-Protestant values. In a series of articles in 1915, philosopher Horace Kallen described, and advocated instead, cultural pluralism. In Kallen's vision, democracy must be founded on self-realization, and a social order that represses cultural difference is antidemocratic. He created a different metaphor: "As in an orchestra, every type of instrument has its specific timbre and tonality . . . ; as every type has its appropriate theme and melody in the whole symphony, so in society each ethnic group is the natural instrument . . . and the harmony and dissonances and discords of them all make the symphony of civilization."[20]

The contribution of Judaism to this symphony was expressed in the rhetoric that accompanied the dedications of new synagogue buildings in East Liverpool in 1922 and in Portsmouth in 1925. In East Liverpool, the principal speaker was Rabbi Isadore Philo of Youngstown, a regionally prominent liberal clergyman. Philo was a vigorous advocate of universalism and social justice for whom the United States was the herald of messianism, and his dedication sermon was full of uplifting thoughts and exhortations to righteousness and brotherhood. He also contributed a hymn to the tune of "America," expressing the senses of Jewish and American pride that he and his hearers felt. "Our temple! 'tis of thee / Fit shrine of liberty / Of thee we sing," it opened, and it ended, "Long may our shrine be bright / With love and truth and light, / Protect it by thy might, / One God our King."[21]

A real measure of progress can be seen in the addresses given at the dedication of the new temple building in Portsmouth. In a striking contrast to the experience of the first synagogue dedication in 1864, this time the local Catholic priest lauded the unity of Protestants, Catholics, and Jews displayed in the ceremony. "No people so much as the chosen people of God are this day doing the will of God by breaking down the walls of social, religious and class prejudice," Father McQuirk declared. "Here, in Portsmouth, you can live your individual and family life as you wish, as long as the rights of God and those of your fellow-citizens are respected. . . . Over this temple floats the Stars and Stripes and back of all this is the spirit of justice and kindness of the whole American people."[22]

For Jews, the hyphenation debate—melting pot versus cultural pluralism—had another aspect as well, that is, Zionism. Jewish nationalism revived in the last quarter of the nineteenth century, first as a cultural movement with both religious and secular elements and then, in the 1890s, as a political movement under Austrian journalist and organizer Theodor Herzl. Although a few Americans had been involved in the organized Zionist movement since its formal inception in 1897, it was only after about 1914 that it blossomed into a broad-based movement in America. One factor was the arrival of the east European Jews, many of whom had been exposed to Zionism in Russia and Poland. Many immigrants understood themselves to have a national as well as—or in place of—a religious identity as Jews. Critical in creating Zionist activism in America was the leadership of Louisville native and Supreme Court justice Louis Brandeis, whose synthesis of Jewish and American values, based on Kallen's philosophy, convinced many that one could be a loyal and authentic Jew and a loyal and authentic American simultaneously.[23]

Not all American Jews were persuaded. In the Pittsburgh Platform of 1889 and again in 1897, the rabbinic leaders of Reform Judaism had explicitly repudiated Jewish nationalism, defining Judaism solely as a religion. American Reform opposition to Zionism was significant, especially among rabbis. It took more than a year for (primarily lay) Zionists in Cincinnati to overcome the objections of anti-Zionist Rabbi David Philipson so they could invite

Brandeis to the city without all-out internecine warfare.[24] Among Orthodox Jews in America, attitudes toward Zionism ranged from hostile to enthusiastic. The greatest opposition came from the ultra-Orthodox, who viewed Zionism as a usurpation of God's prerogative, but these communities were in the largest urban centers.

Not surprisingly, then, small-town Jews responded to Zionism with a range of reactions. Some undertook modest Zionist activity. At the turn of the twentieth century, there was a short-lived Zion Society, affiliated with the national Federation of American Zionists, in Parkersburg. Steubenville, with a large east European population, was extremely active. In 1925, the local chapter of Mizrachi, religious Zionists, claimed seventy members, the Steubenville district of the Zionist Organization of America registered thirty-two men, and Hadassah registered sixty-four women. Teenagers also participated, through the Daughters of Zion and Sons of Zion clubs. In Weirton, Zionist activity was inaugurated in the mid-1920s by several recent arrivals, east Europeans who had spent a few years in Palestine after World War I before joining relatives in the United States.[25]

In many of the towns with older, established, predominantly German Jewish communities, however, Zionism was at best irrelevant, at worst anti-American, and in any event a retreat from the bright promise of universal religion. There were active and even important anti-Zionist rabbis in the Ohio River Valley, even in the 1930s, when for many reasons—not the least of which was the perilous position of Jews in Germany—the Reform movement had become pro-Zionist. Evansville's Reform rabbi Milton Greenwald was a founding member of the anti-Zionist American Council for Judaism, organized in 1943 to protest the Reform movement's recent drift toward pro-Zionism. Four of the approximately seventeen men who served as student rabbis in Portsmouth in the 1920s and 1930s were later associated with the council: Louis Binstock, Julian Feibelman, David Lefkowitz Jr., and Allan Tarshish. Interestingly, both Binstock and Lefkowitz were married to women from Portsmouth: Binstock to Ruth Atlas and Lefkowitz to Leona Atlas, daughters of local merchant Henry Atlas. These familial mergers suggest that rabbinic conviction and congregational predisposition reinforced each other.[26]

Wheeling's Leshem Shomayim, also a bastion of the old, established German Jews, was committed to classical Reform; for example, a 1916 celebratory dinner featured oysters and was preceded, though not followed, by "grace." (In traditional Jewish practice, a short blessing is said before the meal and a much longer prayer of thanksgiving afterward.) Not surprisingly, Leshem Shomayim was predisposed against Jewish nationalism. One of the congregation's young rabbis was Morris Lazaron, a fervent anti-Zionist who, after graduating from

HUC in 1914, spent a year in Wheeling. Lazaron was a founder of the American Council for Judaism and such a vehement detractor of the State of Israel that in 1949 he was forced to retire from his position at the Baltimore Hebrew Congregation, where he had served since 1915.[27]

Ironically, Lazaron was succeeded in Wheeling in 1915–16 by another recent HUC graduate, Abba Hillel Silver. Silver was a lifelong Zionist who spent most of his career as rabbi of a large Reform congregation in Cleveland. A national and international powerhouse in Zionist politics, he presented the case for Jewish statehood at the United Nations in 1947 and was responsible for the strategy that convinced President Harry Truman to support Jewish claims in Palestine and, eventually, to recognize the State of Israel. During his year in Wheeling, Silver was active in social justice and liberal political causes; though his Zionism could not have gone unnoticed, he was extremely popular, especially for his oratory.[28]

This juxtaposition of rabbis suggests that ideological uniformity was perhaps not Leshem Shomayim's highest value in its leadership. In an interesting twist, the two young rabbis of opposite views on nationalism were related through marriage and the Ohio Valley; Lazaron was married to Pauline Horkheimer of Wheeling, and Silver to her sister Virginia. In the end, the Wheeling Reform congregation seems to have maintained the sentiment against Zionism: in April and May of 1948, when the American Council for Judaism sent lecturers to sympathetic congregations around the country in a last-ditch protest against the imminent realization of Jewish political sovereignty, Wheeling hosted one.[29]

One strong motive of Jewish opponents of Zionism was the fear that Jews would be accused of disloyalty to America. This fear for Jewish reputation and safety was not a phantom, for starting in the late nineteenth century, nativism and related prejudices began to gain traction in American popular opinion. There were many ingredients in this stew of prejudice: the social discrimination practiced by status-conscious, upwardly mobile Gentiles; the traditional Judaeophobia of those who advocated for a "Christian America"; the political rhetoric of many Populist radicals; and the "scientific racism" exemplified by Madison Grant's 1913 book *The Passing of the Great Race*, which expressed the fear of many Americans of all classes that the country was being invaded by inferior races that would soon overwhelm the older population of superior Nordics. In each of these manifestations, Americans were looking for a solution to perceived social problems of an era of unprecedented social and economic growth and competition. Taken together, these phenomena account for what one historian calls "the emergence of a full-fledged antisemitic society" by the end of the nineteenth century, lasting until the end of World War II.[30]

The "ambivalent image" continued to operate, of course. One Sunday in 1899, police in Marietta, Ohio, discovered E. M. Mosinter doing business at his grocery in violation of a closing law. Mosinter knew the ways of a small town; he "went to the Mayor and told his troubles, but while he was gone, the police locked up his clerk upon his refusal to close the doors." When Mosinter explained that he closed his store on Saturday in observance of *his* Sabbath, he was given permission to reopen and his clerk was released from custody. The city was certainly under no legal obligation to do this, but perhaps the fact that Mosinter placed high value on his religion swayed the decision of the Protestants in positions of authority. Also, though Mosinter's status as a rabbi was not mentioned in the newspaper account, the authorities may have been aware—and respectful—of that status.[31]

But overall, Jews in the small towns of the Ohio River Valley were not exempt from experiences of antisemitism in its various incarnations. The distrust of immigrants was quite evident, for instance, in the industrial upper Ohio Valley towns such as Steubenville and East Liverpool, where there were substantial immigrant populations. In these towns, Orthodox Jews, who were more likely to be immigrants and who were identifiably ethnic, experienced far more disparagement and discrimination—certainly of the overt kind—than did Reform Jews, whose culture was already highly Americanized. Ironically, the increase in ethnic Catholic immigration also intensified antisemitism of the traditional European Christian variety, which often manifested itself violently in neighborhoods where poor Catholic and Jewish immigrants lived in close proximity.

Already in the Gilded Age of the 1870s and 1880s, status-conscious, upwardly mobile Gentiles had begun to deploy antisemitism as a tool for their own advancement. Soon wealthy and middle-class urban Jews found themselves excluded from clubs and schools to which they had previously had access; by the 1890s, such social ostracism was pervasive. By the 1920s, these attitudes were infecting the social atmosphere of small towns, raising barriers where there had been none. In the opinion of a member of the Gumberts family in Evansville, born in 1912, speaking to an interviewer in 1982, the "limited" socializing between Jews and non-Jews in his youth was "peculiar," seen as a twentieth-century narrowing of expansive nineteenth-century attitudes. Whereas Jews had, in the 1890s, been included in a sort of social register of the city, in the 1920s, Jews, even those of long residence such as the Gumbertses, were excluded from certain social clubs and from the Evansville Country Club. (As in many towns, a Jewish country club was organized in response.)[32]

The intensity—and acceptability—of overt antisemitism increased in the 1920s and 1930s. Many schools, colleges, and professional schools and societies enacted overt or covert limits on the admission of Jewish students. Explicit and implicit employment discrimination was rampant, as were restrictive housing covenants. In an atmosphere of fear of the supposed unassimilability of certain groups, Congress in 1924 passed laws restricting the immigration of southern and eastern Europeans. No less a figure than automotive mogul Henry Ford propagated the libels of "The Protocols of the Elders of Zion," publishing this now-notorious antisemitic forgery in his *Dearborn (MI) Independent* in the 1920s. The Great Depression exacerbated the situation. Between 1933 and 1941, more than a hundred antisemitic organizations were created; some, such as radio demagogue Father Charles Coughlin's Christian Front, had high public profiles and considerable followings. Right-wingers attacked the New Deal as a "Jew Deal," alleging Jewish conspiracy behind Roosevelt's programs. In the years leading up to World War II, isolationists such as Charles Lindbergh often blamed Jews for the international crisis.

In the early 1920s in the Ohio River Valley, a particularly menacing development was the emergence of the Ku Klux Klan as a major social and political force. Taking on the name and organizational trappings of the Reconstruction-era southern resistance group, the revived Klan—some four million members strong across the nation by 1924—railed against the supposed moral collapse of America, its abandonment of Protestant values, and the pernicious influence of African Americans and immigrants. Jews were definitely on the list of the enemies of Christian America.

The Klan was often controversial, however, and there was no single pattern of Klan influence. For instance, in Portsmouth, Ohio, in 1923, after the mayor ordered the arrest of Klansmen marching as a group to a church dedication, he was voted out of office in the next election. On the other hand, in Parkersburg, West Virginia, the anti-Klan mayor and council were reelected that same year.[33]

It is important to remember that the Klan was only one factor in antisemitism and that antisemitism was only one, and not the most important, part of the Klan program. Jews per se were not the main target of the Klan—immigrants in general were—and in some places the Klan was remarkably tolerant of local Jews. Scholars have disagreed about the impact of Klan activity. One writes that in the small towns and industrial big cities of Ohio, where "the Klan held mighty sway," both "Jewish and Catholic-owned businesses were badly hurt in Klan strongholds." But another asserts that "Jews were not generally intimidated by Klansmen in the eastern half of the nation."[34]

Of course, in any event, the Klan's divisive "pro-American," pro-Protestant rhetoric usually included Jews in the category of outsiders, causing considerable anxiety among Jews. Small Jewish communities managed to weather this crisis, even in the two regions of the valley most affected, the industrial upper Ohio Valley and southern Indiana. The Klan phenomenon in each of these places reflected specific local conditions, and local Jews coped as best they could.

The Klan phenomenon was particularly intense, and virulently antiblack, in southern Indiana. Even in a state notorious for spending the entire decade of the 1920s under Klan political control (more than one-quarter of Indiana's native-born white men, from all segments of society, belonged to the Klan in the 1920s), Evansville—on the door to the South—was a standout. Early-twentieth-century Evansville was 12 percent black, and in 1903 it was the scene of a major race riot in which eleven people were killed. The city was home to the first Indiana Klavern in 1920, which claimed five thousand members by 1922, and one of the Klan's most infamous leaders, David Stephenson, began his organizational career there.[35]

These interracial tensions in Evansville diverted much attention from Jews. (This was also the case in Cairo, Illinois, which suffered from severe interracial problems.) The Klan did attempt a not entirely effective boycott of Jewish businesses. One longtime Jewish resident, in business in Evansville in the 1920s, laughingly remembered years later how "fellows would come in to make a purchase and say, 'You know, I'm not supposed to buy anything from you.' I would say, 'Okay, I ain't going to tell anybody.'" Sometimes Jews and Catholics were able to make common cause against the Klan. Across the river from Evansville, in Henderson, Kentucky, Henry Baldauf was reassured that his friend the local priest was keeping an eye on Klan activities.[36] By the end of the 1920s, the Indiana Klan had dwindled to insignificance.

The Klan in the industrial upper Ohio Valley was shaped more by nativism than by racism against native African Americans. The Klan's impact was also shaped by a vigorous—and occasionally violent—response to it on the part of the large communities of immigrant ethnic Catholic industrial workers. In fact, anti-Klan violence by Catholic workers—in Steubenville, Ohio, in August 1923 and in nearby Niles in November 1924—was decisive in weakening the northern Ohio Klan by 1925. Jews too made a public stand for their interests, though in a more restrained manner. In 1923, Steubenville's Orthodox congregation, B'nai Israel, sent a committee to the local school board to protest "children being subjected to the reading of the New Testament in school in violation of the Constitutional guarantee of freedom of religion."[37]

The experience of Marietta illustrates the confluence of various strands in this social conflict. On a Saturday night in February 1923, the recently organized Klan demonstrated with a cross burning on Harmar Hill. The *Marietta Register-Leader* reported that local rumor placed Klan membership at about two hundred. At the time, Helen Josephy, having graduated from Smith College in 1921, was working for the *Marietta Times*. She heard from a Gentile friend, another newspaper reporter, that he had surreptitiously observed the cross burning and rally and had been horrified to hear the Josephys' name brought up as a possible target for Klan harassment. His relief was mixed with other emotions when the focus shifted to the more sizable Catholic community in the area, many of whom were immigrants.[38]

The Klan in the Marietta area grew to about three hundred members in 1925 before gradually losing influence. Though Klan belligerence was more smoke than fire, social antisemitism was a very real factor. In 1929, several of Joseph Josephy's friends nominated him for membership in the Rotary Club, in view of his business success and civic involvements. Josephy's nomination caused a fracas in the club that all but resulted in a schism. So many of the members threatened to resign if a Jew—even one of thirty years' residence—were elected that the nomination was withdrawn. Many who had threatened resignation were prominent Methodist churchgoers (and, perhaps not so coincidentally, business rivals of Josephy). There is no doubt that some prominent Mariettans were involved with the Klan and that the Klan had strong ties with the Methodist Church. A connection with the Rotary incident, though not direct or provable, is certainly conceivable. On the other hand, Jewish Mariettans of the era articulated their feeling that a sense of propriety and noblesse oblige among established Christian families prevented the widespread and blatant expression of prejudices that plagued so many American towns in the 1920s.[39]

In the 1920s and 1930s, Jews in small Ohio River Valley towns might well have said that the most serious challenge for Jewish life was not antisemitism but economic problems. Even in the gung-ho 1920s, erecting a building such as the synagogues in East Liverpool and Portsmouth—central to Jews' feelings of integration and well-being—was a financial stretch for a small community. The Depression was a serious challenge to the stability of many American synagogues and churches, regardless of their size and location, but it was especially daunting for small institutions. The Depression almost killed East Liverpool's B'nai Israel, which seems to have overextended itself in building the new temple and struggled to cover the mortgage. This forced the congregation to sacrifice consistent professional leadership. Student rabbis from HUC were regularly available for the High Holidays, but during the year, East Liverpool relied on rabbis from Wheeling, Youngstown, Steubenville, Akron, and Canton—whoever could be persuaded to visit for a small honorarium.[40]

In the early 1930s, even these small honoraria were impossible for the congregation. The student rabbi for the 1932 High Holidays received only half of what his predecessors had. Trying to figure out how to pay the temple's bills almost completely preoccupied the board, to the point of ritual obsession. Minutes for August 17, 1933, noted, "Due to absence of the Treasurer, the reading of unpaid bills was omitted." A tenth anniversary celebration for the temple that year was cancelled ostensibly because of "the illness of several members," but probably not without some gratitude at avoiding the financial outlay.[41]

The congregation in Portsmouth survived because of some great good luck: a donation in 1929 of $10,000 from the Richmans, a former Portsmouth family by then living in Cleveland, who had become wealthy in clothing manufacture and retail. But most communities struggled to find new solutions to collective problems. In the 1930s, many smaller Jewish communities across the country followed the example of the largest metropolitan areas in establishing a federation of Jewish charities and organizations to centralize fund-raising and coordinate disbursement of funds to various groups and projects. Wheeling and Evansville established federations in 1933 and 1936; Steubenville did so in 1938, and Huntington in 1939. Building on existing intergroup Jewish cooperation, the federation movement gained momentum as American Jews attempted to respond with unity and efficiency to local and national Jewish crises.[42]

Even in the busy years of the 1920s and 1930s, there were signs of long-term trouble in many of the small Jewish communities of the Ohio River Valley. Some communities, especially in the lower valley, began to noticeably lose Jewish population. In some cases, the towns themselves were shrinking, for instance, Madison, Indiana, whose small synagogue closed its doors in 1923, and Mount Vernon, Indiana, where the synagogue closed in 1935. Cairo, Illinois, maintained its population but experienced severe economic problems in the mid-1920s. The congregation collapsed, though it was able to reorganize in the 1930s, and in 1938, it acquired a residence that was remodeled for community use. Jewish population declined even in some localities experiencing growth. Both Owensboro and Henderson, Kentucky, went from more than two hundred Jews in 1917 to fewer than one hundred by 1937, despite increases in the total population. The Jewish population of Parkersburg, West Virginia, dropped by at least half from the 1910s to the late 1930s, while the general population more than doubled.[43]

For other locations, the available Jewish population numbers suggest stability through this period. These include the larger communities of Evansville and Wheeling, as well as East Liverpool and Steubenville, where the organized Jewish community was fairly new. Also stable—or even experiencing slight growth—through this period were the new industrial towns of Aliquippa and Ambridge, Pennsylvania, and Weirton, West Virginia.

Neither the dramatic nature of the Depression nor the virtual cessation of Jewish immigration in 1924 should distract from the fact that larger movements were already well underway that eventuated in the decline of the Jewish population overall in the small towns of the Ohio River Valley. By 1920, more Americans lived in cities or towns (of at least 2,500 population) than on farms or in villages, and the succeeding decade was one of even greater urbanization, as six million Americans moved from farms to cities. The big winners in this demographic shift were the largest cities; those of more than 100,000 population grew twice as fast as the population overall. Thus small towns lost importance as regional centers as their hinterlands declined. As the towns' commercial economies weakened, they became less attractive to Jewish merchants.[44]

There is a second, more specific reason for the decline in Jewish population. Jews had, apparently, always been more inclined to view their small-town homes as temporary rather than permanent settlements. In one example, historian Lee Shai Weissbach was able to quantify the extent to which Owensboro, Kentucky, had always served primarily as a site of sojourn—rather than a multigenerational home—for many Jewish families. "Of the 33 surnames borne by men who joined the Owensboro lodge of B'nai B'rith sometime in the nineteenth century," he notes, "less than half can still be found in the Owensboro city directory of 1922."[45]

Economic realities drove this phenomenon, which continued with the Jewish migrants to small towns in the late nineteenth and early twentieth centuries. From the 1910s through the 1930s, the decline of the local oil economy accelerated the move of the Latvian families from Marietta, Ohio, to the prospering oil centers of Kansas, Oklahoma, and Texas. Shortly after Sarah Rabinowitz's 1909 wedding to Bernard Revel, the *Marietta Register-Leader* reported that her brother Sam had gone to Oklahoma to "attend to business matters for the American Iron and Supply Company." Even with newcomers, by 1935 the Jewish population was half what it had been a decade earlier. By late 1938, the congregation numbered only eleven men, barely more than the minimum required by Orthodoxy for public worship.[46]

Likewise, some Jews in Bellaire who had gotten their starts in the scrap metal business during the turn-of-the-century oil boom followed the industry west in the 1920s. Business success also propelled William Hersch from Parkersburg to a larger city that could provide better contacts and a larger labor market. Hersch, who came to Parkersburg at the turn of the century and built up his United Woolen Mills into a major business, moved his headquarters to

Columbus, Ohio, in the early 1920s. In these towns, the Jewish communities shrank but did not disappear, and their communal institutions continued to function.[47]

In some cases, such movements strengthened larger regional Jewish communities. Jews from New Albany, Indiana, moved south across the river to Louisville; those in Covington and Newport, Kentucky, moved north across the river to Cincinnati, where they had always maintained close connections. Attracting Jews from the declining small towns, Evansville's Jewish population reached almost two thousand as the city topped one hundred thousand by 1930.

For those Ohio River Valley towns where the Jewish population remained stable or grew during and after the 1930s, a new trend was developing: the loss of older population was offset by a new sort of Jewish migration. In 1938, a sociologist, looking specifically at Ohio, predicted a shift in Jewish population away from urban areas where high concentrations of professionals meant more competition. He was optimistic about this trend. "The movement of Jewish professional men toward smaller communities," this sociologist observed, "means that younger men have begun to seek places which have a shortage of practitioners and where their services are needed. In so doing they are at the same time establishing a trend of significance for Jewish life as a whole. These men are perhaps more likely to succeed than their Jewish colleagues of the same age and experience in the larger cities."[48]

The question of whether this perceived movement would have become a significant demographic trend was rendered moot by the intervention of World War II. The military mobilization and war-industry employment of millions of American men and women created new waves of migration that changed the geography of American Jewry profoundly. However, this prewar pattern of new Jewish settlement in small towns did adumbrate the pattern of the postwar period. The families of Jewish doctors, dentists, engineers, and teachers, as well as some businesspeople, filled at least some of the loss of the older generation of Jewish businessmen, extending the life of the organized communities into subsequent decades.

CHAPTER 10

The Demise of Community

In the first half of the twentieth century, most of the small Ohio River towns still provided relatively comfortable contexts for their Jewish residents' social and economic lives and for a modest level of Jewish activity. From the 1950s through the end of the century, however, even this was increasingly unsustainable. By the 1990s, Jewish populations and activity declined irretrievably. Many congregations merged or closed, and those that remained faced further numerical decline and financial difficulties.

For almost all the small Jewish communities of the Ohio River Valley, the 1950s were a decade of change and challenge. The United States was at the time undergoing a remarkable revival of popular interest in religion for a number of reasons: the desire to "nest" and create security in a postwar world that, on the negative side, faced an atomic threat but that, on the positive side, experienced a boom in family formation and baby making. In the 1950s, more Americans than ever before described themselves in terms of organized religious groups—some 96 percent, based on a 1957 survey. Institutional religion benefited, as formal church and synagogue affiliation jumped from 57 percent in 1950 to 63 percent in 1959. Synagogue affiliation alone showed an even greater increase, from about 40 percent of all American Jews in 1950 to about 60 percent a decade later.[1]

At the same time, the demographic base of small-town Jewish communities was eroding. After 1950, the Ohio River Valley began to lose population. In the largest cities of Pittsburgh, Cincinnati, and Louisville, suburbanization in surrounding counties provided an offset to urban depopulation. But throughout the rest of the valley, towns began to shrink.

Outside the big communities of Pittsburgh, Cincinnati, and Louisville, where Jewish life remained vital, the Jewish population was shrinking as well. In this respect, the story of the small Ohio River Valley communities becomes more and more similar to that of Jewish communities in hundreds of small towns elsewhere, especially in the Midwest and the South: population loss, an aging population, congregations merging or closing. The post–World War II increase in formal affiliation, and the baby boom that helped drive it, may have attenuated the effects for a while. But both the changing role of the American small town and the changing profile of American Jewry contributed, ultimately, to serious and usually irreversible decline.

The Jews who lived in the small towns after World War II were both a business and a professional class. Only a very few were recent immigrants, including two rabbis sponsored by the Orthodox congregations in Newport and Covington, Kentucky. For the most part, the European refugees and Holocaust survivors preferred to settle in communities with others of similar background and experience.[2]

Some small-town Jews were natives, such as Herschel Rubin, who was born to immigrant parents in East Liverpool, Ohio, in 1915, grew up in the town's Reform community, and set up his optometry practice there after his graduation from Ohio State University. Irwin Bogarad in 1960 returned from medical training to settle with his young family in his hometown of Weirton, West Virginia. Descendants of nineteenth-century settlers remained in some places. When Temple B'nai Israel of Evansville celebrated its centennial in 1957, there were still several Gumberts families on the membership roster, whose forebears were among the founders of the congregation. At the centennial of Portsmouth's Beneh Abraham the following year, almost one-fourth of the congregation's fifty-eight families had been members since the nineteenth century, and another quarter had been members for at least fifty years. The congregational president was Louis Levi, grandson and namesake of the first president; another member, Sylvan Lehman, was also a grandson of a founder, Simon Lehman.

Some Jewish newcomers followed traditional patterns of business employment. In Ironton, Morris Edelson's clothing store was taken over by his daughter Evelyn and her husband, Martin Weill. The couple met in Dayton, Ohio, but in the mid-1950s, with two small children, they bought her father's store and moved to Ironton. Sam Yablok purchased a junk business in Marietta that had formerly belonged to several other Jewish families. The property for this business included the shell of what was once the fine red brick house of Isaac Hertz Rabinowitz.

Small towns also attracted some Jewish professionals who had been raised in cities. The choice of a small town was even encouraged, in a way, by B'nai

B'rith, which in 1953 published a study of small-town Jewish life intended to serve as a guide for young Jewish men, particularly professionals, considering relocation to a small community. The study noted an overall satisfaction with life on the part of Jews in small towns: half felt that their prospects for economic advancement there were good, two-thirds enjoyed their social lives, and fully 85 percent praised what they perceived as the slower pace of life. At least in 1953, over half of those studied by B'nai B'rith's researcher planned to stay in their small town.[3]

Many Jews in the small towns of the Ohio River Valley echoed this satisfaction. Florence and Max Weinstein moved to Portsmouth in the late 1940s when Max, an optometrist, bought a practice there. Though she had grown up in New York City, Florence longed for a slower pace of life and found Portsmouth congenial. Like other Jews of east European background, the Weinsteins found the cultural transition to Portsmouth's style of Reform Judaism difficult and a bit disconcerting. But they also discovered that the participatory ethos of a small community was quite welcoming, and shortly, they were quite active.

Marty Weill, who was raised in New York City, was initially skeptical about moving to Ironton but was won over. "The people were so nice," he told a local newspaper much later. "They got me involved. . . . In a small town, you're not just a spectator."[4] Weill threw himself into small-town business and social life: the Lions Club, Elks, American Legion, Community Betterment Club, Jaycees, chamber of commerce, and Retail Merchants Association. He received the first Citizen of the Year award in 1963. He took seriously his role as an ambassador of Judaism to non-Jews, and he often spoke on Jewish topics to churches, schools, and civic organizations and published articles in the local newspaper.

Sam Yablok, whose past included a childhood in Russia, education as a teenager in Columbus, Ohio, and several years in Palestine in the tumultuous late 1930s, fit remarkably easily into the milieu in Marietta. In fact, he boasted that "there [wasn't] anyone in six counties who [didn't] know him." A local journalist recalled that "boys of the neighborhood would steal Sam's junk, then would come down Fourth Street carrying it or pulling it in a toy wagon and ask Sam if he wanted to buy it. Sam would pretend he didn't know he was buying his own stuff and give the boys dimes or quarters—whatever the current price of a bottle of pop."[5]

In many ways, life for small-town Jews in the 1950s and 1960s was similar to that of their predecessors a century earlier. They maintained links with other Jewish communities through business and family relations and through institutions like regional federations, B'nai B'rith, and the Reform movement's National Federation of Temple Youth. With the exception of three years in the army in World War II, Herschel Rubin lived life in East Liverpool in much the same way his father had, active in institutions of the business community such as Rotary and the Jaycees. Jews also continued to be active in civic life. Huntington, West Virginia, and Ashland, Kentucky, had Jewish mayors in the twentieth century.[6]

At least in the early postwar period, some small-town Jews continued to adhere to traditional practice. In the late 1940s and early 1950s, observant residents of East Liverpool were still bringing live chickens to a shoḥet who made periodic stops in town. Unannounced changes of schedule were a problem; it was reported to the board of Congregation B'nai Jacob that on several scheduled occasions the shoḥet did not arrive, even though "many people had already bought their chickens, thus creating a bad situation." The board had to run interference with Morris Karp, owner of the City Market, which provided the sheḥitah facilities, when he complained that women were leaving "dirt" after having their chickens killed and cleaned. The solution was to charge an extra fifty cents to those who hadn't bought the live chickens at Karp's market in the first place.[7]

A Jewish woman who grew up in Cairo, Illinois, in the late 1950s remembers her town as the center of an extended but close-knit Jewish community encompassing towns in far western Kentucky, northwestern Tennessee, and southeast Missouri, as well as southern Illinois. Families were connected, in traditional small-town Jewish fashion, throughout the region and were engaged in traditional Jewish small businesses, including clothing and liquor distribution.

Religious life centered in Cairo's small Reform synagogue, and voluntarism continued to be the backbone of institutional life. Fund-raising was done through communal activities, especially "smorgasbord dinners," which were the equivalent of the ubiquitous church suppers. Lay-led Friday evening services were held every other week; occasionally there was a regional circuit-riding rabbi as well. On the High Holidays, the congregation employed a student rabbi and, in lieu of a cantor, played a recording of the chanted "Kol Nidre" prayer.

As in larger communities, educating the Jewish children of the baby boom was a prime concern. The Cairo congregation ran a Sunday school taught by parents. A regional federation sponsored youth groups that met once a month in different towns and a two-week summer camp at which the same group of children spent more intensive Jewish time together. The regional federation director, who ran the camps and youth groups, provided other Jewish education, such as bar mitzvah and (as more attention was paid to girls' Jewish educations) bat mitzvah tutoring, and even officiated at funerals.

An important change in American Jewish life in the 1950s was the improved climate of Jewish-Gentile relations. World War II seemed to have stemmed the tide of antisemitism in America. Nazism raised Americans' consciousness about social bigotry, and the optimism and self-satisfaction of the postwar era focused Americans' minds on building a prosperous and well-adjusted society. Discrimination in education, employment, and housing decreased sharply from the late 1940s on; social exclusion also decreased.

Starting in the early 1960s, Protestant and Catholic thinkers even began to deal systematically with the legacy of Christianity's historical complicity in antisemitism. Religious ecumenism and the community relations movement, vigorously supported by Jewish groups, helped maintain a comfortable—even "patriotic"—context for Jewish integration in postwar society. The cooperative ethos of small towns seems to have accommodated this easily. For example, in 1949, the East Liverpool Ministerial Association made a considerable adjustment to include B'nai Jacob's rabbi: since the rabbi did not eat out, the association agreed to have its annual dinner at the synagogue and pay for kosher food for all.[8]

Another significant feature of post–World War II American Judaism was the growth of Conservative Judaism, which had arisen from tensions within the American Reform movement. In the mid-nineteenth century, Isaac Mayer Wise had envisioned the creation of a minhag Amerika, a unified American Judaism that could encompass a wide range of beliefs and practices. By the 1880s, however, it was clear that the uneasy coalition of traditionalists and radical reformers that had started the UAHC—a union of all "American Hebrews"—was untenable. The momentum of Reform was with the radicals, as illustrated by the famous "treyfe banquet" of 1883 and the Pittsburgh Platform of 1885. Moderate reformers, who agreed that Judaism should be updated but who were still loyal to Jewish law, balked at what seemed to be wholesale abandonment of what they saw as core Jewish beliefs.

A marginalized minority, the traditionalists left the UAHC and HUC and founded a new seminary, the Jewish Theological Seminary, in New York in 1887. Although it was based in Jewish law, the new movement was not traditionally Orthodox, since it acknowledged the reality of historical development in Judaism. In the words of Conservative movement historian Neil Gillman, the seminary's founders "espoused an 'enlightened traditionalism,'" that is, "a willingness to adopt a more modern, critical, open approach to the study of Judaism" and to accept change that was deliberate, but gradual and halakhically justifiable.[9] As uncomfortable as they were with the contemporary Reform movement, the Conservatives (the name finally settled on by the early twentieth century) were also not entirely in sync with the Orthodoxy of the east European immigrants, which clung to old patterns and rejected modernity.

Yet it was in the acculturation of the east European immigrants that Conservative Judaism gained a secure place in American Judaism, eventually equaling that of Reform. As the immigrants and their children adopted American mores, the Conservative movement seemed to offer, in Gillman's words, "an attractive mix of Americanism and classical Judaism." United Synagogue of America, the congregational union of Conservative Judaism, grew from 22 congregations at its founding in 1913 to 229 in 1929. The period after World War II saw even greater growth. Throughout the country, both newly organized and formerly Orthodox congregations moved in large numbers into the camp of a more modern traditionalism. Between 1945 and 1965, United Synagogue grew from 350 to 800 congregations, with 269 joining in 1955–61 alone.[10] The movement reached small as well as large communities: the postwar influx included B'nai Jacob of East Liverpool, B'nai Israel of Steubenville, Adath Israel of Evansville (functionally the successor to B'nai Moshe), Synagogue of Israel of Wheeling (which had in the early 1940s absorbed the members of the disbanded downtown congregation Ohev Sholem), and Beth Israel of Huntington.

The appeal of Conservative Judaism to the laity was largely social and aesthetic rather than ideological; they were more interested in an Americanized style of Judaism, acceptable to the younger generation, than in the particular philosophy of Jewish legal interpretation on which the Conservative movement was founded. In the words of one lay leader, Conservatism was "the solution" because it was "more tasteful to our modern American life, yet not forgetting the fundamentals, the traditions and the ideals of Judaism."[11] In other words, it was not old-fashioned, like Orthodoxy, but not too Protestantized, like Reform.

Steubenville's trajectory was typical. Even before World War II, there was evidence of shifts in members' attitudes at Orthodox Congregation B'nai Israel; as mentioned previously, late Friday night services, in addition to services held at the traditional time of sunset, were introduced in the 1920s. In the 1950s, additional liturgical changes were initiated by the lay board, which directed its president to "meet with the Rabbi and discuss new methods of conducting services. It should be suggested that a few innovations be made, as the members feel that a translation of the important prayers is worth trying." The president promoted other changes as well, including English responsive readings and mixed seating.[12]

The latter innovation was probably the most controversial in Orthodoxy, but as in many congregations, the people of Steubenville voted with their feet. Despite the absence of formal approval, men and women began to sit together at the High Holidays in 1947. Within months, the congregation formally affiliated with the Conservative movement. Religious modernization was accompanied by the modernization of the synagogue building, which was enlarged and remodeled. In 1952, Janet Glick became B'nai Israel's first official bat mitzvah, and by the mid-1950s, women were serving on the board.[13]

The question of women's participation was one of the most troubling issues for congregations transitioning to Conservatism. This was evident in the experience of Congregation B'nai Jacob in East Liverpool. Over the course of several years in the late 1940s and early 1950s, motions were made at board meetings to admit women as members on their own behalf, with independent voting rights. The motions were consistently defeated, which is remarkable because almost every other motion ever made to the board was passed. It seems that meetings revolved around a consensus so that most motions were pro forma; there was clearly no consensus on the women's issue.[14]

The optimism that some Jewish communities felt in the baby boom years of the 1950s and 1960s was, seemingly, a last burst of energy. The Jewish community of Portsmouth, Ohio, seemed on the surface to be maintaining remarkable stability for a town its size. In 1958, it celebrated its centennial, claiming (albeit incorrectly) the title of "the oldest reform congregation between Pittsburgh and Cincinnati." The congregation's secure place among the city's institutions was underscored by the impressive number of local businesses that subscribed to a centennial tribute page in the *Portsmouth Times*; the page was sponsored by "patriotic individuals and institutions interested in building a better community in which to live." Portsmouth's proximity to Cincinnati had always made it a top choice of HUC students looking for student pulpits. Among Beneh Abraham's student rabbis were Solomon Freehof (1914–15), an important Reform thinker; Jacob Rothschild (1935), a central figure in the civil rights struggle in Atlanta; Isaiah Zeldin (1944), a leading rabbi of Los Angeles' post–World War II growth; HUC scholar Eugene Mihaly (1948); and communal leader Balfour Brickner (1951). It would have been a dream come true for the nineteenth-century founders.[15] But the success of integration was not matched by success in demographic continuity. The Jewish population in Portsmouth began to decline slowly after 1930, tracing the slow decline of total population in the county and in the city itself.

The decline was taking place throughout the Ohio River Valley. Part of the problem was the deterioration of the agriculture economy, which was particularly severe in southern Indiana and Illinois. By the 1970s, areas of the valley that relied on heavy industry were also damaged by the general decline of the Rust Belt.[16] At the same time, changes in American commercial life dealt a final blow to the tradition of independent Jewish retail. Downtowns in many places were devastated by the development of regional malls; local Jewish department stores—one of the staples of small-town Jewish life—were unable to compete with increasingly huge retail chains. (Ironically, the chains themselves were often built around urban Jewish department stores, though these were increasingly corporate rather than family owned.)

Decline became evident at different times in locations across the valley. The population of Paducah, Kentucky, like that of Portsmouth, began to drop between 1930 and 1950. Between 1950 and 1970, as these towns' decline continued, other places began to lose population as well: Bellaire, East Liverpool, Steubenville, Wheeling, Covington, Newport, Ashland, and Cairo. After 1970, Weirton, Marietta, Parkersburg, and Evansville were added to the list of ever-shrinking towns. In most of these cases, county population growth did not offset loss within municipal boundaries, or did so only very modestly.

The correlation between general and Jewish population changes is not, however, straightforward. Lee Shai Weissbach has looked specifically at small Jewish communities in the period during which the Jewish population in the United States expanded most dramatically, that is, the mass migration era of the late nineteenth and early twentieth centuries. He discovered that there were certain benchmarks for the maintenance of Jewish life in small communities, even though the demise of Jewish institutions usually lagged Jewish population decline by several decades.

Weissbach looked at two categories of small Jewish communities across the country: those that had more than one hundred Jews in 1878 but fewer than one hundred by 1907, and those that had more than one hundred Jews in 1907 but fewer than one hundred by 1927. Of those communities in the first category (Madison, Indiana, being the only example from the Ohio River Valley), half lost their congregations by 1930 and all but one by 1960; Madison's congregation closed in the 1920s. Of the communities in Weissbach's second category (which included the Ohio River towns of Cairo, Illinois, and Owensboro, Kentucky), two-thirds lost their congregations by 1960 and all but one by the late 1990s. Interestingly, Owensboro is the sole survivor of this group.[17]

Extending this analysis, it becomes clear that many small towns whose Jewish communities did flourish in the era of mass migration still collapsed within the twentieth century if they did not reach a certain size. Weissbach notes that of 135 Jewish communities of over one hundred persons in 1878, nearly half grew to at least one thousand by 1927; therefore more than half did not, and it was these places where Jewish continuity was most in peril. Numerous Ohio River towns experienced Jewish population growth in the mass migration era: East Liverpool, Steubenville, Bellaire, Marietta, and Portsmouth, Ohio; Evansville, Indiana; Wheeling and Huntington, West Virginia; Covington and Newport, Kentucky (combined); and all of the towns in western Pennsylvania. But only Evansville, Wheeling, Huntington, and Covington and Newport reached at least one thousand by 1927; Steubenville was close.

Weissbach sensibly observes that "even communities that were centers of some vitality early in their existence could not survive in places where growth was not sustained and where neither subsequent generations of established families nor new Jewish settlers could find economic opportunity."[18] Of the Ohio River Valley Jewish communities that reached one thousand by 1927, all but Covington and Newport still have congregations. For those that grew but did not reach this benchmark, the future was bleak. Congregations stay afloat in East Liverpool, Parkersburg, Portsmouth, Paducah, and Owensboro, but Marietta, Bellaire, Henderson, Ashland, and Weirton have lost theirs.

Parkersburg's case demonstrates the difficulty of predicting long-term growth and assuring long-term survival. In 1940, Congregation B'nai Israel—or, to be precise, its sisterhood—took the first step toward a synagogue building by purchasing some real estate; the building was completed (though at a different site, on upper Twentieth Street) in 1949. Membership was then no more than fifty families, but optimism seemed reasonable, considering local population growth. In the half-century between 1910 and 1960, Parkersburg's population increased, albeit in uneven spurts, by 151 percent, and the Jewish population increased by an even greater rate—200 percent. But this rate still meant an increase from about 75 individuals to only about 225. In 1960, a congregational planning committee anticipated that they could hire a full-time rabbi by 1965, by which time they expected to have ninety families, with 100 children in the religious school. (The congregation was making do—often well—with part-time student rabbis, one of whom, in 1945, was Eugene Borowitz, now a prominent Jewish thinker.) The estimate of ninety families, the committee reported, "was given to the Community by Mr. Schoen of the Union [UAHC], and he bases his estimates on our Jewish population averages to total Nation-wide."[19] In fact, by 1965, there were still only seventy families, with 40 children in the school.

The problem was that the generation of adults who bolstered small Jewish communities in the immediate postwar period had few successors. Starting in the 1970s, as the adults of the postwar era aged, their children, the "boomer" generation born after the war, moved from their hometowns in droves. In Ashland, Kentucky, for instance, Harold Freedman felt that returning to the family business after college and military service in World War II was a good choice, or at least "the line of least resistance," but he was not surprised that his own son did not follow him, preferring to move to the larger city of Lexington.[20] Marty and Evelyn Weill closed their Ironton store in 1984; none of their children wished to continue it.

Numbers tell only part of the story. In many towns, Jewish institutional life continued only because of structural changes, that is, congregational mergers. As Jewish populations continued to shrink, difficulties of religious difference between Reform and Conservative were eclipsed by economic exigencies. Mergers of Reform and Conservative congregations took place in East Liverpool in 1963, in Huntington in 1973, in Wheeling in 1974, and in Evansville and Steubenville in 1980.

These new entities sometimes took on names that combined their predecessor institutions: in Steubenville, Beth El and B'nai Israel became Beth Israel; in Evansville, Adath Israel and B'nai Israel became Adath B'nai Israel; in Huntington, Ohev Sholom (formerly Ohab Sholem) and B'nai Israel became B'nai Sholom. The Huntington name illustrates another tendency of merged congregations: to give a name that is both hopeful and prescriptive by including some variant of the word "shalom" (peace). Thus East Liverpool's B'nai Israel and B'nai Jacob became Beth Shalom, and in Wheeling, the charming name of Leshem Shomayim was lost in the merger with Synagogue of Israel, giving way to Temple Shalom. (To be sure, the Reform congregation's Hebrew name had already been on its way out. Increasingly through the early twentieth century, the congregation identified itself formally as the Eoff Street Temple; in the mid-1950s, when it moved to a suburban location, it was generally known simply as the Woodsdale Temple.)

The impetus toward merger was gradual but inexorable. Steubenville is a stark example. B'nai Israel, the Conservative congregation, grew from 110 families in the mid-1940s to about 150 in the late 1940s and mid-1950s. Its members were young: 74 children enrolled in the synagogue school in 1955, and 71 in 1961. In 1949, Temple Beth El (Reform) had 125 members, and its Sunday school enrolled more than 50 children. By 1961, there were 90 children in school, and in 1966, a new temple was built in a suburban area of the city. But in the 1950s, Steubenville's population began to slip, taking Jewish population with it. A proposal to merge the two congregations was raised in 1959 and continued to appear at intervals thereafter. By 1970, the city's overall population was down 6 percent from thirty years earlier, but in the following decade, the rate of decline doubled. The two congregations' Sunday school programs were merged on a trial basis in 1972–73 but then separated for what one member of the Conservative group called "religious and social reasons."[21]

By 1976, B'nai Israel's membership had fallen to under 100 families, and many of these consisted of elderly singles and couples. The following year, the congregational historian pointed out that in 1968 the board had worried that only 37 children were enrolled in Hebrew school. Now, nine years later, mourned the writer, "we would happily settle for that amount." The congregation experienced difficulty hiring and retaining rabbis. The synagogue's downtown location was increasingly unappealing. By the late 1970s, membership had sunk to under 40, with no children. Beth El also faced difficulties. In 1970, the congregation had fewer than 100 families, and the number of schoolchildren was dwindling quickly. In 1976, the last full-time rabbi left.[22]

Facing what seemed inevitable, the congregations merged in 1980, creating Beth Israel. One can read the anxiety about the future in the words of B'nai Israel's rabbi Joseph Freedman in submitting the merger agreement to his congregation. Freedman commended the communal unity and combination of "the best of two great traditions of our Jewish Faith" that would result from the union. But most of all, he hoped, it would enable the preservation of "a distinctive Jewish life that will stem the erosion that confronts us by Assimilation of Non-Jewish Values." There is a hint of desperation in his suggestion that "positive action now will save for us and future generations the best of our traditional Jewish Way of Life."[23]

The mergers highlighted the erosion of many differences among Jews in small towns since the east European immigration. In East Liverpool, for example, relations between the Orthodox and Reform communities—which were of more or less equal size—had long been cordial but cautious. Some east Europeans felt strongly that Reform Jews were uppity and assimilated; some older people, even in the late 1990s, referred to them disparagingly as "Deitschen" (Germans, with attendant implications of cultural snobbery). Social interaction increased over the years as the differences between the two communities, primarily economic, lessened. As long as Orthodox families lived in the east end and Reform families in the west end, their children would attend different elementary schools, but over the years, residential segregation lessened. Gradually there was social crossover between the two congregations, and eventually some membership crossover as well, especially after B'nai Jacob become Conservative. B'nai Jacob invited both the Reform rabbi and the temple president to the installation of their new rabbi in 1948 "to promote better feeling in the Jewish community." The temple also invited the synagogue members to events such as confirmation.[24]

As the East Liverpool communities struggled through the 1950s, merger seemed increasingly attractive. When the merger vote was finally taken in 1962, both congregations were virtually unanimous in approving it. At B'nai Israel, there were only two abstentions and no negative votes; at B'nai Jacob, only two negatives. At the organizational level, the deal was a lifesaver for those East Liverpool Jews committed to continued Jewish life. Each old congregation contributed approximately half of the members of the new congregation, Beth Shalom. In 1965 they took the optimistic step of hiring a full-time rabbi. There were about a dozen children in the Hebrew school.[25]

The new congregations that resulted from mergers almost uniformly affiliated with the UAHC.[26] Historically the Reform movement had more experience with small congregations than did the Conservative, but ideological realities were undoubtedly the dominant reason: whereas the Conservative movement could not sanction the significant changes made by Reform to Jewish practice, the Reform movement could tolerate traditional practice as long as it was not controlling. In many cases, the groups used a merger agreement template supplied by the UAHC that was designed to give some room for traditional sensibilities, splitting the difference between Reform and Conservative practice. For instance, the Torah would be read both Friday night and Saturday morning; tallit and *kippa* were optional for the congregation but encouraged on the bimah and even expected of the rabbi. Holidays would be observed both by the Jewish calendar and, if desired, on nearby dates as well; second-day Rosh Hashanah services and bar and bat mitzvah (either Friday evening or Saturday morning) would be made available. In deference to the Conservatives, some version of kashrut was accepted, and smoking was prohibited on Shabbat and holidays. In deference to the Reform members, an organ and a choir were permitted, though perhaps not at all services.[27]

Mergers built in power sharing. Assets, including real estate, were pooled. In East Liverpool, the Reform temple's building became the home of the new congregation, with the sale of B'nai Jacob's properties providing substantial funds for upkeep and operations; in Steubenville, the Conservative synagogue downtown was sold, and its windows and plaques were moved to the existing Reform temple. Political power was carefully balanced: each group provided equal representation to the new congregation's board and committees for two years.

While the fact of mergers indicates a lessening of differences, these carefully constructed agreements highlight the remaining issues, and no mere document could truly deal with the free-floating group and personal jealousies and anxieties released by the changes in congregational identity. Steubenville's merger even required that, during the first High Holidays after the merger, pulpit honors for participation in services be divided equally between the groups to minimize potential jealousies. Several years after the East Liverpool merger, congregant Dr. Alex Fisher analyzed the problem in a letter to the incumbent president concerning reactions to the recent Rosh Hashanah services. "Some [comments] were complimentary and some were critical," Fisher noted. "Some thought the rabbi was too 'orthodox.' Some thought there was not enough English in the service. Some felt that there was too much talking in the audience. Some thought the services were too long. . . . [P]ersonally, I felt that many of these complaints were not offered with a completely unbiased feeling. I'm afraid that there are still many from both former congregations who do not realize that there absolutely must be some give and take. And until this does become a willing reality, I'm afraid there will not be the unity that we all who are really interested in Beth Shalom hope to see." On the other hand, the first student rabbi to serve the merged congregation was profoundly impressed with how hard many people worked to make the merger a success. Yet it was, he remembered, a poignant moment, fatalistic rather than optimistic. Over the years, the press of compromise and the thinning out of the community made the differences of the 1960s irrelevant—at least, despite personal grudges, at the institutional level.[28]

Despite the popularity of mergers, in some towns, a tenacious traditionalist contingent held on to a formal identity until folding. In Ashland, Kentucky, Orthodox congregation House of Israel, formed in the 1920s when Agudath Achim moved toward Reform, closed in 1976. (Agudath Achim held on until 1987.) Traditional synagogues—Orthodox in name, but Conservative in practice—closed in Bellaire in 1986 and in Weirton in the early 1990s. The realignment of American industry in the 1970s and 1980s had a strong impact on the towns in the industrial sections of the Ohio River Valley, which went into decline as the east European Jewish immigrant generation was dying.[29]

Marietta's Orthodox congregation became inactive in the 1970s, as the first generation died or retired to new locations and the second generation settled elsewhere after college. The last rabbi left around 1960. The Beren family transferred the operations of their OKMAR (Oklahoma-Marietta) oil and gas company to Wichita and Denver. The remaining Latvian families and several other east European Orthodox families retained a communal structure, however, and were close socially.

But the remnants of Congregation Binae Israel were aware that their era had passed and made plans for dissolution on their own terms. Among the concerns dealt with at a meeting in spring 1972 was that membership had fallen below the minimum number specified in the congregational charter. Meeting minutes recorded this: "Important! Consideration about transfer or disposition or trusteeship of assets of schul to be effected *before* State has right to step in. Consult lawyer. How many members does it take or what number is minimum required to constitute a congregation. (Include women.)" At the time, there were only eight members (now, by necessity, including the women), all elderly, some of whom lived only part-time in Marietta. The mortgage on the Fourth Street synagogue building had been paid off in the late 1930s. Now arrangements were made for a local bank to pay the bills to maintain it.[30]

One of the most remarkable characteristics of Marietta's Jewish history is the exceptional cohesiveness and tenacity of the east European community. This insularity was created by the community's high degree of interrelatedness and by its durable Orthodoxy. The Marietta Jewish community was almost completely coextensive with their relatives. By maintaining the institutional structure of Congregation Binae Israel (of which they were the only members), the descendants maintained legal control of the synagogue building and the Jewish section of Oak Grove Cemetery. Physical control was maintained by employees of the oil production company office in Marietta, directed by family members in Oklahoma, Texas, Kansas, and Colorado.

For years after services were no longer held at the Fourth Street synagogue, the building was maintained by members of the Beren family. The emotional connection was unbreakable. When he was in town, Adolph Beren would do his morning prayers in the otherwise empty synagogue, rather than at home; he was quoted as saying, "It's a shul—it's so precious to me that I cannot leave it alone—the walls will cry." The Lithuanian Orthodoxy practiced in the Marietta synagogue in the early part of the century had been fixed permanently to the premises. The congregation-family consistently refused use of the building to any non-Orthodox newcomers to Marietta, regardless of the conditions. It belonged to Lithuanian Orthodoxy, not to Marietta.[31]

The end of the era came with the death in December 1994 of the last living son of Wolfe Beren, who, shortly before his death, had returned to Marietta and directed the refurbishing of the synagogue. His funeral was held there, with a rabbi from Telshe Yeshiva in Cleveland officiating. (The Cleveland yeshiva is named for, and is successor to, a famous school in the Lithuanian town of Telshe, which was the spiritual and intellectual center of pre–World War II Lithuanian Orthodoxy.) By January 1995, the only official members of the congregation were Adolph Beren's three children (none of whom lived any closer to Marietta than Wichita, Kansas), who paid for the costs of wrapping up congregational business. The prayer books and Torah scrolls had already been sent from Marietta to Telshe Yeshiva. In 1997, the yeshiva acquired the remaining assets: some religious objects, proceeds from the sale of the synagogue, and the title to the Jewish section of the city cemetery.[32]

In northern Kentucky, too, the tenacious older generation closed the book on Jewish institutional continuity. Despite overall population growth, the Covington and Newport Jewish community's numbers declined through the early postwar years as the towns suffered from a severe blight of organized—

including Jewish—crime. Old-timers like to tell the story that when $1,000 was needed to repair the Newport synagogue's roof, members, in an inventive fund-raising move, went to the gambling establishments and collected the entire amount in half an hour from Jewish gamblers visiting from Cleveland and Detroit.[33]

In the 1970s, however, some uneven gentrification began, and a group of young Jewish suburbanites living in these reviving neighborhoods attempted to found a new Reform congregation. Knowing that they were not the first congregation in Covington, the new group wished to connect with the past by creating itself as the successor to Temple of Israel, even calling the new entity Temple Israel. Leaders approached longtime resident Abe Wander, the nominal president of the old congregation, about the possibility of inheriting the 1939 synagogue. "Under the impression that Mr. Wander would allow them to sell the building and use the proceeds to relocate in a nicer, safer neighborhood," a local historian reported, "the group . . . sought out a prospective buyer." But Wander—who was effectively, and even legally, the congregation—sold the building to a fundamentalist Protestant church and sent the proceeds to Orthodox charities in Israel rather than permit the acquisition of the assets by a liberal Jewish group.[34]

In the upper Ohio Valley, just west of Pittsburgh, one small community has experienced a remarkable turnaround in the past twenty years. The industrial small towns of western Pennsylvania had long been economic colonies of Pittsburgh. In Jewish life, too, these towns were part of the Pittsburgh orbit through business, social, and family contacts. As the city's suburbs expanded and Jews flocked to them, Ambridge was the beneficiary—rather than the victim—of the trend to suburbanization in American Jewish life.

Hemmed in by the Allegheny and Monongahela, Pittsburgh first expanded eastward between the rivers. This was also the direction of the first Jewish residential movements away from older city neighborhoods beginning in the late nineteenth century. By the start of the twentieth century, the city was also reaching northwest, along the Ohio, toward towns such as Sewickley. However, many of these towns resisted and manipulated development to preserve their semirural character, and Sewickley slowly transformed from an upper-class rural retreat in the mid-nineteenth century to an upper-class suburb in the late nineteenth. Not surprisingly, upwardly mobile Jews tended to avoid these towns in the northern and western suburbs, which were seen as exclusive and inhospitable to Jews. In the 1920s, perhaps as few as a dozen Jews lived in nearby suburban Bellevue, Avalon, or Ben Avon, on the Ohio. Because of this residential sparseness, there were no synagogues at all in this area. The few Jews who moved into Sewickley in the 1950s were swimming in distinctly inhospitable waters.[35]

Meanwhile, the small industrial towns such as Coraopolis, Aliquippa, and Ambridge went into decline. They had grown rapidly from the late nineteenth century until immigration restriction in 1924 and experienced modest growth until the 1940s, when it leveled off. In Ambridge, Jews remained a high percentage of the business owners in what was, through the mid-1960s, still a booming steel town. In the late 1960s and early 1970s, as foreign competition and industry restructuring took its toll on the steel industry, Ambridge's Jewish merchants, many of them ready for retirement anyway, began to sell out or, if unable to find any buyer at all, simply close their businesses. Ambridge's town center had more and more boarded-up shop windows.

Ambridge's Congregation Beth Samuel followed this downward trajectory. In the mid-1950s, there were about one hundred families in the congregation, with about seventy children in the school. In the early 1970s, a merger with the Aliquippa synagogue (itself a merger of two earlier Orthodox groups) brought in enough people to sustain the membership level. In the early 1980s, some twenty families joined after the Coraopolis congregation disbanded, but continued population decline seemed inevitable.[36]

In the mid-1980s, though, the decline was reversed with the move of young Jewish families into—strangely enough—the formerly restricted exurban haven of Sewickley. Among other reasons, the Sewickley Valley Hospital, a major regional medical center, attracted young Jewish doctors and administrators who wanted to live near their workplace. Though some new residents commuted to larger congregations in Pittsburgh, others joined the smaller nearby community. By 2000, more than one hundred families belonged to Beth Samuel, which now affiliates with the liberal Reconstructionist movement. Few members actually live in Ambridge; others come from Aliquippa, Coraopolis, and Beaver, and even from the suburban Pittsburgh neighborhood of North Hills. But the majority come from the exurban areas of Sewickley, Moon Township, and even farther out, in less expensive Beaver County. The synagogue's Web site advertises itself as "proudly serving Pittsburgh's northern and western suburbs."[37]

Beth Samuel has profited from its central location and, through a double process of consolidation of small towns and new suburban settlement, has regained its earlier maximum numbers and anticipates further growth. (In contrast to the relationship of Pittsburgh and its western suburbs, the northern Kentucky towns are being left farther behind by Jewish suburbanization in Cincinnati, which has proceeded north away from the central city and the Ohio River.) The shift in constituency has inevitably produced conflict, some of which, as in any congregation, is based on age and class. A high proportion of new residents are physicians and other professionals; the older residents are businesspeople. Parents of young children, who constitute the largest subset in the congregation, have different needs and priorities than do retired members. However, there is also a dynamic resulting from different perceptions of the community. The old-timers view themselves as small-town Jews, residents of their own town; the newer residents consider themselves suburbanites. Older residents fear that their identity will be submerged in the city, whereas the new residents, most not natives of the city or region, celebrate and enjoy the proximity.[38]

In 1952, an article titled "The Disappearing Small-Town Jew: Report on a Dwindling Tribe" appeared in *Commentary* magazine. It was written by Lee Levinger, a Reform rabbi who was born in a small Idaho town in 1890 and whose first pulpit after seminary graduation in 1918 was in Paducah, Kentucky. From his own experience as resident and rabbi, Levinger outlined the characteristics of small-town Jewish life: pioneering spirit, particular economic roles, social familiarity with non-Jews, participation in general community life, networks of Jewish family and friendship encompassing cities and other small towns, the makeshift nature of Jewish life. But Levinger really intended to write the obituary of what he called the small-town Jewish type. "His past is generally colorful," he declared, "his present often shows as successful an integration in American life as is to be found anywhere; but his future raises some troubling questions." Some small-town Jewish communities will survive as their towns become suburbs of large cities, Levinger suggested, but then, he continued, the residents would no longer really be small-town Jews. "Thus as time passes," he concluded, "it seems that we shall soon have to write off most of the 150,000 village Jews from the roster of American Jewry."[39]

In 1952, some Jews in the small communities of the Ohio River Valley would have shared Levinger's prognosis, and many others no doubt would have been less pessimistic about their futures. But his predictions were—regrettably or not—correct.

Conclusion

In many places on the Ohio River, a Jewish presence persists. In some of the larger towns, congregations are still viable, though smaller than in the past. In Evansville—which, with a 2000 population of over 120,000, is distinctly a city—Temple Adath B'nai Israel continued to experience decline in membership: from about 220 families in the late 1980s to under 200 in 1995 to about 130 in 2005. But it maintains a full-time rabbi and a full menu of activities. Likewise, the Huntington congregation, with about 125 families in 2005, has a full-time rabbi. In addition to a congregation, each of these towns claims a Jewish charitable federation, Hadassah chapter (Evansville's with 150 members), and B'nai B'rith lodge (which in Huntington sponsored the erection of a Holocaust memorial on the temple grounds).[1]

Wheeling's Temple Shalom saw membership fall from 150 families in 1976 to about 100 in 1997. "It is no comfort to know it, but what is going on in Wheeling is going [on] in all small towns around the Pittsburgh area," wrote Rabbi Daniel Lowy in 1997. "We have hoped for a change, but there seems to be none in sight."[2] However, with 90 member units in 2005, the congregation still had a full-time rabbi and many programs and services, including a "traditional" Saturday morning minyan. The congregation celebrated its 150th anniversary in 1999.

Steubenville is doing less well. The area continues to lose population; the county has significantly higher than national average unemployment and the highest average age in Ohio. Membership in Temple Beth Israel reflects this demographic reality; it declined from about ninety member units in 1994 (about a third of whom were elderly singles) to fifty-three in 2005. Lay leaders alternated with a student rabbi from HUC until the fall of 1995, when a full-time rabbi was hired; soon, however, the congregation returned to using students.[3]

The smallest, most isolated congregations are smaller than ever. In 2005, according to the Union for Reform Judaism (the new name of the Union of American Hebrew Congregations), Paducah had thirty-six members, Parkersburg thirty, Owensboro fourteen, and East Liverpool only twelve. One source of nourishment for these congregations continues to be HUC's program of pulpit placements, in which all rabbinical students participate. The program not only provides rabbinical services for communities and pulpit experience for rabbis; it keeps Jews in isolated communities directly and personally connected to new ideas and developments in the Jewish institutional world and in the Reform movement, including the ordination of women as rabbis. Drawing on a tradition of welcoming all comers, most small congregations seem to be quite open to women rabbis.

Another important source of continuity for some of these communities is their buildings. East Liverpool Jews maintain their 1926 structure. In Paducah, the ornate 1890s synagogue was razed for a parking lot in 1963, but a smaller, modern building was erected on the outskirts of town, a downtown location no longer being either convenient or an important status statement. Owensboro's 1877 Moorish-style synagogue—"one of Kentucky's most unusual architectural landmarks" in Lee Shai Weissbach's evaluation—is among the fewer than fifty extant nineteenth-century synagogues in the United States and is now on the National Register of Historic Places.[4] A small, generally elderly group still meets there monthly and on High Holidays with "para-rabbinic" leadership trained by the Union for Reform Judaism.

Beneh Abraham of Portsmouth—like Owensboro's Adath Israel a charter member of the UAHC—had in 2005 only thirteen registered members. The congregation's 1958 centennial may have been the high point of its history. By the 1970s, the fifty-year-old synagogue at Eighth and Gay streets was still in fine condition but far too large for the congregation. When they were approached by a fundamentalist Protestant church that was looking for an appropriate site, the time seemed ripe. For the amount received from the sale, the congregation erected—mortgage-free—a new temple, small, modern, and more efficient, on a wooded lot at the edge of town. By the time of the dedication of the new, smaller building in 1975, the stability of Portsmouth's Jewish community had turned into stagnation. Of the forty-two members then, only six had not been members at the time of the centennial seventeen years earlier. Members of the Lehman and Levi families were still on the roster. In 1975, the temple's president was Bernard Levi, the great-grandson of founding president Louis Levi; Bernard's father had also been temple president, during the centennial in 1958. By the 1980s, when Bernard Levi retired to Florida, five generations of the family had lived in Portsmouth for more than 130 years. Some other Jewish families had a third generation remaining in town in the 1990s.[5]

But Portsmouth's prospects are not bright. The poverty rate is double the Ohio state average and 50 percent higher than the national rate. Unemployment is quite high; an indicator of a good economy is when it is down to "only" 8 percent. The *Cincinnati Enquirer* has referred to Portsmouth as "pretty but poor" and a "crack in the world 108 miles from Cincinnati."[6] It has been a long time since another Cincinnatian, Isaac Mayer Wise, praised Portsmouth's Jews as "wide awake for their religion," as the backbone of American Judaism.

For many institutions in very small Jewish communities, the most pressing question in recent years has been how to die with dignity. As his native East Liverpool Jewish community dwindled, Herschel Rubin clipped newspaper articles about dying Jewish communities—in the South, in declining urban areas, even in Ireland—vicariously sharing the experience and emotions of saying good-bye to a beloved institution.

The closing of a synagogue is very difficult emotionally for its survivors. When the Reform synagogue in Ashland, Kentucky, closed in 1986, several members described the experience as traumatic. The temple building was for them a statement of belonging, a physical symbol of American Judaism's parity with Christianity; the decision to close had been delayed as long as possible, one man explained, because "we didn't want to lose our identity in the community." There was grudging recognition of intermarriage and assimilation—someone grumbled, "There are some people in Ashland of Jewish extraction who could belong, but don't." The trustees of the congregation optimistically invested the proceeds of the sale "in case, miraculously, enough Jewish people moved here to start another congregation."[7]

On the face of it, the required miracle might not seem as completely fantastic as it once was. Demographers have recently noted a small reversal in the decline of American small towns: in the 1990s, rural counties experienced a net gain of two million residents, versus a net loss of one and a half million in the 1980s. *Time* magazine even did a cover story on the phenomenon in 1997, and a book titled *The 100 Best Small Towns in America*, intended to help prospective migrants, went through two editions.[8]

Some of the towns on the Ohio River may be beneficiaries to some extent. Newport, Kentucky, with a surge of gentrification in its neighborhoods of Victorian houses, is becoming a middle-class bedroom community for Cincinnati. The "dying downtowns" of the 1970s are now rehabbed as quaint living and shopping spaces in towns like Lawrenceburg and Madison, Indiana, and Marietta, Ohio. But they are hardly boomtowns. In fact, this apparent small-town trend has been quite selective: rural Vermont and Colorado are very popular, for instance. Four Ohio River Valley towns were included in *The 100 Best Small Towns*—Wilmington, Ohio; Bardstown, Kentucky; Jasper, Indiana; and Marion, Illinois—but none are on the river.[9]

American Jews are definitely participating in this migration to small towns. In addition to migrating for economic reasons (recently, of course, for professional rather than business opportunities), most Jews—like most other Americans—who choose this route are also looking for a less stressful lifestyle and stronger sense of community. As one Jewish Mariettan opined, it is "the American dream to live a peaceful life in a small town."[10]

With American Jewry at zero population growth, migration is now "the major dynamic" in a Jewish community's growth or decline, and it is true that more Jews are now living outside the traditional Jewish centers. "In 1936," write demographers Sidney and Alice Goldstein, "90 percent of the country's Jewish population was found in the seventeen largest metropolitan areas; by 1986, the top thirty metropolitan areas had to be considered in order to encompass so high a proportion of American Jewry." The National Jewish Population Survey 2000–2001 found 85 percent of American Jews in the top forty metropolitan areas. The trend, clearly, is "more Jewish population centers than in the past, but with fewer Jews in each center."[11]

Yet dispersion has not meant a general revival of small towns; the new population centers are still urban, and many are in the growth areas of the West and South. Sidney and Alice Goldstein note that "only 5 percent of all Jews were living in nonmetropolitan areas in 1990, that is, not only outside the central cities of the nation's 283 metropolitan areas, but also beyond their suburban areas." Interestingly, "among the small proportion of core Jews living outside metropolitan areas, only 9 percent were nonmigrants." That is, the vast majority of today's small-town Jews were not born and raised there; they have chosen to be small-town Jews.[12]

The impact of mobility altogether on Jewish life and institutions is mixed. In the case of small cities and towns where there is a synagogue, the affiliation rate seems to be slightly higher than it is in the largest metropolitan areas (about 51 percent versus 46 percent). As early as the 1980s, the UAHC noticed that the move of Jewish professionals to new areas of employment in small southern cities was rejuvenating some of the congregations there. However, the smaller the town, the less likely it is to have an organized Jewish community; of the towns listed in *The 100 Best Small Towns*, only eleven claimed organized Jewish congregations, about half unaffiliated with a major national denomination.[13]

Whether this is a cause or an effect, Jews who move to areas with smaller Jewish communities are much more likely to have limited Jewish attachments.

The National Jewish Population Survey found that these Jews were less likely to observe even basic traditions such as fasting on Yom Kippur, attending a Passover seder, or lighting a Hanukkah menorah. Fewer Jews in small communities rated their sense of belonging to the Jewish people as strong or somewhat strong (81 percent versus 89 percent in large communities). Not surprisingly, therefore, fewer said that being Jewish was very important in their lives, though 43 percent (versus 53 percent) did say so. Jews in small communities are more likely to be intermarried—in fact, twice as likely. They are far less likely to raise their children as Jews and give them substantial Jewish educations.

Some of this reflects the trend away from Jewish commitment and behaviors that is affecting the American Jewish population overall. Residence in a major city is certainly no guarantee of Jewish attachment. But this attenuation has made it easier for Jews to live in small towns, and it has made them comfortable enough to eschew the pulls of commonality that created Jewish communities and institutions in the nineteenth century. New small-town Jews may avail themselves of small temples' religious resources, such as Jewish education, but unlike earlier generations, they find adequate social resources among non-Jews.

In this respect, too, it is important to remember that the National Jewish Population Survey's "small community" designation includes many places that are far from being small towns. The study defines as small anything outside the forty largest metropolitan statistical areas defined for the U.S. census. For the Ohio Valley, that would include everything except Pittsburgh and Cincinnati; even Louisville—the fiftieth-largest metropolitan statistical area—is a small community by the National Jewish Population Survey's criteria.

All of these factors combine to suggest that the redistribution of the American Jewish community will almost certainly fail to benefit the Ohio River Valley. It is unlikely that the small communities on the Ohio River will ever again experience the communal vibrancy of the nineteenth and early twentieth centuries; the excitement of pioneering a new Jewish community has moved to other locales. But the demise of Ashland's congregation helped seed another, as they donated a Sefer Torah, *ner tamid*, and siddurim to a new congregation in Iowa, one of whose members had grown up in Ashland. Providing another metaphor of the demographic transformation of American Jewry, the ner tamid from the Weirton temple ended up, like many northern Jews, in the Sun Belt: the lamp now hangs in the new Arizona synagogue of a Weirton native.[14]

With their best days now past, some small Jewish communities seem to serve their dispersed former residents in much the same way the Lower East

Side has served the broader American Jewish imagination: as a mythic "old country" remembered for its closeness, warmth, and supportiveness. In the case of the northern Kentucky towns, proximity to the old hometown—and the intensity of the migration to the urban center—enabled a considerable continuity of community, as people who lived in Covington or Newport from the 1930s through the 1950s transplanted their old friendship networks into new settings. Some of these networks endured for years after their members left Kentucky. In October 1994, two hundred people met at a Cincinnati hotel for a northern Kentucky Jewish "family reunion." Organizers had tracked down hundreds of descendants of former Newport and Covington families. The program book for the event listed nearly five hundred individuals and couples, of whom almost four hundred lived in the Cincinnati area. Many of the attendees were people in their eighties, born as the northern Kentucky community was being born and growing up with it. They spoke of their feelings about the community with unwitting irony—overlooking the fact that urbanization both destroyed their closeness and fostered the construction of their new sense of community.[15]

So do "small towns make good Jews," as American-born Israeli journalist Ze'ev Chafets asserts?[16] It is difficult, if not impossible, to accurately measure assimilation historically. The problems are ones of definition: What is assimilation, after all? When is one no longer to be counted as Jewish? (This is why some scholars avoid the term "assimilation" entirely.) As we are learning now, and as small-town Jewish communities have always known, intermarriage in itself is not determinative. It is true that small-town Jewish communities always had higher levels of intermarriage than did urban Jewish populations. One sociologist studying small towns in Illinois (including Cairo) in the mid-1960s, for instance, found an intermarriage rate of 39 percent among those who married while residing in the small town, about twice the national rate at the time.[17] But it is impossible to know whether the differential always existed at this level. For one thing, in earlier generations, intermarriage was inhibited by social factors: the mutual reluctance of Gentiles and Jews to consider each other as marriage partners, an attitude reinforced by greater parental control of courtship and marriage. As we have seen, many small-town Jews in earlier generations went out of their way to find Jewish potential partners for their children. It is impossible to know how to evaluate the chicken-or-egg effect, for by the 1960s, small-town Jewish communities in many places were already weak and therefore less attractive to committed Jews. Small-town Jewish communities dwindled primarily through out-migration, not through out-marriage. In fact, the meteoric rise of the intermarriage rate since the 1960s coincided with increased Jewish urbanization.

But this suggests an interesting irony. The integration of non-Jewish spouses into the Jewish community was not uncommon in small towns at a time when larger communities were often hostile even to converts. Pointing this out, the sociologist quoted above wrote in 1967, "In fact, most non-Jewish women, after their marriage to a Jew, tend to gravitate toward the Jewish faith and their husbands are thus able to maintain their Jewish identity. One non-Jewish wife, for instance, complained to the interviewer that her husband, even upon her insistence, was not as good a Jew as he ought to be, and said that she would have been much happier if he had attended services more often."[18]

In 1966, a Reform rabbi serving in Huntington predicted, "If the Jewish Community is going to have a future in this country it will have to make it in communities such as Huntington." In this rabbi's analysis, small towns like Huntington are the laboratories for the readjustment of American Judaism: "In the next generation there will be very few [Jewish] families [in Huntington] who will not have non-Jewish relations of a very close degree . . . aunts and uncles, grandparents, etc. It will not be enough for people to be Jews out of habit for they will have to compete with the religious ideas held by the majority."[19] Now this is true not only of small communities like Huntington. Only in the last decade or two has the mainstream American Jewish community begun to grapple with the effects of intermarriage and their implications.

An evaluation of the small-town Jewish experience is a complicated matter. The feelings of individual Jews who have actually lived in small communities are mixed. It is easy to avoid one's Jewishness in a small town, and in many cases, a decision to live there is possible because Judaism is not a high priority for the individual. But Jews who embrace their Jewishness find ways to do so, even when it requires more effort. Like their nineteenth- and early-twentieth-century predecessors, many take to the road for Jewish holidays and celebrations, joining family in cities. Others try to create new networks, such as the Conference on Judaism in Rural New England, which brings together "Jews in the woods" from northern New England and lower Canada at an annual conference, through a newsletter, and with traveling "para-rabbis."

There is no question that in some aspects, small-town Jewish identity is very different from the urban version. Small-town Jews are perforce ambassadors of the Jewish people to the overwhelmingly non-Jewish majority, but this is a function of percentages rather than locale. Likewise, though there is no evidence that small towns are more antisemitic, Jews there cannot be as insulated from it as urban Jews can and therefore have to develop personal means of coping.

Many small-town Jews are very positive about the experience. Elizabeth

Weinberg of Madison argues that the experience of small-town Jews, integrating with the majority while maintaining their Jewishness, demonstrates to "American Jews living in the modern ghettos" how exaggerated their fears for Jewish survival are. Joyce Rubin, who grew up in Cairo in the 1950s and early 1960s, considers the context of her upbringing "very realistic." In other words, she believes the necessary small-town Jewish emphasis on intergroup relations and understanding other religions was more in tune with the requirements of life in America's pluralistic democracy than was the intense Jewish social and cultural life of heavily Jewish urban neighborhoods. Elsa Rubin Efran, who grew up in East Liverpool in the 1940s and 1950s, expressed a similar sense of integration and parity, reinforced by a social familiarity created by the proximity of all classes in the small town. "Our family had friends of all religions and many walks of life—from blue-collar to professional," she remembers. "We went to church dinners, and non-Jews came to Temple dinners. These were *community* events, not religious events." Non-Jewish neighbors met student rabbis at the Rubins' home and also "brought their priests and ministers over. . . . Occasionally I went to church services with my friends, and they came to Temple with me."[20]

The small-town experience was not, however, for everyone. One complaint is the perceived fishbowl environment of a small town, the feeling of living in what one former small-town Jew called "a little Peyton Place," where gossip is the major social activity. Some, upon reflection, began to resent what they perceived as excessive accommodations to Christian sensibilities. Some were absolutely traumatized by the experience. Not a few express regret that they did not grow up in a larger Jewish community, especially given the potential problems of interreligious dating. Expressing her sense of what she missed, one woman, who grew up in the 1960s in the only Jewish family in her town with young children, observed, "As far as I could tell, being Jewish meant being old." She found her way in the Jewish community through years in Israel—and has now moved back to a small city with a small Jewish community not far from where she grew up.

Some enjoyed their small-town Jewishness specifically because of its uniqueness. Young Jews might feel that their world was more cosmopolitan than that of their Christian peers, that through their Jewish contacts outside the small town, they were more sophisticated. New York writer Julie Salamon, who grew up in a small town in inland Adams County, Ohio, relished being exotic, not only as a Jew among small-town Christians but as a small-town Jew among urban Jews. "I often mention my upbringing in this 'colorful' impoverished backwater to let people know I'm not just another Jewish girl from New York," she admits bemusedly. "I have watched myself deliberately bring my parents into conversation, often as comic foils for amusing stories about the adventures of eastern European Jews [her parents were Holocaust survivors] in the American heartland."[21]

The increasing demographic concentration of Jews in urban areas suggests that the small towns that were so important to nineteenth-century Jewish life, and that gained new momentum from the dispersal of east European immigrants, now have a different role in American Jewish life. No longer are they promising economic springboards, so their Jewish communities have lost the vitality that comes with optimism. They are now mostly holding operations.

But it is important to remember that the small-town experience, especially in the nineteenth century, was critical to the maturation of the American Jewish community and to its conversation about the necessary and best ways to be both Jewish and American. The integration of Jews and non-Jews that small-town Jews experienced from the earliest days of the nineteenth century anticipated the experience of late-twentieth-century America. And the willingness to experiment and to take responsibility for the maintenance of Jewish life is an important value for contemporary American Jewish communities. Despite the overall shrinkage of the American Jewish population and quite reasonable fears for the communal future, the fact is that in America, assimilation can go both ways. A Jewish woman who grew up in Bellaire, Ohio, reported that at her fiftieth high school reunion, "one of my non-Jewish friends came to tell me . . . 'I was thinking of you when I attended my grandson's Bar Mitzvah in California.'"[22] Whatever the non-Jewish woman's feelings about her grandchild's religious identity, it is certainly remarkable that today not only may Jews have non-Jewish grandchildren, but non-Jews may have Jewish grandchildren.

If, as Jacob Marcus said, it is impossible to find the first Jew anywhere, it is probably equally impossible to identify the last Jew anywhere. For many reasons, American Jews live in many places, and despite the death of institutions and the fragility of community, American Jews as individuals may carry a spark of Judaism to all these places. Recently, scholars Steven Cohen and Arnold Eisen have described how American Jews carry their identity within themselves, how today Jewishness is what it needs to be for any Jew at any given moment.[23] I think of the girl in my sister's seventh grade class who discovered that her absentee father, divorced when she was a toddler, was Jewish; she then announced that she would not attend school on Hanukkah. I wonder what happened to that girl. She was, of course, mistaken that Jewish practice required her abstention, and clearly all her knowledge of Judaism was filtered through an entirely American lens. In our small town, she had few people of whom to ask her questions and no cadre of Jewish kids with whom to associate. But that Jewish identification set off something in her. Who knows where Jews will continue to be found and what it will mean to American Judaism.

Jews came to the Ohio River Valley at a particular time in its history, which set many of the conditions for—and limits to—the growth of their communities. As ambient conditions changed over almost two centuries, so did the configuration of Jewish life. Remembering that community is both physical place and human relationship, we can expect and accept that change will continue.

As a historian of the region has observed, "Flow, flux, transformation has given the Ohio River and its basin a paradoxical—but somehow abiding—sense of place."[24] This sense of place intersected with a sense of history in pursuit of the future in a speech given by Rabbi Richard Levy in 1999, which he titled "This Judaism Must Flow." The setting was a "second Pittsburgh Conference," the annual convention of the Central Conference of American Rabbis, of which Levy was president, held that year in Pittsburgh. Under discussion was a new statement of principles that advocated a positive reorientation of Reform Judaism to traditional belief and practice, a proposal that stirred controversy just as had the pronouncements of the first conference in the Pittsburgh Platform of 1885.[25]

Levy began with an acknowledgement of that first conference, which, he noted, was as concerned about Jewish continuity as was the contemporary Jewish community. "To reclaim 'our prerogative as a holy nation,' to 'stir our people up from their lethargical slumber' [quotes from Kaufmann Kohler's 1885 opening speech]—these were the motivations that led the radical Reformer Kohler to summon his colleagues here at the junction of three rivers, two of which flowed from the East, where the other radical Reformers lived, forming a third—the great Ohio that would flow west, past the city of Cincinnati where Isaac Mayer Wise, leader of the traditionalists, resided." Kohler's solution for moribund American Jewry was "a sprinkling—indeed, an immersion—in the principles that emerged in this city by the Allegheny and Monongahela [and that] would bring them back to the right path."

In Levy's rhetoric, the flow, flux, and transformation of American Judaism are linked to the Ohio River both metaphorically and historically. Two biblical rivers are two streams of Jewish experience: the Yarden, the river the Jews must cross to become a people in their land (Joshua 1), represents participation in the demands of community; the Yabbok, the river by which Jacob wrestles the adversary (Genesis 32), represents the imperatives of personal autonomy. Presenting the new Pittsburgh Platform, Levy declared,

> Both rivers nurture us, engulf us. . . . The Yabbok runs into the Yarden; the Allegheny and the Monongahela run into the Ohio. For us Reform Jews, both affirming the beliefs of the Jewish people and wrestling as individuals with the meaning of those beliefs in our age are not separate, they are the dialogue which is the stuff of our lives as Reform Jews. The Principles we shall vote on tomorrow commit us to swim in both streams, to swim in that broad channel where the Yabbok and Yarden of Pittsburgh mingle, the Ohio River which in the darkest period of American slavery was the river that meant freedom, the river to which Huck Finn was steering Jim that he might gain his freedom, the river along which Isaac Mayer Wise built the College that, in all its tributaries, has nurtured our understanding that religious freedom means the ability to mingle our people's faith and history with our individual responses to the currents of our times. It was along the Ohio in 1885 that Wise the traditionalist traveled to meet his radical colleagues in this historic city. By passing these Principles, we can reclaim Reform for both Wise and Kohler, for the radicals and the traditionalists, as a movement within which both streams flow seamlessly.[26]

Levy's speech exemplifies the power of place—and the potentialities of a great river, simultaneously stable and moving—to stir the imagination. Ohio Valley Jews of the nineteenth century may well have entertained imaginative flights about such potentialities (if perhaps less theologically lofty) as they settled and made their new homes on the river and considered their futures. But as the Ohio River provided Levy his metaphors, he provided confirmation of the Ohio River Valley's lasting place in American Jewish history. It has been home to many Jews, leaders and followers, and if its cities of Pittsburgh and Cincinnati have played major roles in national Jewish life, the small communities as well have been part of the warp and woof of the American Jewish experience. That there is no renaissance on the horizon for these communities can be seen as testimony to the continued resilience of American Judaism, which will best thrive in new places if we appreciate its past.

Appendix: Population Tables

Table 1. County and Town Populations 1840–1900

	1840	1850	1860	1870	1880	1890	1900
Pennsylvania							
Allegheny	81,235	138,290	178,822	262,204	355,869	551,959	775,058
Pittsburgh[a]	31,204	46,601	49,217	86,076	156,389	238,617	321,616
Ohio							
Columbiana	40,378	33,621	32,836	38,299	48,602	59,029	68,590
East Liverpool	503[b]	1,581	2,051	2,105	5,568	10,956	16,485
Jefferson	25,030	29,133	26,115	29,188	33,018	39,415	44,357
Steubenville	5,203	6,140	6,154	8,107	12,093	13,394	14,349
Belmont	30,901	34,600	36,398	39,714	49,683	57,413	60,875
Bellaire	—	—	1,466	4,033	8,025	9,934	9,912
Washington	20,823	29,540	36,268	40,609	43,244	42,380	48,245
Marietta[c]	2,506	4,185	5,529	6,729	7,016	8,273	13,348

[a]Pittsburgh figures include Allegheny City, which was annexed in 1907.

[b]East Liverpool was at this time Liverpool.

[c]Marietta figures include Harmar village, which was annexed in 1890. The breakdown of the totals is as follows:

	Marietta	Harmar
1840	1,814	692
1850	3,175	1,010
1860	4,323	1,206
1870	5,218	1,511
1880	5,444	1,572

	1840	1850	1860	1870	1880	1890	1900
Meigs	11,452	17,971	26,534	31,465	32,325	29,813	28,620
Pomeroy	—	1,638	6,480	5,824	5,560	4,726	4,639
Gallia	13,444	17,063	22,043	25,545	28,124	27,005	27,918
Gallipolis	1,413	1,686	3,418	3,711	4,400	4,498	5,432
Lawrence	9,738	15,246	23,219	31,380	39,068	39,556	39,534
Ironton	—	—	3,691	5,686	8,857	10,939	11,868
Scioto	11,192	18,428	24,297	29,302	33,511	35,377	40,981
Portsmouth	—[d]	4,011	6,268	10,592	11,321	12,394	17,870
Hamilton	80,145	156,844	216,401	260,370	313,374	374,573	409,479
Cincinnati	46,338	115,435	161,044	216,239	255,139	296,908	325,902
Indiana							
Dearborn	19,327	20,166	24,397	24,116	26,671	23,364	22,194
Lawrenceburg	—	2,651	3,599	3,159	4,668	4,284	4,362
Jefferson	16,614	23,916	25,027	29,741	25,977	24,507	22,913
Madison	3,798	8,012	8,130	10,709	8,945	8,936	7,835
Floyd	9,454	14,875	20,174	23,300	24,590	29,458	30,118
New Albany	4,226	9,859	12,647	15,396	16,423	21,059	20,628
Vanderburgh	6,250	11,414	20,543	33,145	42,193	59,809	71,769
Evansville	—	3,235	11,484	21,830	29,280	50,756	59,007

[d]Portsmouth is not listed separately. Its 1830 population was 1,064.

Table 1 (continued)

	1840	1850	1860	1870	1880	1890	1900
Posey	9,683	12,549	16,158	19,185	20,857	21,529	22,333
Mount Vernon	—	1,120	1,994	2,880	3,730	4,705	5,132
Illinois							
Alexander	3,313	2,484	4,698	10,564	14,808	16,563	19,384
Cairo	—	242	2,188	6,267	9,011	10,324	12,566
(West) Virginia							
Ohio	13,357	18,006	22,422	28,831	37,457	41,557	48,024
Wheeling	7,885	11,435	14,083	19,280	30,737	34,522	38,878
Wood	7,923	9,450	11,046	19,000	25,006	28,612	34,452
Parkersburg	—	1,218	2,493	5,546	6,582	8,408	11,703
Cabell	8,163	6,299	8,020	6,429	13,744	23,595	29,252
Huntington[e]	—	—	—	—	3,174	10,108	11,923
Kentucky							
Boyd[f]	—	—	6,044	8,573	12,165	14,033	18,834
Ashland	—	—	—	2,462	3,280	4,195	6,800
Mason	15,719	18,344	18,222	18,126	20,469	20,773	20,446
Maysville	2,741	4,256	4,106	4,705	5,220	5,358	6,423
Kenton	7,816	17,038	25,467	36,096	43,983	54,161	63,591
Covington	2,026	9,408	16,471	24,505	29,720	37,371	42,938

[e]Huntington was founded in 1871.

[f]Boyd County was created in 1860.

	1840	1850	1860	1870	1880	1890	1900
Campbell	5,214	13,127	20,909	27,406	37,440	44,208	54,223
Newport	—[g]	5,895	10,046	15,087	20,433	24,918	28,301
Jefferson	36,346	59,831	89,404	118,953	146,010	188,598	232,549
Louisville	21,210	43,194	68,033	100,753	123,758	161,129	204,731
Daviess	8,331	12,362	15,549	20,714	27,730	33,120	38,667
Owensboro	—[h]	1,215	2,308	3,437	6,231	9,837	13,189
Henderson	9,548	12,171	14,262	18,457	24,515	29,536	32,907
Henderson	—	1,775	—	4,171	5,365	8,835	10,272
McCracken	4,745	6,067	10,360	13,998	16,262	21,051	28,733
Paducah	—[i]	2,428	4,590	6,866	8,036	12,797	19,446

[g]Newport is not listed separately. Its 1830 population was 715.

[h]Owensboro is not listed separately. Its 1830 population was 229.

[i]Paducah is not listed separately. Its 1830 population was 105.

Sources: County data from University of Virginia Library, Geospatial and Statistical Data Center, http://fisher.lib.virginia.edu/collections/stats/histcensus/. Town data from U.S. Census Office, *Sixth Census or Enumeration of the Inhabitants of the United States, as Corrected at the Department of State, in 1840* (Washington, DC: Blair and Rives, 1841); U.S. Census Office, *The Seventh Census of the United States: 1850* (Washington, DC: R. Armstrong, 1853); U.S. Census Office, *Population of the United States in 1860* (Washington, DC: GPO, 1864); U.S. Census Office, *Ninth Census: 1870,* vol. 1 (Washington, DC: GPO, 1872); U.S. Census Office, *Tenth Census: June 1, 1880,* vol. 1 (Washington, DC: GPO, 1883); U.S. Census Office, *Eleventh Census: 1890,* vol. 1, pt. 1 (Washington, DC: GPO, 1895); U.S. Census Office, *Twelfth Census: 1900,* vol. 1, pt. 1 (Washington, DC: GPO, 1901).

Table 2. County and Town Populations 1900–2000

	1900[a]	1930	1950	1970	2000
Pennsylvania					
Allegheny	775,058	1,374,410	1,515,237	1,605,016	1,281,666
Pittsburgh	321,616	669,817	676,806	520,117	334,563
Beaver	56,432	149,062	175,192	208,418	181,412
Ambridge[b]	—	20,227	16,429	11,324	7,769
Aliquippa[c]	620	27,116	26,132	22,277	11,734
Ohio					
Columbiana	68,590	86,484	98,920	108,310	112,075
East Liverpool	16,485	23,329	24,217	20,020	13,089
Jefferson	44,357	88,307	96,495	96,193	73,894
Steubenville	14,349	35,422	35,872	30,771	19,015
Belmont	60,875	94,719	87,740	80,917	70,226
Bellaire	9,912	13,327	19,573	9,655	4,892
Washington	48,245	42,437	44,407	57,160	63,251
Marietta	13,348	14,285	16,006	16,861	14,515
Meigs	28,620	23,961	23,227	19,799	23,072
Pomeroy	4,639	3,563	3,656	2,672	1,966
Gallia	27,918	23,050	24,910	25,239	31,069
Gallipolis	5,432	7,106	7,871	7,490	4,180
Lawrence	39,534	44,541	49,115	56,868	62,319
Ironton	11,868	16,621	16,333	15,030	11,211
Scioto	40,981	81,221	82,910	76,951	79,195
Portsmouth	17,870	42,560	36,798	27,633	20,909
Hamilton	409,479	589,356	723,952	924,018	845,303
Cincinnati	325,902	451,160	503,998	452,524	331,285
Indiana					
Dearborn	22,194	21,056	25,141	29,430	46,109
Lawrenceburg	4,362	4,072	4,806	4,636	4,685

[a]Data for 1900 also appear in table 1.

[b]Ambridge was first listed in the 1910 census, with a population of 5,205. The population in 1920 was 12,730.

[c]Aliquippa's population in 1910 was 1,743 and in 1920 was 2,931.

	1900	1930	1950	1970	2000
Jefferson	22,913	19,182	21,613	27,006	31,705
Madison	7,835	6,530	7,506	13,081	12,004
Floyd	30,118	34,655	43,955	55,622	70,823
New Albany	20,628	25,819	29,346	38,402	37,603
Vanderburgh	71,769	113,320	160,422	168,772	171,922
Evansville	59,007	102,249	128,636	138,764	121,582
Posey	22,333	17,853	19,818	21,740	27,061
Mount Vernon	5,132	5,035	6,150	6,770	7,478
Illinois					
Alexander	19,384	22,542	20,316	12,015	9,590
Cairo	12,566	13,532	12,123	6,277	3,632
West Virginia					
Brooke	7,219	24,663	26,904	29,685	25,447
Hancock	6,693	28,511	34,388	39,749	32,667
Weirton[d]	—	—	24,005	27,131	20,411
Ohio	48,024	72,077	71,672	64,197	47,427
Wheeling	38,878	61,659	58,891	48,188	31,419
Wood	34,452	56,521	66,540	86,818	87,986
Parkersburg	11,703	29,623	29,684	44,208	33,099
Cabell	29,252	90,786	108,035	106,918	96,784
Huntington	11,923	75,572	86,353	74,315	51,475
Kentucky					
Boyd	18,834	43,849	49,949	52,376	49,752
Ashland	6,800	29,074	31,131	29,245	21,981
Mason	20,446	18,862	18,486	17,273	16,800
Maysville	6,423	6,557	8,632	7,411	8,993
Kenton	63,591	93,534	104,254	129,440	151,464
Covington	42,938	65,252	64,452	52,535	43,370

[d]Weirton overlaps Brooke and Hancock counties. In its early decades, Weirton was an unincorporated entity. The population was about 8,500 in 1930 and about 18,000 in 1940 (Writers' Program of the Works Progress Administration, comp., *West Virginia: A Guide to the Mountain State* [New York: Oxford University Press, 1941], 483). Only a section of the city, Weirton Heights, is listed in the 1940 census, with a population of 2,476.

Table 2. (continued)

	1900	1930	1950	1970	2000
Campbell	54,223	73,391	76,196	88,501	88,616
Newport	28,301	29,744	31,044	25,998	17,048
Jefferson	232,549	355,350	484,615	695,055	693,604
Louisville	204,731	307,745	369,129	361,472	256,231
Daviess	38,667	43,779	57,241	79,486	91,545
Owensboro	13,189	22,765	33,651	50,329	54,067
Henderson	32,907	26,295	30,715	36,031	44,829
Henderson	10,272	11,668	16,837	22,976	27,373
McCracken	28,733	46,271	49,137	58,281	65,514
Paducah	19,446	33,541	32,828	31,627	26,307

Sources: County data for 1900–1970 from U.S. Bureau of the Census, County Population Census Counts 1900–1990, http://www.census.gov/population/www/censusdata/cencounts.html. Town data for 1900–1970 from U.S. Census Office, *Twelfth Census: 1900,* vol. 1, pt. 1 (Washington, DC: GPO, 1901); U.S. Bureau of the Census, *Fifteenth Census of the United States: 1930; Population,* vol. 3, pts. 1–2 (Washington, DC: GPO, 1932); U.S. Bureau of the Census, *Census of Population: 1950; A Report of the Seventeenth Decennial Census of the United States,* vol. 1 (Washington, DC: GPO, 1952); U.S. Bureau of the Census, *1970 Census of Population,* vol. 1, pt. A, secs. 1–2 (Washington, DC: GPO, 1972). All data for 2000 from U.S. Bureau of the Census, American FactFinder, http://factfinder.census.gov/.

Table 3. Jewish Population Estimates

Pennsylvania	Aliquippa	Ambridge	Beaver	Coraopolis	McKees Rocks	Midland	Rochester	Pittsburgh
1852	—	—	—	—	—	—	—	some
1858	—	—	—	—	—	—	—	60
1863	—	—	—	—	—	—	—	150
1870	—	—	—	—	—	—	—	1,000
1878	—	—	—	—	—	—	21	2,000
1889	—	—	—	—	—	—	—	5,000
1897	—	—	—	—	—	—	—	10,000
1905	—	—	—	—	—	—	—	15,000
1912	some	—	some	—	200	—	some	35,000
1917	300	—	—	—	220	94	—	60,000
1927	115	200	—	200	240	—	62	53,000
1937	410	290	30	180	330	100	100	52,000
1947	400	300	—	156	260	—	—	54,000
1953	400	300	—	152	160	—	—	54,000
1960	400	300	—	115	100	—	—	47,000
1967	400	300	115	—	—	—	—	45,000
1978	400	250	115	—	—	—	—	—
1980	400	250	115	—	—	—	—	50,000

Table 3. (continued)

	Aliquippa	Ambridge	Beaver	Coraopolis	McKees Rocks	Midland	Rochester	Pittsburgh
1984	400	250	—	—	—	—	—	50,000
1991	350	—	—	—	—	—	—	—
1999[a]	—	—	—	—	—	—	—	40,000

Ohio									
	East Liverpool	Steubenville	Bellaire	Marietta	Pomeroy	Gallipolis	Ironton	Portsmouth	Cincinnati
1820	—	—	—	—	—	—	—	—	20
1830	—	—	—	—	—	—	—	—	140
1840	—	—	—	—	—	—	—	—	1,250
1850	—	—	—	—	—	—	—	—	2,500
1860	—	—	—	—	—	—	—	—	9,000
1878	—	37	64	—	—	—	47	84	8,000
1905	—	—	140	—	—	—	some	96	17,500
1907	—	200	300	—	some	—	some	114	25,000
1912	some	150	400	some	some	—	some	60	28,000
1917	300	400	440	80	—	—	90	128	25,000
1927	500	920	300	100	—	—	—	200	23,500
1937	535	1,000	275	80	—	14	55	175	21,800
1947	368	780	256	<100	—	—	<100	140	22,000
1953	365	1,000	200	—	—	—	—	120	25,000
1960	365	900	120	—	—	—	—	200	25,000

[a]The data for all Pennsylvania towns are included with Pittsburgh's data.

	East Liverpool	Steubenville	Bellaire	Marietta	Pomeroy	Gallipolis	Ironton	Portsmouth	Cincinnati
1968	290	620	120	—	—	—	—	170	28,000
1974	290	620	120	—	—	—	—	120	30,000
1978	290	405	<100	—	—	—	—	120	30,000
1985	300	200	—	—	—	—	—	120	22,000
1991	200	175	—	—	—	—	—	<100	23,000
1999	<100	125	—	—	—	—	—	—	22,500

Indiana

	Lawrenceburg	Madison	New Albany	Evansville	Mount Vernon
1878	36	253	—	375	86
1905	—	—	—	800	123
1907	—	50	—	750	—
1912	—	32	—	1,000	—
1917	—	70	125	1,500	85
1927	—	24	—	1,800	—
1937	50	15	65[b]	1,765	23
1947	—	—	—	1,350	—
1953	—	—	—	1,450	—

[b]Plus 25 in Jeffersonville (opposite Louisville, KY).

Table 3. (continued)

	Lawrenceburg	Madison	New Albany	Evansville	Mount Vernon
1960	—	—	—	1,225	—
1967	—	—	—	1,125	—
1978	—	—	—	1,200	—
1980	—	—	—	1,200	—
1985	—	—	—	1,200	—
1991	—	—	—	520	—
1999	—	—	—	400	—

Illinois	
	Cairo
1878	57
1905	98145.451
1907	150
1912	—
1917	375
1927	75
1937	60

West Virginia	Wheeling	Weirton	Parkersburg	Huntington
1854	17	—	—	—
1878	300	—	77	—
1905	400	—	150	71
1907	550	—	50	100
1912	500	—	400	150
1917	1,000	69	440	310
1927	750	—	98	1,125
1937[c]	1,150	—	125	810
1947	800	300	100	700
1953	800	300	100	700
1960	800	265	100	925
1967	700	300	170	750
1974	775	—	170	350
1978	650	—	155	350
1980	650	150	155	450
1985	650	150	155	450
1991	300	<100	—	275
1999	275	—	110	250

[c]Plus 25 in Chester, 35 in Wellsburg, 16 in Moundsville, and 15 in New Martinsville.

Table 3. (continued)

Kentucky	Ashland	Maysville	Covington/ Newport	Louisville	Owensboro	Henderson	Paducah
1830	—	—	—	20	—	—	—
1860	—	—	—	2,000	—	—	—
1875	—	—	—		—	—	170
1878	—	18	—	2,500	213	79	203
1905	—	—	—	7,000	155	189	234
1907	—	—	—	8,000	—	150	260
1912	some	—	some	10,000	—	250	250
1917	—	—	650[d]	9,000	230	275	250
1927	170	—	1,100[e]	12,500	49	93	800
1937	150	28	850[f]	13,800	65	88	600
1947	200	—	—	9,000	—	140	150
1953	175	—	—	7,900	125	140	150
1960	175	—	—	8,500	—	140	275
1967	150	—	—	8,500	—	—	175
1974	150	—	—	9,200	—	—	175

[d]Covington 350, Newport 300.

[e]Covington 500, Newport 600.

[f]Covington 350, Newport 475, Fort Thomas 25.

	Ashland	Maysville	Covington/ Newport	Louisville	Owensboro	Henderson	Paducah
1978	—	—	—	9,200	—	—	175
1980	—	—	—	9,200	—	—	175
1985	—	—	—	9,200	—	—	175
1991	—	—	—	8,700	—	—	—[g]
1999	—	—	500	8,700	—	—	—

[g]Included with southern Illinois. Weissbach estimates 150 for 1994. Lee Shai Weissbach, *The Synagogues of Kentucky* (Lexington: University Press of Kentucky, 1995), 149.

Sources: Data for 1907 and 1912 from Herman Bernstein, ed., *American Jewish Yearbook 5675*, vol. 16, September 21, 1914–September 8, 1915 (Philadelphia: Jewish Publication Society, 1914). Data for 1917 from Samson D. Oppenheim, ed., *American Jewish Yearbook 5679,* vol. 20, September 7, 1918–September 24, 1919 (Philadelphia: Jewish Publication Society, 1918). Data for 1947 from Henry Schneiderman and Morris Fine, eds., *American Jewish Yearbook 5709, 1948–49,* vol. 50 (Philadelphia: Jewish Publication Society, 1949). Data for 1953 from Morris Fine, ed., *American Jewish Yearbook 1954,* vol. 55 (Philadelphia: Jewish Publication Society, 1954). Data for 1967 from Morris Fine and Milton Himmelfarb, eds., *American Jewish Yearbook 1968,* vol. 69 (Philadelphia: Jewish Publication Society, 1968). Data for 1974 from Morris Fine and Milton Himmelfarb, eds., *American Jewish Yearbook 1976,* vol. 76 (Philadelphia: Jewish Publication Society, 1975). Data for 1978 from Morris Fine and Milton Himmelfarb, eds., *American Jewish Yearbook 1979,* vol. 79 (Philadelphia: Jewish Publication Society, 1978). Data for 1985 from Milton Himmelfarb and David Singer, eds., *American Jewish Yearbook 1986,* vol. 86 (Philadelphia: Jewish Publication Society, 1986). Data for 1991 from David Singer, ed., *American Jewish Yearbook 1992,* vol. 92 (Philadelphia: Jewish Publication Society, 1992). Data for 1999 from David Singer and Lawrence Grossman, eds., *American Jewish Yearbook 2000,* vol. 100 (Philadelphia: Jewish Publication Society, 2000). All other data from Jacob Rader Marcus, *To Count a People: American Jewish Population Data, 1585–1984* (Lanham, MD: University Press of America, 1990).

Notes

Introduction

1. Lee Shai Weissbach, *Jewish Life in Small-Town America* (New Haven, CT: Yale University Press, 2005), 4–5. Weissbach and I were working on small-town Jews simultaneously for a while. His work takes a national scope and concentrates on the years from about 1880 through the 1920s. The largest proportion of my regional work is focused on the nineteenth century. Any reader with an interest in small-town Jewish life should read Weissbach.

2. Frederick Jackson Turner, "The Significance of the Section in American History," in *History, Frontier, and Section: Three Essays* (Albuquerque: University of New Mexico Press, 1993), 93–116, 100 (Cutler quote).

3. Frederick Jackson Turner, *The Frontier in American History* (New York: Holt, Rinehart and Winston, 1962), 162.

4. Andrew R. L. Cayton and Peter S. Onuf, *The Midwest and the Nation: Rethinking the History of an American Region* (Bloomington: Indiana University Press, 1990), 126.

5. Kenneth Gladish, foreword to *Always a River: The Ohio River and the American Experience*, ed. Robert L. Reid (Bloomington: Indiana University Press, 1991), vii.

6. Jonathan D. Sarna and Nancy H. Klein, *The Jews of Cincinnati* (Cincinnati, OH: Center for the Study of the American Jewish Experience, Hebrew Union College, 1989), 1.

7. See, for example, H. Bennett Abdy, *On the Ohio* (New York: Dodd, Mead, 1919), 193–96; John Uri Lloyd, *Felix Moses: The Beloved Jew of Stringtown on the Pike* (Cincinnati, OH: Caxton Press, 1930); R. E. Banta, *The Ohio* (New York: Rinehart, 1949), 278–79; and examples cited in Maxwell Whiteman, "Notions, Dry Goods, and Clothing: An Introduction to the Study of the Cincinnati Peddler," *Jewish Quarterly Review* 53, no. 4 (April 1963): 319, 321.

1. On the Frontier

A version of this chapter appeared as "'Richest and Best Is the Wine of the West': The Ohio River Valley and the Jewish Frontier," *Ohio History* 112 (Winter–Spring 2003): 4–18.

1. Representatives of the Hebrew congregation in Cincinnati, OH, to the elders of the Jewish congregation at Charleston, SC, July 3, 1825, Bertram W. Korn Collection, American Jewish Archives, Hebrew Union College Jewish Institute of Religion, Cincinnati, OH (hereafter cited as AJA).

2. The term "frontier" has been the subject of much challenge and reinterpretation in academic circles in recent years. For a good summary of the controversy, see Patricia Nelson Limerick, "Frontier," in *A Companion to American Thought*, ed. Richard Wightman Fox and James T. Kloppenberg (Oxford: Blackwell, 1995), 255–59. Works on the Ohio Valley as well as on the classic American West (i.e., the western third or so of the continent) engage this controversy.

3. Frederick Jackson Turner, "The Significance of the Frontier in American History," in *History, Frontier, and Section*, 60, 69.

4. Gregory Nobles, *American Frontiers: Cultural Encounters and Cultural Conquest* (New York: Hill and Wang, 1997), xii.

5. Elizabeth Perkins, *Border Life: Experience and Memory in the Revolutionary Ohio Valley* (Chapel Hill: University of North Carolina Press, 1998), 78–79, 174.

6. Kim Gruenwald, *River of Enterprise: The Commercial Origins of Regional Identity in the Ohio Valley, 1790–1850* (Bloomington: Indiana University Press, 2002); Joe William Trotter Jr., *River Jordan: African American Urban Life in the Ohio Valley* (Lexington: University Press of Kentucky, 1998).

7. Jacob Rader Marcus, *The Colonial American Jew* (Detroit: Wayne State University Press, 1970), 3:1338–40.

8. Among the works that develop the idea of "Jewish frontiers" is Sander Gilman and Milton Shain, eds., *Jewries at the Frontier: Accommodation, Identity, Conflict* (Urbana: University of Illinois Press, 1999).

9. Captain Harry Gordon of the British Army's Western Department in Pennsylvania, 1766, quoted in Walter Havighurst, *River to the West: Three Centuries of the Ohio* (New York: Putnam, 1970), 20.

10. The story of the early Ohio River Valley is outlined in various standard state histories: George W. Knepper, *Ohio and Its People* (Kent, OH: Kent State University Press, 1989); James H. Madison, *The Indiana Way: A State History* (Bloomington: Indiana University Press, 1986); Lois A. Carrier, *Illinois: Crossroads of a Continent* (Urbana: University of Illinois Press, 1993); Otis K. Rice and Stephen W. Brown, *West Virginia: A History*, 2nd ed. (Lexington: University Press of Kentucky, 1993); and Lowell H. Harrison and James C. Klotter, *A New History of Kentucky* (Lexington: University Press of Kentucky, 1997). Important, more detailed studies are Andrew R. L. Cayton, *Frontier Indiana* (Bloomington: Indiana University Press, 1996); Stephen Aron, *How the West Was Lost: The Transformation of Kentucky from Daniel Boone to Henry Clay* (Baltimore: Johns Hopkins University Press, 1996); and R. Douglas Hurt, *The Ohio Frontier: Crucible of the Old Northwest, 1720–1830* (Bloomington: Indiana University Press, 1996).

11. Quoted in Eric Hinderaker, *Elusive Empires: Constructing Colonialism in the Ohio Valley, 1673–1800* (New York: Cambridge University Press, 1997), 174.

12. Darrel E. Bigham, "River of Opportunity: Economic Consequences of the Ohio," in Reid, *Always a River*, 135.

13. Quoted in Knepper, *Ohio and Its People*, 47.

14. Quoted in ibid., 61. For the ordinance generally, see Peter S. Onuf, *Statehood and Union: A History of the Northwest Ordinance* (Bloomington: Indiana University Press, 1987).

15. Hinderaker, *Elusive Empires*, 260.

16. St. Clair quoted in ibid., 245.

17. Hurt, *Ohio Frontier*, 160–86.

18. James P. Miller, *The Genesis of Western Culture: The Upper Ohio Valley, 1820–1825* (New York: DaCapo Press, 1969), x.

19. Not that the colonial Dutch authorities were pleased with these new arrivals. Governor Peter Stuyvesant and his council attempted to exclude Jews, first from residence and then from other rights and privileges, but these moves were blocked by the intervention of Dutch Jews who were investors in the Dutch West India Company.

20. Needless to say, the Jewish involvement in slave trading was nowhere near monopolistic or even significant, either to Jewish business or to the slave trade as a whole. See Eli Faber, *Jews, Slaves, and the Slave Trade* (New York: New York University Press, 1998).

21. The story of these Philadelphia-based merchants is told in Edwin Wolf II and Maxwell Whiteman, *The History of the Jews of Philadelphia from Colonial Times to the Age of Jackson* (Philadelphia: Jewish Publication Society, 1957); Sidney M. Fish, *Barnard and Michael Gratz: Their Lives and Times* (Lanham, MD: University Press of America, 1994); and Marcus, *Colonial American Jew.*

22. Some of these Jewish families were also intermarried with wealthy Christian families. David Franks married Margaret Evans, from a well-connected political family in Philadelphia; David's sister Phila, in New York, married Oliver DeLancey. They raised their children as Christians.

23. Myers's advertisement, *Pittsburgh Gazette*, October 14, 1793, reprinted in Allon Schoener, *The American Jewish Album: 1654 to the Present* (New York: Rizzoli, 1983), 39.

24. Quoted in Fish, *Barnard and Michael Gratz*, 155.

25. Jacob Feldman, *The Jewish Experience in Western Pennsylvania: A History, 1755–1945* (Pittsburgh: Historical Society of Western Pennsylvania, 1986), 3–6; Marcus, *Colonial American Jew*, 1:331. The hamlet of Gratz, Kentucky, about twenty miles from the Ohio River down the Kentucky River, is but a small indication of that family's importance in Kentucky history.

26. Bigham, "River of Opportunity," 130–79.

27. Malcolm J. Rohrbough, *The Trans-Appalachian Frontier: People, Societies and Institutions, 1775–1850* (New York: Oxford University Press, 1978), 104–38; Richard C. Wade, *The Urban Frontier: The Rise of Western Cities, 1790–1830* (Urbana: University of Illinois Press, 1996), 47; Cayton, *Frontier Republic*, 113.

28. Wade, *Urban Frontier*, 323–26, 324 (quote).

29. Rice and Brown, *West Virginia*, 81–85.

30. Cayton and Onuf, *Midwest and the Nation*, 53.

31. Estimates of American Jewish population in the eighteenth and nineteenth centuries cover a broad range because the records are insufficient to establish more exact numbers. The estimates in this chapter are from Ira Rosenwaike, *On the Edge of Greatness: A Portrait of American Jews in the Early National Period* (Cincinnati, OH: American Jewish Archives, 1985).

32. Eli Faber, *A Time for Planting: The First Migration, 1654–1820* (Baltimore: Johns Hopkins University Press, 1992), 142.

33. Quoted in Wade, *Urban Frontier*, 195.

34. David Philipson, "The Jewish Pioneers of the Ohio Valley," *Publications of the American Jewish Historical Society* 8 (1900): 43–57, 44 (quote).

35. Jacob Rader Marcus, ed., *Memoirs of American Jews, 1775–1865* (Philadelphia: Jewish Publication Society, 1955), 1:205.

36. Ibid., 1:208. The story of the Quaker was first told to David Philipson by Jonas's daughter. It is retold by Marcus in his introduction to Jonas's memoir. Ibid., 1:203.

37. The Seixas family had come to America from Portugal in 1730. Gershom Mendes Seixas was not an ordained rabbi, and he had only a modest Jewish education. His role was that of ḥazan (cantor), who led prayers. He was often referred to as the "minister" of New York City's Congregation Shearith Israel.

38. Philipson, "Jewish Pioneers of the Ohio Valley," 47.

39. The list is reprinted in Sarna and Klein, *Jews of Cincinnati*, 28. Entries for two of the men list no occupation.

40. Bene Israel means "sons (or children) of Israel." There are a wide variety of transliterations of the Hebrew word for "sons/children." I use the form that was used by each congregation itself.

41. Feldman, *Jewish Experience in Western Pennsylvania*, 12.

42. Surnames are not error-free markers. It is possible that Peter and Reuben Israel were non-Jews. Rabbi Morris Feuerlicht of Indianapolis, in an article about Indiana for the *Universal Jewish Encyclopedia*, claimed that the first Jewish settlement in the state was at Rising Sun, about twenty miles west of Cincinnati, in about 1825. Since Rising Sun had only six hundred inhabitants by 1833, it seems improbable that there was a Jewish community in a meaningful sense. However, it is not improbable that there was a single Jewish man or two—especially given the proximity to Cincinnati—and perhaps Feuerlicht was acquainted with a relative of one of these men. Morris Feuerlicht, "Indiana," in *Universal Jewish Encyclopedia* (New York: Universal Jewish Encyclopedia, 1941), 5:557.

43. See, for example, Stanley Chyet, "The Political Rights of the Jews in the United States, 1776–1840," *American Jewish Archives* 10 (April 1958): 14–75.

2. From Europe to the Ohio River Valley

1. The classic works on this transitional period are Jacob Katz, *Tradition and Crisis: Jewish Society at the End of the Middle Ages* (New York: New York University Press,

1993), and Jacob Katz, *Out of the Ghetto: The Social Background of Jewish Emancipation, 1770–1870* (Syracuse, NY: Syracuse University Press, 1998).

2. Katz, *Tradition and Crisis*, 41.

3. The changing situation in Germany, as summarized in the following paragraphs, is detailed in Steven M. Lowenstein, *The Mechanics of Change: Essays in the Social History of German Jewry* (Atlanta, GA: Scholars Press, 1992). For Alsace, see Paula Hyman, *The Emancipation of the Jews of Alsace: Acculturation and Tradition in the Nineteenth Century* (New Haven, CT: Yale University Press, 1991). Hasia Diner summarizes the background of Jewish emigrants in *A Time for Gathering: The Second Migration, 1820–1880* (Baltimore: Johns Hopkins University Press, 1992), 6–35.

4. Avraham Barkai, *Branching Out: German-Jewish Immigration to the United States* (New York: Holmes and Meier, 1994), 11.

5. Ibid., 9; Jonathan Sarna, *American Judaism: A History* (New Haven, CT: Yale University Press, 2004), 64. The course of the migration is outlined in Diner, *Time for Gathering*, 36–59.

6. Barkai, *Branching Out*, 9–10 (Germany); Diner, *Time for Gathering*, 56 (Bavaria and Poznań).

7. Lowenstein, *Mechanics of Change*, 136.

8. Data in this and the subsequent paragraph are from *Pinkas ha-kehilot: Entsiklopedyah shel ha-yishuvim ha-Yehudim le-min hivasdam ve-ad le-ahar Sho'at Milhemet ha'Olam ha-Sheniyah* [Record-book of the Communities: Encyclopedia of Jewish Communities from Their Founding until after World War II] (Jerusalem: Yad Va-Shem, 1969–1996). This series contains histories of all towns with Jewish populations in central and eastern Europe and a few other places. Unfortunately, it does not include Alsace.

9. Jonathan Sarna, ed., *The American Jewish Experience* (New York: Holmes and Meier, 1997), 359.

10. Knepper, *Ohio and Its People*, passim.

11. Jacob Rader Marcus, *To Count a People: American Jewish Population Data, 1585–1984* (Lanham, MD: University Press of America, 1990), 172–73.

12. Sarna and Klein, *Jews of Cincinnati*, 38.

13. Harrison and Klotter, *New History of Kentucky*, 99–103; Lewis N. Dembitz, "Jewish Beginnings in Kentucky," *Publications of the American Jewish Historical Society* 1 (1893): 100.

14. Feldman, *Jewish Experience in Western Pennsylvania*, 9, 15–30.

15. *Ohio Gazetteer* cited in William Alexander Mabry, "Industrial Beginnings in Ohio," *Ohio State Archaeological and Historical Quarterly* 55 (July–September 1946): 250–53; Madison, *Indiana Way*, 95–96; John Alexander Williams, *West Virginia: A Bicentennial History* (New York: Norton, 1976), 50.

16. Marcus quoted in Sarna and Klein, *Jews of Cincinnati*, 24.

17. A good study of peddling is Whiteman, "Notions, Dry Goods, and Clothing," 306–21. Also see Rudolf Glanz, "Notes on Early Jewish Peddling in America," *Jewish Social Studies* 7 (April 1945): 119–36.

18. Isaac Wolf Bernheim, *The Story of the Bernheim Family* (Louisville, KY: Morton, 1910).

19. Mary E. Thomas, comp., *Licenses to Travelling Merchants, Boat Stores, and Pedlars in Ohio, Taken from Records in the Jefferson County Court House, Steubenville, Ohio* (Reynoldsburg, OH: Research Unlimited, n.d.).

20. Estate of Moses (Morris) Frank, journals and wills book, vol. D, p. 163, Gallia County Probate Court, Gallipolis, OH.

21. Richard Warren Welch, "The Assimilation of an Ethnic Group: The German-Jewish Peddlers in the Upper Ohio Valley, 1790–1840" (master's thesis, Michigan State University, 1972), 39, 68, 86. Hyman Lazarus was Welch's great-great-grandfather.

22. For early Jews in Wheeling, see Harry Levi, *A Brief History of Congregation Leshem Shomayim, Wheeling, West Va.* (Wheeling, WV: Bullard Printing House, 1899). The Gumberts and Heiman families settled in Evansville. Congregation B'nai Israel, Washington Avenue Temple, one hundredth anniversary, 1857–1957, Evansville, IN, nearprint file, AJA. Two Jews who settled in Owensboro were Marcus Suntheimer and Samuel Moise. Paducah's pioneer Jewish families were those of Morris and Abraham Uri, D. Loewenstein, and Leopold Klaw. Morris Kahn was in Golconda, Bernard Baer and Lehman Tannhauser in Metropolis. Isaac Wolfe Bernheim, *History of the Settlement of Jews in Paducah and the Lower Ohio Valley* (Paducah, KY: Temple Israel, 1912), 14–22. Henry and Leon Adler settled in Lawrenceburg. *History of Dearborn, Ohio and Switzerland Counties, Indiana* (Chicago: Weakley, Harraman, 1885), 259. Mount Vernon's early Jewish residents were Moses and Daniel Rosenbaum, Levi Hartung, David and Louis Mendel, Sampson Oberdorfer, and Emanuel Wolf. Bernheim, *Jews in Paducah*, 17; W. P. Leonard, *History and Directory of Posey County* (Evansville: A. C. Isaacs, 1882), n.p.. Charles and Solomon Coblenz became citizens while living in Marietta. Journal of Court of Common Pleas, September 11, 1845, Washington County, Ohio, vol. 10, p. 214. The first burial in the Jewish section of Cairo's Villa Ridge cemetery was that of Harmon Rosenwater in 1853. Isaac Walder had a clothing store at the corner of Sixth Street and Ohio Levee in Cairo by 1857. Irene Hodge to Al Cohen (State Historical Records Survey), October 18, 1939, Cairo, IL, SC-206, folder 1, AJA. Samuel Newberger settled in Parkersburg around 1853. Abraham Shinedling, *West Virginia Jewry: Origins and History, 1850–1958* (n.p., 1963), 1127. For Bellaire, see Larry Good, "Brief Histories of All Synagogues in the City of Wheeling," 1989, SC-12958, AJA. Subscribers to the *Israelite* included the Wise brothers in Ironton, A. Epstein in Aurora, and E. Frohman and Frederic Gutman in Steubenville. *Israelite*, September 8, 1854, 72, September 22, 1854, 88, February 2, 1855, 240. J. Levinson of New Albany subscribed to the *Occident*. *Occident*, April–May 1855, 2A.

23. *Vorstands-Bericht des Deutschen Pionier-Vereins von Cincinnati, Ohio* [Report of the Board of Directors of the German Pioneer Society of Cincinnati, Ohio] (Cincinnati, OH: Rosenthal, 1892), 24; Whiteman, "Notions, Dry Goods, and Clothing," 314 (quote).

24. Barkai, *Branching Out*, 72.

25. Moch family, genealogies file, AJA.

26. Henrietta Evans and Mary P. Wood, eds., *Early Gallia County Court Records, 1846–1899* (Gallipolis, OH: Gallia County Historical and Genealogical Society, 1984); *Gallipolis (OH) Daily Tribune*, September 17, 1900; *Gallipolis (OH) Bulletin*, April 22, 1868; *Gallipolis (OH) Journal*, March 4, 1869.

27. Caryn Shoemaker, comp., Greenlawn Cemetery census, 1983, Portsmouth Historical Society, Portsmouth, OH; Elizabeth Weinberg, "Hoosier Israelites on the Ohio," *Indiana Jewish History* 27 (July 1991): 23a–23b, 44a–44b; Elizabeth Weinberg, "Bernhard Felsenthal's Madison," *Indiana Jewish History* 24 (October 1988): 8–10.

28. Stephen G. Mostov, "A 'Jerusalem' on the Ohio: The Social and Economic History of Cincinnati's Jewish Community, 1840–1875" (PhD diss., Brandeis University, 1981), 83; Henderson County cemetery censuses, n.d., Henderson County Public Library, Henderson, KY.

29. Barkai, *Branching Out*, 92–99 .

30. Bernheim, *Story of the Bernheim Family*, 13, 97.

31. *Portsmouth City Directory and Advertiser for 1856; Williams' Portsmouth City Directory for 1864–5* (Portsmouth: Stephenson and Patterson, 1864); *Portsmouth (OH) Times*, October 22, 1864, 4.

32. U.S. Census Office, manuscript census of the United States, publications M653-1008 (Meigs County, OH, 1860), M593-1242 (Meigs County, OH, 1870), and T9-1047 and 1048 (Meigs County, OH, 1880), National Archives and Records Administration, Washington, DC; *Pomeroy (OH) Tribune-Telegraph*, April 8, 1903, 4.

33. *Gallipolis (OH) Daily Tribune*, September 17, 1900, 1; *Gallipolis (OH) Journal*, February 9, 1854, 58; Evans and Wood, *Early Gallia County Court Records, 1846–1899*; *Die Deborah* (Cincinnati), February 22, 1861, 136, July 1, 1864, 4, September 15, 1865, 44, November 3, 1865, 71.

34. *Gallipolis Journal*, August 20, 1863, 99; *Die Deborah* (Cincinnati), July 29, 1864, 20; *Gallia County, Ohio, Birth Records*, vol. 1, 1864–81 (Gallipolis, OH: Gallia County Genealogical Society, 1993); U.S. Bureau of the Census, State of Ohio, 1860, 1870, 1880.

35. Shinedling, *West Virginia Jewry*, 1127; *Israelite*, September 8, 1854, 72; William A. Marsh, comp., *1880 Census of West Virginia* (Baltimore: Gateway Press, 1991), 12:167; *Gallipolis (OH) Daily Tribune*, September 17, 1900, 1.

36. Weinberg, "Bernhard Felsenthal's Madison," 2; *Portsmouth (OH) Times*, September 4, 1875, 3; Ruth Baldauf Levi, interview by the author, June 14, 1995; Arthur Baldauf, interview by Darrel Bigham, Evansville, IN, 1974, transcript, University of Southern Indiana Special Collections and University Archives, Evansville, 4; Herman Landau, *Adath Louisville: The Story of a Jewish Community* (Louisville, KY: Landau, 1981), 6, 22; Dinkelspiel genealogical charts provided by Ned Lewison, Baltimore, MD, July 2000.

37. Moch family, genealogies file; *American Israelite*, September 26, 1889, 2; *History of Lower Scioto Valley, Ohio* (Chicago: Interstate, 1884), 259–60; Shoemaker, Greenlawn Cemetery census.

38. Baldauf, interview, 3–4. Some writers have reported that the tiny town of Bran-

denburg, some thirty-five miles downstream from Louisville, was named for Colonel Solomon Brandenburg, a Jewish hero of the War of 1812. See Herman Landau, "Jews," in *The Kentucky Encyclopedia*, ed. John E. Kleber (Lexington: University Press of Kentucky, 1992), 470. However, there is no solid evidence of this.

39. Mostov, "'Jerusalem' on the Ohio," 238.

40. Diner, *Time for Gathering*, 85.

3. Finding and Founding Communities

1. Karl Raitz, ed., *The National Road* (Baltimore: Johns Hopkins University Press, 1996); Bigham, "River of Opportunity," 141–42.

2. "Railroads," in *The Reader's Companion to American History*, ed. Eric Foner and John A. Garraty (Boston: Houghton Mifflin, 1991), 906–7; Bigham, "River of Opportunity," 153; Michael Allen, "The Ohio River: Artery of Movement," in Reid, *Always a River*, 120.

3. See Charles Sellers, *The Market Revolution, 1815–1848* (New York: Oxford University Press, 1991).

4. Thomas, *Licenses to Travelling Merchants*. Needless to say, many peddlers probably tried to work without licenses when they could. For context, see Glanz, "Notes on Early Jewish Peddling," 119–36, and Whiteman, "Notions, Dry Goods, and Clothing," 306–21.

5. Virginia, vol. 34, p. 173 (1845), R. G. Dun & Co. Collection, Baker Library, Harvard Business School, Boston, MA; Shinedling, *West Virginia Jewry*, 1368.

6. Feldman, *Jewish Experience in Western Pennsylvania*, 15; Virginia, vol. 34, p. 121 (1857, 1861), R. G. Dun & Co. Collection.

7. Shinedling, *West Virginia Jewry*, 43.

8. Quoted in Glanz, "Notes on Early Jewish Peddling," 124.

9. *Occident*, November 1846, 405.

10. Marcus, *Memoirs of American Jews*, 3:3.

11. Merchants of Wheeling, WV, June 1891, SC-12959, AJA; Shinedling, *West Virginia Jewry*, 1563.

12. U.S. Census Office, manuscript census of the United States, publications M432-712 (Monroe County, OH, 1850) and M432-738 (Washington County, OH, 1850), National Archives and Records Administration. The following three paragraphs are also partially based on these censuses and on U.S. Census Office, manuscript census of the United States, publications M653-1048 and 1049 (Washington County, OH, 1860), National Archives and Records Administration.

13. Declarations of intention, May 23, 1842, Journal of the Court of Common Pleas, Washington County, OH, vol. 9, p. 195; naturalizations, September 11, 1845, Journal of the Court of Common Pleas, Washington County, OH, vol. 10, p. 214; Landau, *Adath Louisville*, 6; Weinberg, "Hoosier Israelites," 23a; *Marietta (OH) Intelligencer*, June 30, 1844 (quote).

14. Naturalizations, February 24, 1854, Journal of the Court of Common Pleas,

Washington County, OH, vol. 12, p. 318; marriage licenses, December 24, 1854, Washington County, OH.

15. Weinberg, "Hoosier Israelites," 33a.

16. Andrew R. L. Cayton and Paula R. Riggs, *City into Town: The City of Marietta, Ohio, 1788–1988* (Marietta, OH: Dawes Memorial Library, 1991), 129.

17. Cayton and Riggs, *City into Town*, 124.

18. Isaac Leeser, *Occident*, April 1852, 50–51.

19. *Indiana Gazetteer, or Topographical Dictionary of the State of Indiana* (1850; Knightstown, IN: Bookmark, 1977), 297.

20. Weinberg, "Hoosier Israelites," 22–24.

21. Ibid., 23a, 36a–b.

22. Weinberg, "Bernhard Felsenthal's Madison," 8–10, 18; Weinberg, "Hoosier Israelites," 6; *Israelite*, August 6, 1855, 39.

23. Weinberg, "Bernhard Felsenthal's Madison," 2; Weinberg, "Hoosier Israelites," 35, 26a–b.

24. Elizabeth Weinberg, "Visitor's Tour: Madison, Indiana's Jewish Community, 1849–1923," *Indiana Jewish History* 23 (April 1988): 11.

25. *Israelite*, January 29, 1869, 6.

26. Barkai, *Branching Out*, 78–79.

27. Weinberg, "Hoosier Israelites," 26a–b, 44a–b; U.S. Census Office, manuscript census of the United States, publication M653-1368 (Ohio County, VA, 1860), National Archives and Records Administration.

28. Ned Lewison, personal correspondence with the author, July 11, 2000 (Coblenz); Joseph P. Elliott, *A History of Evansville and Vanderburgh County, Indiana* (Evansville, IN: Keller, 1897), 467 (Gumberts).

29. *History of Posey County, Indiana* (1886; Evansville, IN: Unigraphic, 1967), 377–78.

30. The extensive literature on the development of the middle class and the effect on the family includes Nancy Cott, *The Bonds of Womanhood: "Woman's Sphere" in New England, 1780–1835* (New Haven, CT: Yale University Press, 1977); Mary P. Ryan, *Cradle of the Middle Class: The Family in Oneida County, New York, 1790–1865* (Cambridge: Cambridge University Press, 1981); and Glenna Matthews, *"Just a Housewife": The Rise and Fall of Domesticity in America* (New York: Oxford University Press, 1987). See also Nancy Cott's excellent article, "Domesticity," in *A Companion to American Thought*, ed. Richard Wightman Fox and James T. Kloppenberg (Cambridge, MA: Blackwell, 1995), 181–83.

31. For religious developments of the time, see Leon Jick, *The Americanization of the Synagogue, 1820–1870* (Hanover, NH: University Press of New England / Brandeis University Press, 1976).

32. This controversy is discussed in chap. 4.

33. Barkai, *Branching Out*, 82–83; Weinberg, "Bernhard Felsenthal's Madison," 18; *Israelite*, January 28, 1859, 238.

34. Diner, *Time for Gathering*, 88.

35. Ibid., 94–99.

36. Landau, *Adath Louisville*, 9, 181; Feldman, *Jewish Experience in Western Pennsylvania*, 19.

37. Lee Shai Weissbach, "Stability and Mobility in the Small Jewish Community: Examples from Kentucky History," *American Jewish History* 79 (1990): 360 (Owensboro); Bernheim, *History of the Settlement of Jews*, 29, 56, 62, 69 (Paducah); Levi, *Brief History of Congregation Leshem Shomayim*, 8 (Wheeling).

38. *Occident*, October 1855, 369 (Portsmouth); "Portsmouth, Ohio—Dedication—Lectures," *Israelite*, December 24, 1858, 199 (Portsmouth); *Israelite*, January 28, 1859, 238 (Pomeroy); Ohave Scholom Church, incorporation papers, February 19, 1868, photocopy from Meigs County recorder's office provided by Margaret Parker, Meigs County Historical Society, Pomeroy, OH (Pomeroy); *Chicago Reform Advocate*, "The Jews of Illinois—Part Second—Jewish Communities outside Chicago," May 4, 1901, 378 (Cairo); Congregation B'nai Israel, Washington Avenue Temple, one hundredth anniversary, 1 (Evansville); *Occident*, February 16, 1860, 281 (Evansville).

39. *Israelite*, February 26, 1864, 277, September 23, 1864, 101; Henny Evans (Gallia County Genealogical and Historical Society) to author, February 3, 1995; Congregation Beneh Abraham, congregational minute book, October 1878, Portsmouth, OH, AJA; Moch family, genealogies file.

40. Levi, *Brief History of Congregation Leshem Shomayim*, 16; Hebrew Lodge [Ladies'] Benevolent Association, incorporation papers April 15, 1868, photocopy from Meigs County recorder's office provided by Margaret Parker, Meigs County Historical Society.

41. Stanley R. Brav, "The Jewish Woman, 1861–1865," *American Jewish Archives* 17, no. 1 (April 1965): 50, 52. The gradual accession of women to synagogue membership is described in Karla Goldman, *Beyond the Synagogue Gallery: Finding a Place for Women in American Judaism* (Cambridge, MA: Harvard University Press, 2000), 55–59, 192–96.

42. The standard history is Deborah Dash Moore, *B'nai B'rith and the Challenge of Ethnic Leadership* (Albany: State University of New York Press, 1981).

43. Sarna and Klein, *Jews of Cincinnati*, 44 (Cincinnati); Landau, *Adath Louisville*, 181 (Louisville); Feldman, *Jewish Experience in Western Pennsylvania*, 42 (Pittsburgh); Congregation B'nai Israel, Washington Avenue Temple, one hundredth anniversary, 2 (Evansville); *Directory of the Lodges and Officers of the Independent Order of B'ne B'rith* (New York: n.p., 1900), 6 (Madison); *Chicago Reform Advocate*, "Jews of Illinois," 378 (Cairo); *Directory of the Lodges and Officers*, 6 (Paducah); Weissbach, "Stability and Mobility," 360 (Owensboro).

44. Bernheim, *History of the Settlement of Jews*, 56–61 (Paducah); *Chicago Reform Advocate*, "Jews of Illinois," 378 (Cairo).

45. Diner, *Time for Gathering*, 107–8; *Israelite*, March 19, 1869, 6 (Parkersburg).

46. *Parkersburg State Journal*, January 21, 1875, 4; *Historical Hand-Atlas [with] Outline Maps and Histories of Wood and Pleasants Counties, West Virginia* (Chicago: Hardesty, 1882), 226.

4. Religious Conflicts and Congruity

1. The exchange appears in the *Occident*, February 16, 1860, 281, March 22, 1860, 309–10, and May 17, 1860, 45–46, and in the *Israelite*, March 2, 1860, 275.

2. A. Irma (Mrs. Samuel) Cohon to Jacob R. Marcus, Max Del Banco, biographies file, AJA.

3. Congregation B'nai Israel, Washington Avenue Temple, one hundredth anniversary, 1.

4. The material on Reform in this and the following paragraphs is from the authoritative history of the movement, Michael A. Meyer, *Response to Modernity: A History of the Reform Movement in Judaism* (Detroit, MI: Wayne State University Press, 1988). For Berlin, see Steven Lowenstein, *The Berlin Jewish Community: Enlightenment, Family, and Crisis, 1770–1830* (New York: Oxford University Press, 1994).

5. Jews living outside Israel have, since the first century C.E., celebrated the major Jewish holidays of Pesaḥ (Passover), Shavuot, and Sukkot for two days, for reasons having to do with uncertainties about the Jewish lunar calendar. The second day is known as *yom tov sheni shel galuyot* (the Diaspora's second holiday).

6. See the discussion in chap. 2.

7. Meyer, *Response to Modernity*, 225.

8. Jick, *Americanization of the Synagogue*, 190–91.

9. Ibid., 45–57; Diner, *Time for Gathering*, 127–40.

10. Werner Cahnmann, "Village and Small Town Jews in Germany: A Typological Study," in *Leo Baeck Institute Year Book 19* (London: Secker and Warburg, 1974), 120.

11. See Lance Sussman, *Isaac Leeser and the Making of American Judaism* (Detroit, MI: Wayne State University Press, 1995).

12. Jick, *Americanization of the Synagogue*, 58–78.

13. Weinberg, "Hoosier Israelites," 1–47; *Die Deborah* (Cincinnati), January 18, 1856, 176, May 2, 1856, 302.

14. Bernhard Felsenthal, nearprint file, AJA; Weinberg, "Hoosier Israelites," 23a–23b, 26a–26b.

15. Emma Felsenthal, *Bernhard Felsenthal: Teacher in Israel* (New York: Oxford University Press, 1924), 15–17, 21.

16. The first article appeared in *Die Deborah* (Cincinnati), March 13, 1857, 237–38. All translations from the German are mine.

17. The second article appeared in *Die Deborah* (Cincinnati), March 20, 1857, 242–43. The words in italics appear in Hebrew characters in Felsenthal's article.

18. The final article appeared in *Die Deborah* (Cincinnati), March 27, 1857, 253–54.

19. *Madison (IN) Daily Evening Courier* quoted in Elizabeth Weinberg, "Adas Israel's First Teacher—Bernhard Felsenthal," *Indiana Jewish History* 24 (October 1988): 26; Moritz Mayer (rabbi in Charleston, SC) to Bernhard Felsenthal, 1856, cited in Victor Ludlow, "Bernhard Felsenthal: Quest for Zion" (PhD diss., Brandeis University, 1979), 23.

20. Ludlow, "Bernhard Felsenthal," 12, 23 (Frank); *Israelite* quoted in Weinberg, "Hoosier Israelites," 39.

21. Josephine Goldmark, *Pilgrims of '48* (New Haven, CT: Yale University Press, 1930), 195–225.

22. Wehle quoted in Gershom Scholem, *The Messianic Idea in Judaism* (New York: Schocken, 1971), 170.

23. Weinberg, "Hoosier Israelites," 23a–b, 26a–b, 36a–b; Elizabeth Weinberg, "August 3, 1855—The Dedication, Synagogue in Madison, Indiana," *Indiana Jewish History* 21 (August 1986): 11–22.

24. Karl Raitz, "The Face of the Country," in Raitz, *National Road*, 62.

25. Shinedling, *West Virginia Jewry*, 1327–31.

26. Isaac M. Fein, *The Making of an American Jewish Community: The History of Baltimore Jewry from 1773 to 1920* (Philadelphia: Jewish Publication Society, 1971), 90–91 (Wiesenfelds); Sonneborn family, genealogies file, Jewish Museum of Maryland, Baltimore (Sonneborns). The social and business connections between Wheeling residents and Baltimoreans are suggested in Levi, *Brief History of Congregation Leshem Shomayim*, 14, and confirmed by numerous social announcements in the contemporary Jewish press.

27. Meyer, *Response to Modernity*, 244–50.

28. Fein, *Making of an American Jewish Community*, 18, 38–41, 93.

29. Richard Walsh and William Lloyd Fox, eds., *Maryland: A History, 1632–1974* (Baltimore: Maryland Historical Society, 1974), 334, 413.

30. Isaac M. Fein, "Baltimore Jews during the Civil War," *American Jewish Historical Quarterly* 51 (December 1961): 69–75.

31. Ibid., 83–84.

32. *Sinai*, February 1859, 26–27; Har Sinai records, Jewish Museum of Maryland.

33. John Alexander Williams, *West Virginia: A Bicentennial History* (New York: Norton, 1976), 49; Kenneth W. Noe, *Southwest Virginia's Railroad: Modernization and the Sectional Crisis* (Urbana: University of Illinois Press, 1994), 2, 15–17; Charles H. Ambler, *Sectionalism in Virginia from 1776 to 1861* (Chicago: University of Chicago Press, 1910), 125 (quote).

34. Williams, *West Virginia*, 50, 82, 84 (quotes); Kenneth Nodyne, "Ohio County and the Election of 1860: A Preliminary Study," *Journal of the West Virginia Historical Association* 4 (Spring 1980): 20–21. In both 1850 and 1860, Ohio County (of which Wheeling is the seat) had the highest percentage of foreign-born residents of any Virginia county. See University of Virginia Library, Geospatial and Statistical Data Center, Historical Census Browser, http://fisher.lib.virginia.edu/collections/stats/histcensus/.

35. Lawrence Fuchs, *The Political Behavior of American Jews* (Glencoe, IL: Free Press, 1956), 35; Bertram Korn, "Jewish '48'ers in America," *American Jewish Archives* 2 (June 1949): 11–15; Fein, *Making of an American Jewish Community*, 99 (soldiers); Shinedling, *West Virginia Jewry*, 27 (soldiers). The editor of *Der Patriot* was Ph[ilip?] Rapport. Carol A. Scott, *Marriage and Death Notices of Wheeling, West Virginia, and the Tri-State Area, 1866–1870* (Apollo, PA: Closson Press, 1988), 3:29. Baltimore Jews split between the Union and Confederate armies.

36. George Atkinson and Alvaro Gibbens, *Prominent Men of West Virginia* (Wheeling, WV: Callin, 1890), 770–71.

37. Ibid., 770–71.

38. *Sinai*, October 1862, 257–58, November 1862, 287 (quote).

5. A Judaism for the Middle Class

1. Isaac Mayer Wise, *Israelite*, November 26, 1858, 166.

2. Richard L. Bushman, *The Refinement of America: Persons, Houses, Cities* (New York: Knopf, 1992), xiii.

3. Ibid., 347–48.

4. Jick, *Americanization of the Synagogue*, 82. For examples of synagogue buildings, see Diner, *Time for Gathering*, 167, 183–84.

5. Jick, *Americanization of the Synagogue*, 115–16, 182, 183 (quote).

6. Robert Wiebe, *The Search for Order, 1877–1920* (New York: Hill and Wang, 1967), 2, 4.

7. Jick, *Americanization of the Synagogue*, 151.

8. Meyer, *Response to Modernity*, 239. The full-length biography of Wise is Sefton D. Temkin, *Creating American Reform Judaism: The Life and Times of Isaac Mayer Wise* (London: Littman Library, 1998). More fun to read is Wise's own marvelously energetic *Reminiscences*, edited by his disciple Rabbi David Phillipson (Cincinnati, OH: Wise, 1901).

9. Wise, *Reminiscences*, 330–32.

10. Wise quoted in Temkin, *Creating American Reform Judaism*, 29.

11. Howe quoted in Sarna and Klein, *Jews of Cincinnati*, 4.

12. R. Carlyle Buley, *The Old Northwest: Pioneer Period, 1815–1840* (Bloomington: Indiana University Press, 1950), 1:423.

13. Eugene H. Roseboom, *A History of the State of Ohio*, vol. 4, *The Civil War Era: 1850–1873* (Columbus: Ohio Historical Society, 1944), 10.

14. *Israelite*, December 24, 1858, 199.

15. Diner, *Time for Gathering*, 160–62.

16. See Mary Ann Clawson, *Constructing Brotherhood: Class, Gender, and Fraternalism* (Princeton, NJ: Princeton University Press, 1989), and Steven C. Bullock, *Revolutionary Brotherhood: Freemasonry and the Transformation of the American Social Order, 1730–1840* (Chapel Hill: University of North Carolina Press, 1996).

17. Wise quoted in Diner, *Time for Gathering*, 162 (first quote); Wise quoted in *Israelite*, December 24, 1858, 199 (second quote).

18. Hasia Diner and Beryl Lieff Benderly, *Her Works Praise Her: A History of Jewish Women in America from Colonial Times to the Present* (New York: Basic Books, 2002), 113.

19. Karla Goldman, *Beyond the Synagogue Gallery: Finding a Place for Women in American Judaism* (Cambridge, MA: Harvard University Press, 2000), 78–99; Jonathan Sarna, "Mixed Seating in the American Synagogue," in *The American Synagogue: A Sanctuary Transformed*, ed. Jack Wertheimer (Hanover, NH: Brandeis University Press, 1987), 363–94; *Israelite*, October 7, 1864, 116 (Portsmouth).

20. Diner and Benderly, *Her Works Praise Her*, 114.

21. *Israelite* quoted in Brav, "Jewish Woman," 47.

22. *Israelite*, October 5, 1860, 106.

23. *Die Deborah* (Cincinnati), November 30, 1855, 120.

24. *Israelite*, September 27, 1861, 98.

25. *Israelite*, October 18, 1861, 125, May 2, 1862, 350. Traditionally, the Torah (the five books of Moses, in scroll form) is read in one year, in weekly installments. The practice of a triennial reading completes the Torah reading in three years; each week's portion is shorter.

26. *Israelite*, September 23, 1864, 101.

27. Ibid.; *Israelite*, March 5, 1869, 2.

28. *Israelite*, September 27, 1861, 98; Judith E. Endelman, *The Jewish Community of Indianapolis, 1849 to the Present* (Bloomington: Indiana University Press, 1984), 17–18.

29. *Israelite*, September 18, 1868, 5; Weinberg, "Visitor's Tour," 1–17. Weinberg, "Hoosier Israelites," 40; Weinberg, "Adas Israel's First Teacher," 32.

30. Bernheim, *History of the Settlement of Jews*, 65.

31. Congregation B'nai Israel, Washington Avenue Temple, one hundredth anniversary, 2. In the years before adequate (and adequately secular) public schools, many American Jewish communities supported their own full-day schools.

32. Ibid., 1.

33. *Israelite*, January 2, 1874, 6; K. K. Ansche Israel, constitution, [ca. 1912], microfilm 816, AJA.

34. *American Israelite*, April 23, 1875, 6. Wise changed the name of the paper from the *Israelite* to the *American Israelite* in July 1874, in a fit of optimism that "Americanized Judaism [was] now prevailing over the length and breadth of this country." Wise quoted in Temkin, *Creating American Reform Judaism*, 266.

Wise's account of the Parkersburg events reveals something intriguing about nineteenth-century American Judaism. According to halakhah, matrilineality determines Jewish identity; that is, the child of a Jewish father and non-Jewish mother is not considered Jewish, though the child of a Jewish mother and non-Jewish father is. However, there is no reference to Lilly Rauch's being converted before her wedding. The prevalence of such incidents in nineteenth-century America suggests widespread de facto recognition of patrilineality as well as matrilineality long before the practice was validated de jure by the Reform movement in 1983. See Dana Kaplan, "Conversion to Judaism: A Historical Perspective," *Judaism* 48 (Summer 1999): 259–74.

35. *American Israelite*, April 23, 1875, 6.

36. Quoted in Alan Silverstein, *Alternatives to Assimilation: The Response of Reform Judaism to American Culture, 1840–1930* (Hanover, NH: University Press of New England, 1994), 49.

37. Silverstein, *Alternatives to Assimilation*, 49; *Proceedings of the Union of American Hebrew Congregations*, vol. 1, 1873–1879 (Cincinnati, OH: Bloch, 1879), 8, 15, 30.

38. Congregation Beneh Abraham, congregational minute book, June 29, 1874.

39. *Proceedings of the Union of American Hebrew Congregations*, 20, 66, 81, 137.

40. Arthur Hertzberg, *The Jews in America: Four Centuries of an Uneasy Encounter* (New York: Simon and Schuster, 1989), 112, 117; Henry Feingold, *Zion in America* (New York: Hippocrene, 1974), 112. As far as Hertzberg's biases, his subtitle says it all. Despite what Feingold asserts, no historian has demonstrated that German American Jews took up Christianity—even in its Unitarian form—in large numbers.

41. Diner, *Time for Gathering*, 141.

42. Congregation Oheb Shalom, articles of incorporation, Lawrence County, OH, corp. book 1, 1874, Ironton, OH, histories file, AJA (Ironton); S. O. Heilbronner, "History of the Jews and the Congregation Adas Israel" (manuscript, 1942), SC-4902, AJA (Henderson); *American Israelite*, September 12, 1879, 3 (Gallipolis).

43. Jick, *Americanization of the Synagogue*, 191–93.

6. The Community within a Community

1. U.S. War Department, *The War of the Rebellion: A Compilation of the Official Records of the Union and Confederate Armies* (Washington, DC: GPO, 1887), ser. 1, vol. 17, pt. 2, p. 424, quoted in Bertram W. Korn, *American Jewry and the Civil War* (New York: Atheneum, 1970), 122–23.

2. Korn, *American Jewry and the Civil War*, 122.

3. The most detailed and contextualized analysis of this incident is Stephen V. Ash, "Civil War Exodus: The Jews and Grant's General Orders No. 11," *Historian* 44, no. 4 (August 1982): 505–23.

4. Korn, *American Jewry and the Civil War*, 159–63; Ash, "Civil War Exodus," 508.

5. Ash, "Civil War Exodus," 511.

6. Korn, *American Jewry and the Civil War*, 124–26.

7. Bernheim, *History of the Settlement of Jews*, 33; Grant quoted in Ash, "Civil War Exodus," 511; Korn, *American Jewry and the Civil War*, 122 (quote). Interestingly, Isaac Wolfe Bernheim's local history mentions the "period of unrest and insecurity" but not the expulsion. Perhaps, as a lifelong Republican, he was embarrassed by Grant's actions.

8. Korn, *American Jewry and the Civil War*, 16.

9. Bernheim, *History of the Settlement of Jews*, 18, 37–46, 52, 78.

10. Wise quoted in Temkin, *Creating American Reform Judaism*, 174.

11. Ibid., 180–83.

12. Ibid., 183–84.

13. *Cincinnati Daily Enquirer* quoted in Korn, *American Jewry and the Civil War*, 43. The term "shoddy" originally meant "short wool carded or worn from the inside of the cloth, without fibre or tenacity, and with no capability of wear, and yet easily made into the semblance of more durable goods." With the outbreak of the Civil War, the term was applied to inferior goods foisted on the federal government by unscrupulous war profiteers; it then also became a pejorative nickname for these alleged profiteers. By further extension, the term was soon used broadly to include, in contemporary words, "swindling and humbug of every character." Since many Jewish firms contracted to

provide army supplies, especially uniforms, the dynamic of antisemitism quickly turned "shoddy" into a synonym for "Jew." Gary L. Bunker and John Appel, "'Shoddy,' Anti-Semitism and the Civil War," *American Jewish History* 82 (1994): 43–71.

14. *Portsmouth (OH) Times*, October 1, 1864, 3.

15. *Cincinnati Enquirer* quoted in Korn, *American Jewry and the Civil War*, 130.

16. Jonathan Sarna, "Anti-Semitism and American History," *Commentary*, March 1981, 42–47.

17. For the competitiveness perspective, see John Higham, *Send These to Me: Immigrants in Urban America* (Baltimore: Johns Hopkins University Press, 1984), esp. chaps. 5 and 6; for the religious developments perspective, see Naomi Cohen, *Encounter with Emancipation: The German Jews in the United States, 1830–1914* (Philadelphia: Jewish Publication Society, 1984), 249–85, and Leonard Dinnerstein, *Antisemitism in America* (New York: Oxford University Press, 1994), xix–xxviii.

18. Louise Mayo, *The Ambivalent Image: Nineteenth-Century America's Perception of the Jew* (Rutherford, NJ: Fairleigh Dickinson University Press, 1988); Jonathan Sarna, "The 'Mythical Jew' and the 'Jew Next Door' in Nineteenth-Century America," in *Anti-Semitism in American History*, ed. David A. Gerber (Urbana: University of Illinois Press, 1986), 57–78.

19. Sarna, "'Mythical Jew,'" 70–73.

20. Ibid., 68–70.

21. *Portsmouth (OH) Times*, October 18, 1873, 3, February 27, 1886, 3.

22. Ilse Dorsch Horacek, ed., *It Was Written* (Mount Vernon, IN: Posey County Historical Society, 1983), 12, 163, 47, 11, 79.

23. Bernheim, *History of the Settlement of Jews*, 53 (Weil); *Portsmouth (OH) Times*, April 10, 1875, 3 (Mayer); Samson D. Oppenheim, ed., *American Jewish Year Book 5679*, vol. 20, September 7, 1918–September 24, 1919 (Philadelphia: Jewish Publication Society, 1918), 228 (Kahn); Baldauf, interview (Baldauf); Shinedling, *West Virginia Jewry*, 1169 (Zilenziger).

24. Bernard Allen, *Parkersburg: A Bicentennial History* (Parkersburg, WV: Bicentennial Committee / Woodroof Enterprises, 1985), 49 (Prager); *Portsmouth (OH) Times*, July 5, 1873, 3; Bernard Mandel, "Religion and the Public Schools of Ohio," *Ohio State Archaeological and Historical Quarterly* 58, no. 2 (April 1949): 185–206.

25. Barkai, *Branching Out*, 175–90; Carl Wittke, "Ohio's Germans, 1840–1875," *Ohio Historical Quarterly* 66, no. 4 (October 1957): 339–54. Statistics for Portsmouth and Scioto County calculated from U.S. Census Office, *Ninth Census: 1870*, vol. 1 (Washington, DC: GPO, 1872).

26. Ohio, vol. 70, p. 96 (1871), R. G. Dun & Co. Collection (Emsheimer); Virginia, vol. 34, p. 173 (1845), R. G. Dun & Co. Collection (Ballenberg).

27. Indiana, vol. 50, p. 109 (1862), R. G. Dun & Co. Collection (Moses); Indiana, vol. 50, p. 108 (1861), R. G. Dun & Co. Collection (Hoffstadt); Ohio, vol. 110, p. 84 (1858), R. G. Dun & Co. Collection (Newberger); West Virginia, vol. 34, p. 173 (1845), R. G. Dun & Co. Collection (Graff); Ohio, vol. 70, pp. 11, 33 (1863), R. G. Dun & Co. Collection (Franks).

28. Ohio, vol. 110, pp. 112, 216 (1876), R. G. Dun & Co. Collection (Weiler); Ohio, vol. 110, p. 148 (1879), R. G. Dun & Co. Collection (Newberger:); Ohio, vol. 110, p. 146/6 (1877), R. G. Dun & Co. Collection (Newman); David Gerber, "Ethnics, Enterprise, and Middle-Class Formation: Using the Dun and Bradstreet Collection for Research in Ethnic History," *Immigration History Newsletter* 12, no. 1 (May 1980): 4.

29. West Virginia, vol. 34, p. 121 (1864), R. G. Dun & Co. Collection.

30. David Gerber, "Cutting Out Shylock: Elite Anti-Semitism and the Quest for Moral Order in the Mid-Nineteenth-Century American Marketplace," in Gerber, *Anti-Semitism in American History*, 217.

31. Ohio, vol. 70, p. 77 (1865), R. G. Dun & Co. Collection (Emsheimer); Ohio, vol. 70, p. 202 (1884), R. G. Dun & Co. Collection (Moch).

32. West Virginia, vol. 34, p. 9 (1860, 1867), vol. 35, p. 303 (1879), R. G. Dun & Co. Collection.

33. *Portsmouth (OH) Times*, April 10, 1875, 3, August 12, 1871, 3.

34. *Owensboro (KY) Examiner*, August 17, 1877, quoted in Lee Shai Weissbach, *The Synagogues of Kentucky* (Lexington: University Press of Kentucky, 1995), 168.

35. This style was also popular in Europe at the time. See Geoffrey Wigoder, *The Story of the Synagogue* (San Francisco: Harper and Row, 1986). For the cultural roots of this aesthetic, see Ismar Schorsch, "The Myth of Sephardic Supremacy," in *Leo Baeck Institute Year Book 34* (London: Secker and Warburg, 1989), 47–66.

36. *Israelite*, September 16, 1864, 93.

37. *Israelite*, October 7, 1864, 116; *Portsmouth (OH) Times*, September 10, 1864, 3.

38. *Israelite*, October 7, 1864, 116.

39. *Portsmouth (OH) Times*, October 1, 1864, 3.

40. *Gallipolis (OH) Dispatch*, March 26, 1869, 4; *Gallipolis (OH) Bulletin*, May 5, 1869, 3; *Gallipolis (OH) Dispatch*, May 7, 1869, 4.

41. *Gallipolis (OH) Bulletin*, March 3, 1869, 3; *Gallipolis (OH) Dispatch*, March 5, 1869, 3.

42. *Israelite*, February 5, 1869, 5. Anne C. Rose, *Beloved Strangers: Interfaith Families in Nineteenth-Century America* (Cambridge: Harvard University Press, 2001), looks at Jewish-Christian and Protestant-Catholic marriages in the context of changing American culture. She emphasizes how these families and others viewed the phenomenon; her goal is to "describe thoughts and feelings," not to "chart quantifiable trends" (12).

43. *Israelite*, December 9, 1864, 189.

44. Hasia Diner is skeptical when assessing local reports about Jewish communal activity. She argues that nineteenth-century newspaper articles constantly "gauged the worth of Judaism": that is, complimentary remarks subtly implied negative judgments—for example, mentions of the "grandeur" of Jewish weddings reflected suspicion of an alleged Jewish "tendency to flaunt wealth." She suggests Protestants viewed any praise of Judaism or its institutions as a critique of Christianity. Diner, *Time for Gathering*, 183, 184, 196. But in the local Ohio River Valley papers, such stories do not stand out from their context (in subject or writing style) in any negative way. Especially when Diner suggests that newspaper reporters' praises of new synagogues (as, for

example, "most superior") contained an implicit critique of Jewish ostentation, she underestimates the importance of booster rhetoric in small-town newspapers. Almost everything in small towns was "superior" in local eyes—from the new store on Main Street to the size and quality of farmer Smith's eggs. A case in point is the description of Portsmouth's Catholic churches in a local history, which uses similarly extravagant language: the churches "present a worthy and lasting monument to the enterprise and religious zeal of the people of that religion," and one of these Portsmouth edifices is "among the finest in the state." Costs for everything—construction, pipe organ, altars—are included. *History of Lower Scioto Valley*, 217–19. When costs are mentioned in stories about synagogues, Diner interprets it as an obsession with Jewish wealth. Diner here treats Jews as curiously passive objects—not at all her usual approach.

45. Higham, *Send These to Me*, 126.

46. Ibid., 141, 144.

47. *Sheppard's Marietta City Directory for 1873 and 1874* (Cincinnati, OH: J. S. Sheppard, 1873); Ohio, vol. 193, p. 236 (1878), and vol. 194, p. 333 (1876), R. G. Dun & Co. Collection.

48. Ohio, vol. 194, p. 318 (1875), R. G. Dun & Co. Collection (Hurwitz); Ohio, vol. 194, p. 425 (1882), R. G. Dun & Co. Collection (Luchs); *Marietta (OH) Register*, September 16, 1887, 1 (Sulzbacher).

49. Ohio, vol. 194, pp. 425, 496 (1886), R. G. Dun & Co. Collection; *Marietta (OH) Times*, May 15, 1907, 1; Great Council of Ohio Improved Order of Red Men, fifty-fifth great sun session, Marietta, OH, May 13–16, 1907, souvenir program; L. G. Austin, comp., *Illustrated History and Business Review of Washington County, Ohio, for the Year 1891* (Coshocton, OH: Union, 1891).

50. *Marietta (OH) Register*, September 16, 1887, 1; Ohio, vol. 98, p. 170 (1888), R. G. Dun & Co. Collection; Austin, *Illustrated History and Business Review*, 166–67.

51. *Marietta (OH) Times*, July 19, 1888; *Marietta (OH) Weekly Leader*, July 17, 1888.

52. Quoted in Cayton and Riggs, *City into Town*, 170–71, 172.

53. Diner, *Time for Gathering*, 229.

7. Maintaining Community

1. Bigham, "River of Opportunity," 155–57.

2. Diner, *Time for Gathering*, 80–81.

3. Lee Shai Weissbach, "The Jewish Communities of the United States on the Eve of Mass Migration: Some Comments on Geography and Bibliography," *American Jewish History* 78 (1988): 83 (quote), 87, 89.

4. This analysis is based on the same data set that Weissbach used, with the addition of some Ohio River towns not listed there.

5. Weissbach, "Jewish Communities of the United States," 92.

6. Weissbach, "Stability and Mobility," 372.

7. Weissbach, "Jewish Communities of the United States," 91.

8. *American Israelite*, April 5, 1900 (Ironton); Eugene B. Willard, *A Standard History of the Hanging Rock Iron Region of Ohio* ([Chicago?]: Lewis, 1916), 775–76 (Ironton); *American Israelite*, September 26, 1889 (Gallipolis); *Gallipolis (OH) Bulletin*, September 23, 1884, 3 (Gallipolis; quote); *Pomeroy (OH) Tribune-Telegraph*, April 8, 1903, 4 (Pomeroy).

9. Heilbronner, "History of the Jews"; Frieda J. Dannheiser, *The History of Henderson County, Kentucky* (Henderson, KY: Henderson County Genealogical and Historical Society, 1978), 302 (quote).

10. Bernheim, *History of the Settlement of Jews*, 73.

11. *Chicago Reform Advocate*, "Jews of Illinois," 378.

12. Congregation Beneh Abraham, congregational minute book, April 27, 1867, October 9, 1870.

13. Diner, *Time for Gathering*, 134–35, 217–18.

14. Congregation Beneh Abraham, congregational minute book, November 4, 1877, April 23, 1876, October 28, 1877.

15. Ibid., January 7, 28, 1872, April 27, 1874, August 29, 1875; *Portsmouth (OH) Times*, September 4, 1875, 3 (Mayer's obituary).

16. *American Israelite*, October 3, 1879, 2, October 17, 1879, 7.

17. Congregation Beneh Abraham, one hundredth anniversary, 1858–1958, 8, Portsmouth, OH, nearprint file, AJA; Simon Gerstmann, biographies file, AJA.

18. Congregation Beneh Abraham, congregational minute book, December 21, 1873, June 11, 1876; Wise quoted in *Portsmouth (OH) Times*, August 8, 1874, 3; *Portsmouth (OH) Times*, June 17, 1876, 2 (gift).

19. Congregation Beneh Abraham, congregational minute book, July 2, November 12, 1876, February 11, March 11, April 22, May 6, June 17, 1877, March 3, April 21, 1878, May 11, June 1, 1879.

20. Congregation Beneh Abraham, congregational minute book, June 15, 1879, May 23, 1880; *Portsmouth (OH) Times*, September 18, 1886, 3 (Eichelstein obituary).

21. *History of Lower Scioto Valley*, 219, 132.

22. Congregation Beneh Abraham, congregational minute book, September 9, 1889; *Portsmouth (OH) Times*, August 15, 1874, 3, November 13, 1880, 3.

23. Congregation Beneh Abraham, congregational minute book, [July?] 1882, October 14, 1883, June 8, July 11, December 6, 1884.

24. Ibid., November 14, 21, December 5, 12, 1886, January 7, December 11, 20, 1887, January 22, August 12, 27, 1888.

25. Ibid., September 9, 1888; Maurice Shapiro to Jacob R. Marcus, December 11, 1968, SC-10904, AJA.

26. Congregation Beneh Abraham, congregational minute book, May 17, 1889, November 11, 1900, October 13, 1901; Shapiro to Marcus, December 11, 1968.

27. Silverstein, *Alternatives to Assimilation*, 135–36.

28. Congregation Beneh Abraham, congregational minute book, November 10, 1901, October 14, 1906; Heilbronner, "History of the Jews" (Henderson).

29. Silverstein, *Alternatives to Assimilation*, 125–26, 185–89; *American Israelite*, "Circuit Work in West Virginia," November 26, 1903, 5.

30. Shinedling, *West Virginia Jewry*, 874, 963–64; *Chicago Reform Advocate*, "A History of the Jews of Huntington," October 7, 1916, 4–11; *Israelite*, August 8, 1873, 6 (quote).

31. Shinedling, *West Virginia Jewry*, 874–75, 891, 899; *American Israelite*, "Circuit Work in West Virginia," 5; *Chicago Reform Advocate*, "History of the Jews of Huntington," 4–11.

32. Congregation B'nai Israel, program for centennial service, May 11, 1956, Parkersburg, WV, manuscript collection 427, AJA. It is possible that this Jewish community was more closely inbred than other Ohio Valley communities. Of the twelve identifiably Jewish women who married in Wood County between 1880 and 1925, four married Jewish men from Wood County, and four others married Jewish men from other places in West Virginia. All married Jewish men. Wes Cochran, ed., *Wood County, W.V., Marriages 1880–1925* (n.p., n.d.). Given the difficulty of establishing exact and meaningful quantification in the case of small communities, I cannot claim too much, but these are interesting numbers considering the small Jewish marriage pool in West Virginia.

33. *Menorah*, October 1896, 250.

34. *American Israelite*, "Circuit Work in [West] Virginia," December 10, 1903, 5.

35. Ibid.

36. Congregation B'nai Israel, program for centennial service; town data card—Parkersburg, 1909, box 123, Industrial Removal Office papers, American Jewish Historical Society (hereafter cited as IRO papers).

37. Congregation B'nai Israel records, October 29, November 10, 1909, April 11, November 26, 1910, February 15, 1912, Parkersburg, WV.

38. Ibid., January 10, 1910, January 23, 1916, April 3, 1930, June 20, 1935.

39. Ibid., correspondence file (pledges); Congregation B'nai Israel, program for centennial service.

40. Moch family, genealogies file; *Gallipolis (OH) Daily Tribune*, February 15, 1960 (obituary of Emma Moch Ingels), June 28, 1965 (obituary of Blanche Moch Smith), March 16, 1967 (obituary of Joe Moch).

41. Dreyfuss family, genealogies file, AJA. Even in the nineteenth century, some American rabbis performed intermarriages. Meyer, *Response to Modernity*, 290. For example, in 1893, Rabbi Emil Hirsch of Chicago married Marcus Sulzer of Madison, Indiana, and Lida Griffith, whose father was a Baptist minister in the nearby town of Vevay. The couple's children were raised observing some of both religions; at least one eventually chose Christianity. Elizabeth Weinberg, "Families and Personalities' (typescript, 1998), 8, small collections 14470, AJA.

42. *Marietta (OH) Register*, March 3, 1898, 7.

43. *Die Zeitung* (Marietta, OH), March 10, 1898, 1; *Marietta (OH) Times*, March 9, 1898, 1.

44. *Marietta (OH) Times*, March 9, 1898, 1; *Marietta (OH) Register*, March 3, 1898, 7; *Die Zeitung* (Marietta, OH), March 10, 1898, 1; *American Israelite*, March 17, 1898, 6; *American Israelite*, June 9, 1898, 7; *Die Zeitung* (Marietta, OH), March 10, 1898, 2.

45. U.S. Census Office, manuscript census of the United States, publications T623-1330 and 1331 (Washington County, OH, 1900), National Archives and Records Administration. Between 1881 and 1910, more than a quarter-million Jews from the Austro-Hungarian Empire immigrated to the United States; 85 percent of them came from Galicia. Arieh Tartakower, "Jewish Migratory Movements in Austria in Recent Generations," in *The Jews of Austria: Essays on their Life, History, and Destruction*, ed. Josef Fraenkel (London: Valentine, Mitchell, 1967), 285–310. Galicia is now split between western Poland and eastern Ukraine.

8. The East European Immigration and the Reconfiguration of Community

1. For the east European Jewish immigration and acculturation to America, see Gerald Sorin, *A Time for Building: The Third Migration, 1880–1920* (Baltimore: Johns Hopkins University Press, 1992). In *The Jews of the United States* (Berkeley: University of California Press, 2004), Hasia Diner views the central and east European migrations as two peaks in a larger wave of European Jewish migration from 1820 to 1920, thus emphasizing commonalities. Basic works on the mass migration in general include John Bodnar, *The Transplanted: A History of Immigrants in Urban America* (Bloomington: Indiana University Press, 1985), and Walter Nugent, *Crossings: The Great Transatlantic Migration, 1870–1914* (Bloomington: Indiana University Press, 1992).

2. Lee Shai Weissbach demonstrates in the case of Kentucky how the Jewish populations of cities benefited more from the east European migration than did those of small towns. More than half of the post-1880 Jewish immigrants in Kentucky settled in Louisville. Lee Shai Weissbach, "Kentucky's Jewish History in National Perspective: The Era of Mass Migration," *Filson Club History Quarterly* 69, no. 3 (July 1995): 255–74.

3. Ibid., 263; Feldman, *Jewish Experience in Western Pennsylvania*, 180–86. The east European immigration to Cincinnati is covered in Sarna and Klein, *Jews of Cincinnati*, 61–83. An excellent discussion of German-Russian tensions is in Moses Rischin, *The Promised City: New York's Jews, 1870–1914* (Cambridge, MA: Harvard University Press, 1962), 95–111.

4. Feldman, *Jewish Experience in Western Pennsylvania*, 143; Sarna and Klein, *Jews of Cincinnati*, 64–66; Weissbach, "Kentucky's Jewish History," 263.

5. The original "treyfe banquet" menu, in all its Victorian glory, is reproduced in Sarna, *American Judaism*, 146.

6. The complete text of the Pittsburgh Platform of 1885 appears in Meyer, *Response to Modernity*, 387–88; it is discussed on 264–70.

7. This defection led to the creation of a new American Jewish religious movement, eventually to become known as Conservative. This movement is discussed in chap. 10.

8. Meyer, *Response to Modernity*, 270.

9. Congregation Beneh Abraham, congregational minute book, May 26, June 30, 1895.

10. Feldman, *Jewish Experience in Western Pennsylvania*, 68–88 (Pittsburgh); Sarna and Klein, *Jews of Cincinnati*, 79 (Cincinnati); Weissbach, "Kentucky's Jewish History," 264 (Louisville); Meyer, *Response to Modernity*, 292 (UAHC).

11. Elliott, *History of Evansville and Vanderburgh County*, 275; *History of Vanderburgh County, Indiana* (Madison, WI: Brant and Fuller, 1889), 304.

12. Elliott, *History of Evansville and Vanderburgh County*, 275.

13. Town data card—Evansville, 1907, box 123, IRO papers; town data report—Evansville, 1912, box 83, IRO papers; William Gumberts, interview by Darrel Bigham, 1982, transcript, 3, 11–12, University of Southern Indiana Special Collections and University Archives, Evansville. The materials in the IRO collection at the American Jewish Historical Society, which provide the information in this chapter, include town data cards (summaries of data on local communities) and correspondence from traveling agents, prospective and actual "removals," and local employers and Jewish community leaders.

14. Merchants of Wheeling, WV, June 1891; Levi, *Brief History of Congregation Leshem Shomayim*, 17–18, 20–22.

15. Levi, *Brief History of Congregation Leshem Shomayim*, 23.

16. Town data card—Wheeling, 1909, box 123, IRO papers; Oppenheim, *American Jewish Yearbook 5679*, 344; Good, "Brief Histories of All Synagogues"; Shinedling, *West Virginia Jewry*, 1492–95. For a general view of the cigar industry and Jewish involvement in it, see Patricia Cooper, *Once a Cigar Maker: Men, Women, and Work in American Cigar Factories, 1900–1919* (Urbana: University of Illinois Press, 1987).

17. Congregation B'nai Israel, constitution and bylaws, 1946, Huntington, WV, AJA; Shinedling, *West Virginia Jewry*, 875, 883, 961. Ohab Sholem did not join the UAHC until 1935. Shinedling quotes one observer who suggested that only then could they "safely 'join the Union' without arousing too much ill will and disfavor on the part of the Orthodox membership" (894). It is unclear why this would have been the case, since by then there was an Orthodox option in town. Perhaps some people maintained memberships in both, for historical reasons or for the sake of communal unity, and until the Orthodox community was firmly established, the radical step of formally affiliating with the very liberal UAHC was too alienating.

18. Shinedling, *West Virginia Jewry*, 876, 963–64, 918.

19. The general population of Paducah grew from 4,500 in 1860 to 19,000 in 1900, but the Jewish population grew from about 200 in 1870 to only about 250 in 1900. Weissbach, "Stability and Mobility," 357–58, 363, 372; Weissbach, "Kentucky's Jewish History," 267.

20. Congregation Beneh Abraham, congregational minute book, January 6, February 16, April 8, 1906, October 5, 1919; Congregation Beneh Abraham, one hundredth anniversary.

21. Congregation Beneh Abraham, congregational minute book, October 6, 1893,

March 31, May 26, 1895, January 26, August 2, September 20, 1896, February 5, 1926. The *American Jewish Yearbook* lists Portsmouth's total Jewish population as 128 in 1918. Oppenheim, *American Jewish Yearbook 5679*, 53.

22. Congregation Beneh Abraham, congregational minute book, August 12, September 16, 1894.

23. *Portsmouth (OH) Daily Times*, "Men Who Helped Make Portsmouth," March 6, 1924, 1.

24. *Portsmouth (OH) Daily Times*, "Samuel Horchow Passes Away in Columbus Hospital," March 21, 1924, 3.

25. Henry Goldstein to David Bressler, May 19, 1908, traveling agents, box 19, IRO papers.

26. *Menorah*, April 1897, 238 (Newport); Weissbach, *Synagogues of Kentucky*, 153, 155 (Newport); Leslie Lassetter, "The Story of Covington's Schule, The Temple of Israel," 7–8, nearprint—geography file, AJA (Covington); Weissbach, *Synagogues of Kentucky*, 151 (Covington).

The Covington congregation's fund-raising approach was unique: they enlisted the help of Covington's (non-Jewish) mayor, George Phillips, who agreed without knowing quite what to do. He turned for advice to a prominent local Jewish leader, Rabbi David Philipson at HUC. "The Jewish people of this City have honored me by making me Chairman of a campaign for the purpose of raising the amount of $3,000.00 to pay off the indebtedness of the new Church they are building here," the mayor wrote to Philipson, asking for his help in "speaking to some influential Jewish person for a liberal donation." The rabbi was not amused. Although it was welcome and praiseworthy for non-Jews to contribute to such causes, he noted in reply, it was certainly not usual for a non-Jew to be a campaign chairman: "This work should be done by Jews." In a postscript, Philipson asked Phillips for the address of the congregational treasurer so that he himself might forward a donation—and, perhaps, also a rebuke. In Philipson's eyes, the request to the mayor may have smacked of a ghetto mentality of appealing to the ruler for favors. Or perhaps it smacked of the embroilment of immigrant Jews in the corruption-ridden hurly-burly of early-twentieth-century city politics. One can only speculate on the Covington community's motives. George Phillips to Rabbi David Philipson, September 13, 1915, photocopy in Northern Kentucky Jewish family reunion file, AJA; Rabbi David Philipson to George Phillips, September 21, 1915, Rabbi David Philipson papers, manuscript collection 35, box 1, file 15, AJA (photocopy in Northern Kentucky Jewish family reunion file, AJA).

27. Congregation Beneh Abraham, congregational minute book, June 29, 1873; town data card—Ashland, 1909, box 123, IRO papers; Shinedling, *West Virginia Jewry*, 52, 57, 61, 1082, 1357.

28. Dave Rabinovitz to David M. Bressler, January 21, 1910, traveling agents, Ohio file, IRO papers; *Pinkas ha-kehilot*, 6:75 (Plavinas); *Marietta (OH) Times*, May 6, 1907, 1.

29. Henry Goldstein [to David Bressler?], May 28, 1908, traveling agents, box 19, IRO papers.

30. Congregation Binae Israel, congregational minute book, April 23, September 8,

October 14, 1900, July 23, 1901, October 1, 1905, February 24, 1902, May 17, 1903, September 7, 1907, Marietta, OH, photocopy and translation from the Yiddish provided by Robert Beren; *American Israelite*, June 9, 1898, 7 (cemetery).

31. Aaron Rothkoff, *Bernard Revel* (Philadelphia: Jewish Publication Society, 1972), 143; *Marietta (OH) Register-Leader*, June 25, 1909, 4–5; *Marietta (OH) Daily Times*, June 25, 1909, 5. In the 1910s and 1920s, Sarah Rabinowitz's family provided substantial support for Revel's project of reviving the institution that became, under his leadership, Yeshiva University.

32. Some steel and coal companies even employed Jewish immigrants directly to run their company stores when those Jews spoke the dominant language of the non-Jewish east European workers. Robert Perlman, *From Shtetl to Milltown: Litvaks, Hungarians, and Galizianers in Western Pennsylvania, 1875–1926* (Pittsburgh: Historical Society of Western Pennsylvania, 2001), xii, 32.

33. Ewa Morawska, *Insecure Prosperity: Small-Town Jews in Industrial America, 1890–1940* (Princeton, NJ: Princeton University Press, 1996).

34. Feldman, *Jewish Experience in Western Pennsylvania*, 100, 156.

35. Herschel Rubin, "Notes for Program for Kiwanis Club of East Liverpool, Ohio" (typescript, August 22, 1991). I used this and several other related items while they were in the possession of Herschel Rubin of East Liverpool; they were subsequently forwarded (with a considerable amount of other material) to AJA, where they are available under Congregation Beth Shalom, manuscript collection 602 (hereafter cited thus).

36. James Alfred White, "Immigrants and Immigrant Groups in Steubenville: 1860–1920" (master's thesis, Ohio State University, 1967), passim; town data report—Steubenville, 1906, box 123, IRO papers; Paul Tobin, interview by the author, August 1994.

37. Congregation B'nai Israel, golden anniversary jubilee, 1902–52, Steubenville, OH, provided by Jerome Endich.

38. Ibid., 5; "History of Congregation B'nai Israel to 1976," 5–6, provided by Jerome Endich; Feldman, *Jewish Experience in Western Pennsylvania*, 259, 272–75.

39. Edward Muller, "Metropolis and Region: A Framework for Enquiry into Western Pennsylvania," in *City at the Point: Essays on the Social History of Pittsburgh*, ed. Samuel P. Hays (Pittsburgh: University of Pittsburgh Press, 1989), 197; Feldman, *Jewish Experience in Western Pennsylvania*, 195–96, 204–6; Sons of Israel Congregation, charter, 1918, Midland, OH, histories file, AJA (Midland); Ladies' Aid Society, minutes, 1921–1935, microfilm 1029, AJA (Coraopolis); Oppenheim, *American Jewish Yearbook 5679*, 62 (Aliquippa). It is unclear how long Sons of Israel Congregation lasted; after it folded, Midland Jews affiliated with the Orthodox Congregation B'nai Jacob in East Liverpool, Ohio.

40. Feldman, *Jewish Experience in Western Pennsylvania*, 205; Perlman, *From Shtetl to Milltown*, 62.

41. Nandor Marton, "The Jewish History of Weirton, W. Va." (typescript, 1953), 1, 3, histories file, AJA; Irwin Bogarad, interview by the author, February 25, 1996;

Shinedling, *West Virginia Jewry*, 1256; Oppenheim, *American Jewish Yearbook 5679*, 54, 64.

42. Eva Wasbutzky, "Remembrances of East Liverpool's Early Jewish Community" (typescript, April 5, 1976); Congregation B'nai Israel, articles of incorporation, June 27, 1919; Temple B'nai Israel, dedication booklet, May 14, 1922; Rubin, "Notes for Program for Kiwanis Club," all in Congregation Beth Shalom, manuscript collection 602, AJA.

43. *American Israelite*, November 14, 1889, 6, February 28, 1901, 2; *Menorah*, August 1896, 109; Laurance F. Good, "Brief History of the Sons of Israel Congregation" (typescript, 1989), SC-823, AJA; Good, "Brief Histories of All Synagogues." Rabbi Judah Wechsler was married in Bellaire in 1855 to Jeannette Rosenbach of Cumberland, Maryland; Isaac Strouse, who served as ḥazan in Wheeling a few years later, performed the ceremony. *Die Deborah* (Cincinnati), November 30, 1855, 120.

44. Town data card—Bellaire, 1907, box 123, IRO papers; Herman Bernstein, ed., *American Jewish Yearbook 5675*, vol. 16, September 21, 1914–September 8, 1915 (Philadelphia: Jewish Publication Society, 1914), 372.

45. Jacob A. Riis, *How the Other Half Lives* (1901; New York: Dover, 1971), 19; Dinnerstein, *Antisemitism in America*, 61 (quote).

46. The history of the IRO is detailed in Jack Glazier, *Dispersing the Ghetto: The Relocation of Jewish Immigrants across America* (Ithaca, NY: Cornell University Press, 1998). Robert Rockaway focuses on the "removals" themselves, largely in their own words, in *Words of the Uprooted: Jewish Immigrants in Early Twentieth-Century America* (Ithaca, NY: Cornell University Press, 1998). Unfortunately, Rockaway does not give an unbiased view of German-Russian relations: he blames antagonisms on Germans' "arrogance" and "hysterical reactions," in response to which Russians reacted only with "dignity and [an] assertive manner" (205–7).

47. Glazier, *Dispersing the Ghetto*, 143, 196.

48. Henry Goldstein to David Bressler, May 19, 1908, traveling agents, box 19, IRO papers.

49. Stanley Bero to David Bressler, January 29, 1910, traveling agents, box 19, IRO papers.

50. Town data card—Bellaire, 1907, box 123, IRO papers; Stanley Bero to David Bressler, November 3, 1907, traveling agents, box 19, IRO papers.

51. Bero to Bressler, November 3, 1907; Henry Goldstein to David Bressler, June 2, 1908, traveling agents, box 19, IRO papers.

52. Stanley Bero to David Bressler, June 18, 1910, traveling agents, box 19, IRO papers. This Luchs was a relative of the Luchs brothers in Marietta.

53. M. Leschinsky to IRO, December 1904, Gershon Sibulsky to IRO, May 1905, and C. H. Edelman to IRO, January 1905, in immigrant correspondence, Ohio, IRO papers; Charles Lando to IRO, April 17, 1904–November 11, 1904, local agents, Bellaire, OH, IRO papers; Goldstein to Bressler, June 2, 1908. Some documents were translated from the original Yiddish by the IRO.

9. Communities at Maturity

1. For American Jewish life and culture after the east European mass migration, see Henry L. Feingold, *A Time for Searching: Entering the Mainstream, 1920–1945* (Baltimore: Johns Hopkins University Press, 1992). A colorful look at New York's defining Jewish cultural milieu is Irving Howe, *World of Our Fathers* (New York: Harcourt Brace, 1976).

2. Moore, *B'nai B'rith and the Challenge*, 101.

3. "Purim Entertainment Given by the Religious Schools of Congregation B'nai Israel, Steubenville, Ohio, 1925" souvenir program, 25, provided by Jerome Endich.

4. Works Progress Administration, Historical Records Survey—church survey forms of Ohio, 1978, box 6, Ohio Historical Society, Columbus (Bellaire); Feldman, *Jewish Experience in Western Pennsylvania*, 204–6 (Coraopolis and Rochester); Good, "Brief Histories of All Synagogues" (Coraopolis and Rochester).

5. "History of Agudas Achim Synagogue," Bellaire, OH, SC-12958, AJA; "Sons of Israel Congregation," Bellaire, OH, SC-823, AJA.

6. Pamela S. Nadell, *Women Who Would Be Rabbis: A History of Women's Ordination, 1889–1985* (Boston: Beacon Press, 1998), 138–41; Sisterhood of Temple B'nai Israel, minute book, December 9, 1929, [1919]–1933, East Liverpool, OH, small collections 3012, AJA.

7. Ewa Morawska notes this also with respect to Johnstown, Pennsylvania. Morawska, *Insecure Prosperity*, 138.

8. The material on the East Liverpool sisterhood is drawn from the Sisterhood of Temple B'nai Israel minute book. For more about sisterhoods, see Jenna Weissman Joselit, "The Special Sphere of the Middle-Class American Jewish Woman: The Synagogue Sisterhood, 1890–1940," in Wertheimer, *American Synagogue*, 206–30.

9. Sisterhood of Temple B'nai Israel, minute book, November 1, 1923.

10. Ibid., April 30, 1923.

11. Lassetter, "Story of Covington's Schule," 9.

12. *Chicago Reform Advocate*, "History of the Jews of Huntington"; *Ashland (KY) Daily Independent*, religion supplement, December 6, 1994.

13. Temple Beth El, silver anniversary, 1924–1949, 4, Steubenville, OH, AJA

14. "Purim Entertainment Given," 6. For more about the development of late Friday services, see Silverstein, *Alternatives to Assimilation*, 105, and Meyer, *Response to Modernity*, 219.

15. Meyer, *Response to Modernity*, 264.

16. Congregation B'nai Israel, golden anniversary jubilee, 6.

17. William R. Hutchison, *Religious Pluralism in America* (New Haven, CT: Yale University Press, 2003), 196.

18. *East Liverpool (OH) Evening Review*, January 4, 21, 24, 25, 26, 1916.

19. *East Liverpool (OH) Evening Review*, January 28, February 1, 1916. For the importance of this relief drive to American Jewish unity, see Sorin, *Time for Building*, 208.

20. Horace Kallen, "Democracy versus the Melting-Pot," *Nation*, February 25, 1915, 220.

21. "Order of Service at the Dedication of the Temple B'nai Israel," May 14, 1922, Congregation Beth Shalom, manuscript collection 602.

22. *Portsmouth (OH) Daily Times*, "Fitting Excercises [*sic*] Mark the Dedication of the New Temple," January 5, 1925.

23. This background is detailed in Melvin I. Urofsky, *American Zionism from Herzl to the Holocaust* (Garden City, NY: Anchor Press, 1975), 44–163.

24. *Letters of Louis D. Brandeis*, ed. Melvin I. Urofsky and David W. Levy (Albany: State University of New York Press, 1973–75), 3:316, 415, 441, 4: 4–7.

25. Shinedling, *West Virginia Jewry*, 1120; "Purim Entertainment Given" (Steubenville); Marton, "Jewish History of Weirton," 4 (Weirton).

26. Thomas A. Kolsky, *Jews against Zionism: The American Council for Judaism, 1942–1948* (Philadelphia: Temple University Press, 1990), 206–7. Another rabbi-congregant marriage was that of Ruth Wolf of Wheeling and Harry Levi, who was rabbi there at the turn of the twentieth century. Shuly Rubin Schwartz, *The Rabbi's Wife: The Rebbetzin in American Jewish Life* (New York: New York University Press, 2006), 246–47.

27. Congregation Leshem Shomayim, sixtieth anniversary celebration booklet, 1916, nearprint file, AJA.

28. Marc Lee Raphael, *Abba Hillel Silver: A Profile in American Judaism* (New York: Holmes and Meier, 1989). Silver was also a student rabbi in Huntington, where the local newspapers praised his sermons (14–15).

29. Kolsky, *Jews against Zionism*, 187. Many supporters abandoned the American Council for Judaism after the establishment of the State of Israel; those who remained were increasingly on the fringe of American Judaism. After 1967, the organization was effectively defunct.

30. Dinnerstein, *Antisemitism in America*, 35. Dinnerstein's is the best history of the topic.

31. *Marietta (OH) Daily Times*, December 18, 1899, 1.

32. Gumberts, interview.

33. David Chalmers, *Hooded Americanism: The History of the Ku Klux Klan* (New York: Watts, 1981), 156, 177–78, 176, 180.

34. Ibid., 176, 180; Dinnerstein, *Antisemitism in America*, 98.

35. Chalmers, *Hooded Americanism*, 163–64; Robert M. Taylor Jr., ed., *Indiana: A New Historical Guide* (Indianapolis: Indiana Historical Society, 1989), 191.

36. Gus Cohen, interview by Darrel Bigham, 1982, University of Southern Indiana Special Collections and University Archives; Baldauf, interview.

37. William Jenkins, *Steel Valley Klan: The Ku Klux Klan in Ohio's Mahoning Valley* (Kent, OH: Kent State University Press, 1990), 39–54, 117–39; Congregation B'nai Israel, golden anniversary jubilee. This document does not tell the outcome of the meeting.

38. *Marietta (OH) Register-Leader*, February 26, 1923; Helen Josephy Robeson, interview by the author, 1977, White Plains, NY. After her postcollege stint with the

Marietta (OH) Times, Josephy went to Paris to write for *Vogue*. She made a terrific impression in Marietta when, in 1929, she published a travel book, *Paris Is a Woman's Town*, in collaboration with Mary Margaret McBride, later a well-known radio personality. Bookstores in Marietta filled their windows with copies of the book, and Josephy spoke at numerous gatherings. The *Times* modestly carried the story of the publication on page five of its June 6, 1929, edition but could not help printing a laudatory article about its former employee two days later, proclaiming, "Anything Miss Josephy writes should be well worth reading." The book was, in fact, a best seller.

39. Allen Rupp, "A History of the Marietta Rotary Club" (typescript, 1970), 31, in the author's possession; *Marietta (OH) Times*, February 26, 1923.

40. Congregation B'nai Israel, congregational minute book, 1927–1935, East Liverpool, OH, SC-1513, AJA.

41. Ibid., March 8, 1932, August 17, 1933.

42. Congregation Beneh Abraham, congregational minute book, June 7, 1929; Daniel Elazar, *Community and Polity: The Organizational Dynamics of American Jewry*, rev. ed. (Philadelphia: Jewish Publication Society, 1995), 213–14.

43. Elizabeth Weinberg, "Then There Was One" (typescript, n.d.), 1, SC-14682, AJA; Congregation Ansche Israel, constitution and minutes, 1839–1981, Mount Vernon, IN, microfilm 816, AJA; Works Progress Administration, Historical Records Survey, Cairo, IL, [1938 or 1939], SC-206, AJA. Members of the Kronenberg and Hoffstadt families remained in Madison for over a century; a third-generation Hoffstadt (a single woman) died in the family home in 1986 at age ninety-three. Weinberg, "Visitor's Tour," 8.

44. Bernard Bailyn, Robert Dallek, David B. Davis, David Herbert Donald, John L. Thomas, and Gordon S. Wood, *The Great Republic: A History of the American People*, 4th ed. (Lexington, MA: D. C. Heath, 1992), 2:355.

45. Weissbach, "Stability and Mobility," 365.

46. *Marietta (OH) Register-Leader*, June 30, 1909; Congregation Binae Israel, congregational minute book, December 29, 1938. These minutes are recorded in English and Yiddish on facing pages; the English improved considerably in thirty years.

47. Dr. Jules Duga (Columbus, OH; formerly of Bellaire, OH) to the author, July 31, 1994; Marc Lee Raphael, *Jews and Judaism in a Midwestern Community: Columbus, Ohio, 1840–1975* (Columbus: Ohio Historical Society, 1979), 164–65.

48. Lee Levinger, "Jews in the Liberal Professions in Ohio," *Jewish Social Studies* 2, no. 4 (October 1940): 434.

10. The Demise of Community

1. John Corrigan and Winthrop Hudson, *Religion in America: An Historical Account of the Development of American Religious Life* (Upper Saddle River, NJ: Pearson/Prentice-Hall, 2004), 385; Robert S. Ellwood, *The Fifties Spiritual Marketplace: American Religion in a Decade of Conflict* (New Brunswick, NJ: Rutgers University Press, 1997), 5; Sarna, *American Judaism*, 277.

2. For the story of one survivor couple who did choose a small town (in the Ohio River Valley, close to—though not on—the river), see Julie Salamon, *The Net of Dreams: A Family's Search for a Rightful Place* (New York: Random House, 1996).

3. Robert Shosteck, *Small-Town Jewry Tell Their Story: A Survey of B'nai B'rith Membership in Small Communities in the United States and Canada* (Washington, DC: B'nai B'rith Vocational Service Bureau, 1953), 20–21, 36, 48.

4. *Ironton (OH) Tribune*, February 23, 1990, 3E.

5. *Marietta (OH) Times*, August 16, 1980, 1+.

6. Shinedling, *West Virginia Jewry*, 917; *Ashland (KY) Daily Independent*, religion supplement, December 6, 1994, 30.

7. Congregation B'nai Jacob, congregational minute book, March 8, 1949, Congregation Beth Shalom, manuscript collection 602. What is apparently the last reference to paying a communal shoḥet is in the meeting minutes of late 1955.

8. B'nai Jacob record book, May 2, 1949. For ecumenism in this era, see Ellwood, *Fifties Spiritual Marketplace*; for the community relations movement, see Stuart Svonkin, *Jews against Prejudice: American Jews and the Fight for Civil Liberties* (New York: Columbia University Press, 1997). The classic analysis of American society's "three great faiths" is Will Herberg, *Protestant, Catholic, Jew: An Essay in American Religious Sociology* (Garden City, NY: Doubleday).

9. Neil Gillman, *Conservative Judaism* (New York: Behrman House, 1993), 34.

10. Ibid., 91; Jack Wertheimer, "The Conservative Synagogue," in Wertheimer, *American Synagogue*, 116, 123.

11. Quoted in Wertheimer, "Conservative Synagogue," 118.

12. "History of Congregation B'nai Israel," 11.

13. Ibid., 12–14. It is not clear if these women were members on their own or through their husbands' memberships, or if their board membership included voting privileges.

14. See Jonathan Sarna, "The Debate over Mixed Seating in the American Synagogue," in Wertheimer, *American Synagogue*, 379–86.

15. *Portsmouth (OH) Times*, October 13, 1958, 16. Beneh Abraham is the oldest only on the north side of the river; the Reform congregation in Wheeling is older.

16. In the case of Marietta, important segments of civic leadership were ambivalent about industrialization and growth, and there seems to have been a very definite decision to remain a small town. See Paula Roush Riggs, "Marietta, Ohio: A Town and Its Images, 1888–1938" (PhD diss., Case Western Reserve University, 1975). Also see Cayton and Riggs, *City into Town*, 245–49.

17. Lee Shai Weissbach, "Decline in an Age of Expansion: Disappearing Jewish Communities in the Era of Mass Migration," *American Jewish Archives* 49, nos. 1–2 (1997): 39–61. Cairo acquired a building for a new synagogue in the late 1950s, but still the congregation did not last past the mid-1970s. Janey Solomon (Cairo, IL), in telephone conversation with the author, January 2005.

18. Weissbach, "Decline in an Age of Expansion," 54.

19. Congregations B'nai Israel, minutes and correspondence, correspondence

folder, Report of Planning Committee, March 6, 1960, Parkersburg, WV, manuscript collection 427, AJA.

20. Quoted in *Ashland (KY) Daily Independent*, December 6, 1994, 25.

21. "History of Congregation B'nai Israel," 14–21; Temple Beth El, silver anniversary; "A Salute to Our Past Presidents," twentieth anniversary of temple building, November 21, 1986, typescript provided by Jerome Endich.

22. "History of Congregation B'nai Israel," 18.

23. Preamble to merger agreement, January 8, 1980, Temple Beth Israel files, Steubenville, OH, photocopy provided by Rabbi Kenneth Milhander.

24. Congregation B'nai Jacob, congregational minute book, February 2, 1948.

25. Congregation B'nai Israel, congregational minute book, October 1, 1962; Congregation B'nai Jacob, congregational minute book, October 1, 1962; Beth Shalom, trustees minute book, March 9, 1965, June 16, 1965.

26. The Huntington and Evansville congregations are in functional respects Reform but remain, for historical reasons, affiliated with both the Union for Reform Judaism (successor to the Union of American Hebrew Congregations) and the United Synagogue of Conservative Judaism (successor to the United Synagogue of America). These dual affiliations should technically be impossible because of several critical and irreconcilable differences between the movements, even (since 1983) with respect to the definition of who is a Jew.

27. Temple Shalom (Congregation L'Shem Shomayim), articles of merger, Temple Shalom files, Wheeling, WV, photocopy provided by Rabbi Daniel Lowy; merger agreement, January 8, 1980, Temple Beth Israel files, photocopy provided by Rabbi Kenneth Milhander; Congregation Beth Shalom, constitution, regulations, and bylaws, 1963 draft, East Liverpool, OH. Many Reform congregations celebrate Jewish holidays not on their actual date but on the nearest Friday evening. It is unclear when and where this practice originated.

28. Dr. Alexander S. Fisher to Beth Shalom trustees, September 25, 1966, in Beth Shalom, trustees minute book, 1964–69; Rabbi Richard Levy, in telephone conversation with the author, 1996.

29. *Ashland (KY) Daily Independent*, religion supplement, December 6, 1994, August 17, 1986 (Ashland); Good, "Brief History of the Sons of Israel Congregation" (Bellaire); Bogarad, interview (Weirton).

30. Congregation Binae Israel, congregational minute book, March 12, 1972.

31. Quoted in *Denver Intermountain Jewish News*, May 19, 1989, B1.

32. Congregation Binae Israel, congregational minute book, January 12, 1995; Robert Beren (Wichita, KS) to the author, 1997; Lela Gae Beren Jacoby, interview by the author, Encino, CA, 1997.

33. "The Jewish Community of Northern Kentucky: A Brief History," Northern Kentucky Jewish family reunion file.

34. Lassetter, "Story of Covington's Schule," 23–25.

35. Muller, "Metropolis and Region," 200–204; Feldman, *Jewish Experience in Western Pennsylvania*, 185–86.

36. Lou Zell (Ambridge, PA), in telephone conversation with the author, 1995.

37. Beth Samuel Jewish Center, http://www.bethsamuel.org/.

38. Rabbi Shalom Bell, in telephone conversation with the author, 1995; Rabbi Shoshana Kaminsky, in telephone conversation with the author, 2002; Beth Samuel Jewish Center, http://www.bethsamuel.org/.

39. Lee Levinger, "The Disappearing Small-Town Jew: Report on a Dwindling Tribe," *Commentary*, August 1952: 157–63.

Conclusion

1. Union for Reform Judaism, http://www.urj.org/. In 2003, the Union of American Hebrew Congregations voted to replace its historically significant nineteenth-century name, which had idealistic—and never-realized—overtones of national Jewish unity, with one that more explicitly refers to its religious philosophy. The same consideration prompted the United Synagogue of America to change its name to the United Synagogue of Conservative Judaism in 1992.

2. Rabbi Daniel Lowy to the author, 1997.

3. Jerome Endich to the author, 1994.

4. Lee Shai Weissbach, "Bearing Witness," *Kentucky Humanities*, Winter 1994, 3. Attempting to explain the weakness of Jewish life in Owensboro today, Weissbach hypothesizes that although Owensboro currently has a substantial population, the small size of the pre–World War II Jewish community discouraged chain migration and other Jewish settlement. Weissbach to the author, March 2002.

5. Congregation Beneh Abraham, new temple dedication, April 25, 1975, near-print file, AJA.

6. *Cincinnati Enquirer*, "Upstart Dueling a Daily," July 30, 1995, G1–3.

7. *Ashland (KY) Sunday Independent*, August 17, 1986; *Ashland (KY) Daily Independent*, religion supplement, December 6, 1994.

8. *Time*, "The Great Escape," December 8, 1997, 54; Norman Crampton, *The 100 Best Small Towns in America* (New York: Prentice Hall, 1993, 1995). Crampton uses 5,000–15,000 population as his definition of a small town.

9. *New York Times*, January 16, 2000, Y41 (Newport), November 7, 1999, Y48 (Lawrenceburg); Taylor, *Indiana*, 123 (Madison).

10. *Jewish Week*, "Movement of Jews into Small Cities Puts New Life into Congregations," July 13, 1984; Evelyn Pitasky, "The Jewish Community: Marietta, Ohio (1970–1980)" (paper, Marietta College, 1983), 1–2.

11. Sidney Goldstein and Alice Goldstein, *Jews on the Move: Implications for Jewish Identity* (Albany: State University of New York Press, 1996), 48.

12. Ibid., 49, 87.

13. National Jewish Population Survey 2000–2001, available from United Jewish Communities, http://www.ujc.org/ (affiliation data); *Jewish Week*, "Movement of Jews into Small Cities."

14. Marty Weil (Ironton, OH) to the author, 1994 (Ashland); Bogarad, interview (Weirton).

15. "Celebration of the Century: Northern Kentucky Jewish Families," program book, October 9, 1994, provided by Rita Goldhoff; Rita Goldhoff (Cincinnati) to the author, 1994.

16. Ze'ev Chafets, *Members of the Tribe: On the Road in Jewish America* (New York: Bantam Books, 1988), 93.

17. Eugen Schoenfeld, "Small-Town Jews: A Study in Identity and Integration" (PhD diss., Southern Illinois University, 1967), 175.

18. Ibid., 178.

19. Rabbi Larry Kaplan to Zelma, August 12, 1966, Rabbi Larry Kaplan papers, AJA.

20. Weinberg, "Hoosier Israelites," 3; Joyce Rubin, interview by the author, Los Angeles, March 25, 1997; Efran quoted in Howard V. Epstein, *Jews in Small Towns: Legends and Legacies* (Santa Rosa, CA: Vision Books International, 1997), 493.

21. Salamon, *Net of Dreams*, 6.

22. Quoted in Epstein, *Jews in Small Towns*, 542.

23. Steven M. Cohen and Arnold M. Eisen, *The Jew Within: Self, Family, and Community in America* (Bloomington: Indiana University Press, 2000).

24. Robert L. Reid, introduction to *Always a River*, xv–xvi.

25. Both Levy's speech and the statement of principles are available at Central Conference of American Rabbis, http://www.ccarnet.org/. Levy was a student rabbi in East Liverpool in 1963–64.

26. The statement of principles that Levy supported passed the conference in the face of fierce opposition from elements who saw it as Reform's caving in to resurgent Orthodoxy. Only time will tell if this turn to tradition is as significant a juncture as the turn away from tradition in the original Pittsburgh Platform.

Bibliographic Essay

American Jewish History

The most complete resource is the first four volumes of a five-volume set, *The Jewish People in America*, published by Johns Hopkins University Press in 1992. These volumes include Eli Faber, *A Time for Planting: The First Migration, 1654–1820*; Hasia Diner, *A Time for Gathering: The Second Migration, 1820–1880*; Gerald Sorin, *A Time for Building: The Third Migration, 1880–1920*; and Henry L. Feingold, *A Time for Searching: Entering the Mainstream, 1920–1945*. A recent, comprehensive history is Hasia Diner, *The Jews of the United States* (Berkeley: University of California Press, 2004). Jonathan Sarna's *American Judaism: A History* (New Haven, CT: Yale University Press, 2004) is a masterful study emphasizing religious life.

Regional History

My basic sources included the following state histories: George W. Knepper, *Ohio and Its People* (Kent, OH: Kent State University Press, 1989); James H. Madison, *The Indiana Way: A State History* (Bloomington: Indiana University Press, 1986); Lois A. Carrier, *Illinois: Crossroads of a Continent* (Urbana: University of Illinois Press, 1993); Otis K. Rice and Stephen W. Brown, *West Virginia: A History*, 2nd ed. (Lexington: University Press of Kentucky, 1993); and Lowell H. Harrison and James C. Klotter, *A New History of Kentucky* (Lexington: University Press of Kentucky, 1997). There is a new history of Ohio, written for the state's bicentennial by Andrew R. L. Cayton, titled *Ohio: The History of a People* (Columbus: Ohio State University Press, 2002).

This book is part of the Ohio River Valley Series. The first publication in the series, which includes studies of aspects of the Ohio River as a geographic, economic, and cultural entity, is Robert L. Reid, ed., *Always a River: The Ohio River and the American Experience* (Bloomington: Indiana University Press, 1991). Two other works in the series were very useful. Joe William Trotter Jr.'s *River Jordan: African American Urban Life in the Ohio Valley* (Lexington: University Press of Kentucky, 1998) is an overview of one ethnic group's experience. For the small-town experience generally and the role of the river in local development, a good study is Darrel Bigham's *Towns and Villages of the Lower Ohio* (Lexington: University Press of Kentucky, 1998).

I found the following useful in understanding the nature of American regionalism: *All over the Map: Rethinking American Regions* by Edward L. Ayers, Patricia Nelson Limerick, Stephen Nissenbaum, and Peter S. Onuf (Baltimore: Johns Hopkins University Press, 1996); "Regionalism," on the changing uses of regionalism, by John L. Thomas, in Stanley I. Kutler, ed., *Encyclopedia of the United States in the Twentieth Century* (New York: Charles Scribner's Sons, 1996); and, of course, the classic essays of Frederick Jackson Turner collected in *History, Frontier, and Section: Three Essays* (Albuquerque: University of New Mexico Press, 1993). Specific works relevant to my area of study were Andrew R. L. Cayton and Peter S. Onuf, *The Midwest and the Nation: Rethinking the History of an American Region* (Bloomington: Indiana University Press, 1990); Nicole Etcheson, *The Emerging Midwest: Upland Southerners and the Political Culture of the Old Northwest, 1787–1861* (Bloomington: Indiana University Press, 1996); and Kim Gruenwald, *River of Enterprise: The Commercial Origins of Regional Identity in the Ohio Valley, 1790–1850* (Bloomington: Indiana University Press, 2002).

Small-Town Life

A good general work on American urban development is Eric H. Monkkonen, *America Becomes Urban: The Development of U.S. Cities and Towns, 1780–1980* (Berkeley: University of California Press, 1988). Lewis Atherton's classic study *Main Street on the Middle Border* (Bloomington: Indiana University Press, 1954) deals with midwestern small towns under five thousand population. Another study, Richard O. Davies's *Main Street Blues: The Decline of Small-Town America* (Columbus: Ohio State University Press, 1998), examines an Ohio town where the peak total population barely exceeded two thousand.

The definitive work on small-town Jews is Lee Shai Weissbach's comprehensive *Jewish Life in Small-Town America* (New Haven, CT: Yale University Press, 2005). He pulls together information from small communities across the nation and describes the patterns of life that emerged. Another important work is Ewa Morawska, *Insecure Prosperity: Small-Town Jews in Industrial America, 1890–1940* (Princeton, NJ: Princeton University Press, 1996), about Johnstown, Pennsylvania, which had a Jewish population over one thousand.

Interesting memoirs of small-town Jewish life abound. Some that I looked at were Brenda Weisberg Meckler, *Papa Was a Farmer* (Chapel Hill, NC: Algonquin Books, 1988), about Jewish farmers in southwest Ohio; Stella Suberman, *The Jew Store: A Family Memoir* (Chapel Hill, NC: Algonquin Books, 1998), about a storekeeping family in western Tennessee in the 1920s; Howard V. Epstein, *Jews in Small Towns: Legends and Legacies* (Santa Rosa, CA: Vision Books International, 1997), an anthology of short memoirs from around the country; and Julie Salamon's wonderful *The Net of Dreams: A Family's Search for a Rightful Place* (New York: Random House, 1996), about her childhood in tiny Seaman, in Adams County, Ohio. See also some of the stories in Ze'ev Chafets, *Members of the Tribe: On the Road in Jewish America* (New York: Bantam Books, 1988), and Dan Rottenberg, ed., *Middletown Jews: The Tenuous Survival of an American Jewish Community* (Bloomington: Indiana University Press, 1997), a collection of oral histories from Muncie, Indiana.

Of course of greatest use in researching communities about which little if anything has been written were the collections of the state and local historical societies and the major Jewish repositories, the American Jewish Archives (located at Hebrew Union College in Cincinnati) and the American Jewish Historical Society (formerly located on the campus of Brandeis University, Waltham, MA, and now in New York City).

Regional Jewish Studies

Regionalism is a concept that has been applied quite productively to American Jewish history in recent years. There has long been interest in the experience of Jews in the South, and there is a burgeoning literature on Jews in the West. Two early models are William Toll, *The Making of an Ethnic Middle Class: Portland Jewry over Four Generations* (Albany: State University of New York Press, 1982), and Judith E. Endelman, *The Jewish Community of Indianapolis, 1849 to the Present* (Bloomington: Indiana University Press, 1984).

Two essays in Sander Gilman and Milton Shain's collection *Jewries at the Frontier: Accommodation, Identity, Conflict* (Urbana: University of Illinois Press, 1999) illustrate how the conversation between ethnic group and region has played out in two of the more colorful American regions. These demonstrate how place is an integral part of Jewish identity: "Bifocality in the Texas-Jewish Experience" by Seth Wolitz and "Alaskan Jews Discover the Last Frontier" by Bernard Riesman.

Landscape and Geography

Geographic theory is an intriguing subject relevant to regional studies. Useful to me were Kent C. Ryden, *Mapping the Invisible Landscape: Folklore, Writing, and the Sense of Place* (Iowa City: University of Iowa Press, 1993), and, especially, Yi-Fu Tuan, *Space and Place: The Perspective of Experience* (Minneapolis: University of Minnesota Press, 1977).

One study that brings these theories to practical fruition is John Berry's *Rising Tide: The Great Mississippi Flood of 1927 and How It Changed America* (New York: Simon and Schuster, 1997), which explores the interaction between humans and landscape. Berry's narrative is built around human actions with respect to the river: acting on the physical landscape (the engineering question: how do we prevent damaging floods?) and acting with and against other people (the resources question: whose interests are served, and whose are sacrificed, when political decisions are made about flood control?). Landscape studies is applied to the Ohio River Valley in John Jakle, *Images of the Ohio Valley: A Historical Geography of Travel, 1740–1860* (New York: Oxford University Press, 1977). Geographic theory is also making some headway in Jewish studies, as evidenced in Harold Brodsky, ed., *Land and Community: Geography in Jewish Studies* (Bethesda: University Press of Maryland, 1997).

Index